Suzuki GSX-R750

SUZUKI
GSX-R750

Gary Pinchin

The Crowood Press

Dedication

To Angela and our boys.

First published in 1997 by
The Crowood Press Ltd
Ramsbury, Marlborough
Wiltshire SN8 2HR

British Library Cataloguing in Publication Data

A catalogue record for this book is available from the British Library.

ISBN 1 86126 082 2

Typeset by Swindon Press Limited, Swindon, Wiltshire.

Printed and bound in Great Britain by the Bath Press

Contents

Acknowledgments   6

Foreword   8

1   Birth of a Legend   9

2   Making Its Mark – Launch of the GSX-R   28

3   America On-Line   41

4   Suzuki – Endurance World Champions   57

5   Slingshot into the Second Generation   78

6   RR for Real Race Bike   100

7   Return of the Long-Stroke   108

8   Final Makeover   120

9   Grant's Team Suzuki   127

10   Water-Cooling for the Third Generation   141

11   Supersport Swan Song   160

12   New Design – New Benchmark   174

13   Tough Track Baptism   185

Index   202

Acknowledgements

First of all thanks to my wife Angela and our four boys, Joe, Tyler, Kelly and Zak, for putting up with me being in the office during weekends and evenings whilst researching and writing this book. Without Angela's support and understanding it simply would not have happened.

I also must thank three of my closest friends in the road racing world, Colin Fraser, Alan Cathcart and Kel Edge. Their unbounded enthusiasm for all things bikes and racing provided much-welcomed encouragement.

Colin not only helped by digging out all the Suzuki brochures I could not obtain from sources closer to home, he also emptied his vast archive of North American Suzuki racing photos to provide many never-seen-before pictures for the book. And he helped fill in gaps with riding impressions from his own personal experiences of GSX-Rs – and with racing background information to give a true North American perspective.

If that was not enough, he led me around the Daytona garages in March 1997, introducing me to anyone he felt might be able to contribute snippets of information from GSX-R750 history!

Alan also opened his extensive archives to provide not only pictures, but much needed technical information. It meant giving up valuable time – and having me working in his office, pestering him when he had much more important things to do like earning a living! He never complained; in fact he actively encouraged me to ask for help if needed. A true friend. And his family put up with me stopping over and scrounging meals.

Thanks also go to my Superbike travelling partner, Kel Edge. Despite an intensive schedule in the early part of 1997 that took him around the world (literally) chasing Superbike tests, Daytona and the early World races, he still found time to raid his extensive files and come up with many of the superb images in this book. And just when I thought he had exhausted the files, another batch followed in the post a few days later. Thanks, mate!

Two other friends, very well-known British-based lensmen 'Cliveyboy' Clive Challinor and Terry Howe, supplied the balance of the racing shots: Clive's from the British tracks, and Terry's from the TT and some British short-circuits. Great stuff!

Something that has always impressed me about this sport is the willingness of people to just kick back and talk bikes. Even people at the top level are all enthusiasts, just like me and you. So thanks to Fujio Yoshimura, Don Sakakura, Doug Polen, Bill Syfan, Anders Andersson, Rex White, Mick

Grant and James Whitham. Not only were those special interviews informative, they were so much fun too!

And if it was not for Japanese photo-journalist Kyoichi Nakamura there would be no background to Yoshimura's Japanese racing efforts. Bradley Dixon, marketing manager at Yoshimura R & D, kindly provided me with the excellent Yoshimura Racing History with the message to use what I needed, but the reference work was printed in Japanese! I have trouble with English, let alone hieroglyphics. Naka came to rescue.

I'm indebted also to star-man Gordon Ritchie at Superbike magazine for digging out heaps of trade-supplied pictures that Suzuki were unable to come up with and to Paul Fowler for supplying a mountain of information, including all the GSX-R World Cup notes.

Thanks also to Redcat, particularly Mark Tyler, Lester Harris and the lads on the Suzuki WSB team, plus all the Suzuki racing people (riders and mechanics) who have given me their time and patience over the years.

Information Sources

Motocourse, Cycle World, Sport Rider, Cycle, Motorcyclist, American Road Racing, Road Racing World, Yoshimura Racing History, Yoshimura: The Book, Daytona 200, RPM, Superbike magazine, Road Racing Monthly, Road Racer, and MCN.

Foreword

Back in 1986 when I was hitting the road week in, week out, chasing Suzuki GSX-R Cup points and cash I had no idea I was laying the groundwork for a couple of World Superbike titles.

But that's how my career panned out and I've got to say the Suzuki GSX-R750 played a big part in changing my fortunes in the sport of road racing.

It was a punishing schedule back then but it put me where I am today. So it's an honour to be sitting here writing the Foreword for a book that charts the history of the machine from both road and racing perspectives.

I'd reached a difficult period in my career in the early eighties. I was breaking lap records and winning races but finances prevented me from racing too far outside of Texas, and there wasn't enough racing within the state for me to sustain a full season.

I was unsure of my future and even quit racing for a while but then the GSX-R Cup was launched in 1986 when the new Suzuki first arrived in the States. I looked at the schedule and there were several races at tracks where I already held lap records. I knew the series was made for me and after my first time on the GSX-R I realized the bike had been too.

The GSX-R Cup helped me into a situation where I could secure a factory Superbike ride with Yoshimura, the type of deal every racer with World Championship aspirations dreams of. What wonderful times I and my wife Dianne had with the team in the States and in Japan. And their GSX-Rs were so good, good enough for me to win the All Japan TTF1 title, the first non-Japanese rider to do so.

Ultimately, Suzuki and I went separate ways after that but I've always held a special affection for the people at Suzuki, at Yoshimura and, of course, the GSX-R750.

The launch of the all-new GSX-R750 allowed me to go back to my roots. By year end we had gotten our kitted privateer bike bang on the pace and I'm looking forward to a great season in the States, running my own operation in AMA Superbike and Formula USA.

I'm also looking forward to another season in the World Endurance Championship with the French-based Suzuki factory. We had some bad luck last year but still got second places at Spa and the Bol.

Right now, I'm sitting back home here in Texas writing this a few days after winning the first World Endurance race of 1997 at Le Mans on the Suzuki.

You know, when Suzuki launched the GSX-R750 back in 1985 it was a revolutionary motorcycle. Twelve years later they've created another benchmark machine. It's kind of neat to have had the chance to race, and be victorious, with both.

Doug Polen
1997

1 Birth of a Legend

'A Legend Now Begins.' That is how Suzuki's 1985 sales brochure heralded the all-new Suzuki GSX-R750 Hyper Sports. Glossy literature featured the new sportsbike in the foreground, with the French-based, alloy-framed, TTF1-spec GSX-750 factory Suzuki at the rear. The backdrop was the Paul Ricard circuit in southern France.

Suzuki's sportsbike reputation was built on racing. The birth of the GSX-R750 was the outcome of years of track action with factory race bikes like the 1977 GS750, 1978 GS1000, 1980 GS1000R – and the 1984 TTF1 spec GSX-750.

The brochure screamed its message to eager enthusiasts: 'This is a sportsbike derived from our works race bikes.' It was a sportsbike with ultimate race track pretensions: a sportsbike to set new standards.

In fact, the race bike pictured was the Patrick de Radigues/Jean-Pierre Oudin works machine run by Dominique Meliand's Le Mans-based, semi-factory supported team in the World Endurance Championship.

Meliand masterminded Suzuki's 1983 title-winning effort in World Endurance (the last year of the 1,000cc limit before the regulations reduced engine capacity to 750cc) with riders Frenchman Herve Moineau and Belgian Richard Hubin clinching the title. For the 1984 season Meliand kept the 1983 XR41 chassis

The HB Suzuki World Endurance machine at the non-championship Bol d'Or in 1983 – the final year of the 1,000cc capacity limit. It did not win this particular battle but Herve Moineau and Richard Hubin won the war, the World Endurance title. Compare similarities in frame design to the road-going 1985 GSX-R750. (Kel Edge)

that had housed the all-conquering 1,000cc GSX engines and convinced Suzuki to supply him with Yoshimura-tuned GSX-750 motors to slot in the 1,000cc frames.

Against the odds his team, with Patrick de Radigues and Jean-Pierre Oudin in the saddle, scooped the prestigious *Bol d'Or* over the better-financed Japanese rivals at the famous Ricard track.

Suzuki had also entered the first year of the new 750cc limit World TTF1 championship in 1984 at a disadvantage. Arch-rivals Honda had used the final year of the one-litre formula to develop their new 750cc V4 in over-bored 860cc and 920cc guises. While Suzuki lifted the Endurance title, Honda won both the 1983 World and British TTF1 championships.

Then Suzuki officially pulled out of all competition for 1984 and only some hard talking from the Meliand corner in France, and Heron Suzuki boss Denys Rohan in England, persuaded Suzuki to relent and support a scaled-down racing effort.

The British team, chasing TTF1 glory, was also supplied with Yoshimura-prepared, 16-valve, short-stroke (67mm x 53mm) GSX-750R engines, which fitted into the 1983 square-tube chassis used previously with GS1000-based XR69 one-litre units. With a dry weight of 328lb (149kg), the Suzuki was the lightest in its class, and with 40mm Kayaba forks up front and a heavily braced swing-arm, White Power shock and Full Floater rising-linkage rear suspension, handling was exemplary.

Cutaway of the original air/oil-cooled GSX-R750 motor. (Glenn Bayly Collection)

The Yoshimura Suzuki prepared by Suzuki GB, utilizing a TTF1 frame, displayed at a major Malaysian bike show by Yoshimura's UK distributor, David Dixon. The bike was intended for a limited production run – this was before Suzuki Japan announced plans to launch the GSX-R750. The Yosh project was stillborn. (Rex White Collection)

But the bikes were down on power, and reliability problems wreaked havoc: the bikes suffered a string of engine seizures without anyone really knowing why. Several crashes occurred too as riders Mick Grant and Rob McElnea were forced to ride beyond the capabilities of the machines in order to try to beat the Hondas.

Yoshimura had optimistically quoted the engines as producing 120bhp, promising another five for later in the year. In Suzuki's lightweight chassis this would have been a race-winning power-to-weight ratio with which to beat the Hondas. In fact the air-cooled engines never delivered anything like that: 'The highest we ever saw was 106bhp by the end of the season, measured at the gear-box – and on top of that we had major reliability problems,' admitted Suzuki's Team Manager Rex White during a track test of the machine to journalist Alan Cathcart.

In the US the Yoshimura team was also struggling in the AMA Superbike Production series. American Honda fielded Fred Merkel on a VF750F. Honda had also sold their factory 1993 VF750F Superbikes to ex-team members Sam McDonald and Venezuelan Roberto Pietri, while privateers like Canadian Reuben McMurter and Ricky Orlando raced similar machines with factory RSC kits.

The American-based Yoshimura R & D, with little support from Suzuki America, fielded Wes Cooley on a GS750 and, while Cooley rode the wheels off his bike to finish on the podium several times, Merkel ran away with the series as VF750Fs dominated the result sheets. Only Dale Quarterley (GPZ750) and Rich Oliver (KZ7540) occasionally broke the monotony – and finished in the top six – with Kawasakis.

Back on the world and British stage, despite all the problems, Heron Suzuki

Rob McElnea's 1984 factory Suzuki TTF1 bike. He won the Premier Classic 1,000cc TT on this bike – and finished second to Wayne Gardner in the British TTF1 series. (Alan Cathcart Archive)

kept plugging away. Rex White explained the reason for staying in the series when it would have been easy to stage a tactical withdrawal:

There were more reasons for staying in than pulling out, even though we were getting licked. We felt we had a commitment not just to the factory but also to the organizers, our sponsors and to the spectators to stick with it.

Plus, if we'd pulled out, the prestige of F1 would have taken a big bashing, with just one Japanese works team left in for an unchallenged walkover. We believe that TTF1 is bound for great things and also helps us to sell large-capacity road bikes. To have left Honda to have even more of a walkover than they did in the end would have been bad for the class.

And White knew that the new oil-cooled GSX-R750 was on the way, powering a street motorcycle with a very similar state-of-the-art chassis closely modelled on the alloy one fitted to the 1984 F1 racer …

In fact, Heron Suzuki had pre-empted the Japanese company's GSX-R750 launch. In the winter of 1983–4 the British company built a road-going sportsbike based on a factory aluminium XR69 chassis with the old GS750 engine slotted in. Yoshimura's UK distributor, Dave Dixon, took the bike to a major bike show in Malaysia. Heron had hoped to market a production version of the bike, but the project never got off the ground. Rohan travelled to Japan early in 1984 and was presented with details of the GSX-R750 then.

A NEW RACER

From the picture in Suzuki's 1985 advertising literature, the shiny new GSX-R750 frames bore an uncanny resemblance to the old 1,000cc race frames – box-section aluminium – but while the technologies might have looked similar, little else was in common with the racer, as one might expect in a street bike.

If Suzuki's new GSX-R750 did not borrow too much from the race bike it certainly broke new ground in virtually every department, especially in technology employed and performance delivered. The 'R' (for Racer) simply took the sportsbike ethic to a new level: lighter, faster, quicker – no compromises.

When American monthly magazine *Cycle World* reviewed the new machine in their March 1985 issue, the headline boldly stated: 'Changing the rules – sportsbikes will soon be divided into two categories: Before the GSX-R, and after.' Steve Anderson's opening gambit added: 'There's a revolution under way, and you've likely never heard of its architect. His name is Etsuo Yokouchi and his blueprint for change is the Suzuki GSX-R750.'

Prophetic words indeed, borne out by the way motorcycling evolved in the decade or so following the introduction of the GSX-R. So what about Mr Yokouchi's vision?

When the GSX-R750 was conceived the target was 100Ps from a 750cc engine. But the biggest problem facing Etsuo Yokouchi, Suzuki's chief engineer and development team leader of the GSX-R750 project, was overcoming the handicap of weight. The new bike would have to weigh much less than any of the existing 750cc machines on the market. The bottom line? This bike had to boast the most awesome power-to-weight ratio ever quoted for a 750-class machine.

According to in-house Suzuki magazine, *Tech News*, detailing the engine development of the new machine, Yokouchi reasoned that Suzuki's GSX-R400, the 400 sportsbike class leader of the time, was 19 per cent lighter than its rivals. He therefore opined that the 750 should be 20 per cent lighter than anything in its sector. Since the average weight of rival 750 machines was around 484lb (220kg), this meant Suzuki would be shooting for a maximum weight of 387lb (176kg) for the new GSX-R750. An extraordinary target for the era!

Original concept drawing on the 1985 GSX-R750. (Glenn Bayly Collection)

AN OIL-COOLED ENGINE

It was then down to Tansunobu Fuji, the man responsible for engine development, to design an engine to produce 100Ps – and make a major contribution in the weight-saving programme in the process.

The GSX-R750 concept was for a four-cylinder, double-ohc, four-valve-per-cylinder engine unit. This was conventional enough, but the problem was that, given the target of 100Ps, air-cooling would not be sufficient to maintain an efficient working temperature, while water-cooling would add too much weight to the motorcycle.

The story is that during the engineers' protracted discussions regarding this engine-cooling headache, conversation drifted to aircraft engines, specifically reciprocating engines – and their cooling systems. The fastest of these was the World War II P51 Mustang, which research showed had a liquid-cooling system – liquid, but not water. Yokouchi discovered the P51 had an oil-cooled engine!

Such an idea had never been tried in motorcycle engine design. Suzuki quickly discovered, after experimenting with dyed water to simulate oil, that it was not going to be possible simply to run oil through conventional water jackets. The jacket did not give the oil sufficient cooling surface. It was also established that using the cam-chain tunnel area for rerouting the return of the oil from the top end of the engine was not possible either. There was too much foaming effect of the oil as it came in contact with the reciprocating cam chain and valves.

However, the engineers calculated it would be possible to gain enough surface cooling area by redesigning the cylinder head finning. On the bench, this appeared to work. Furthermore, it was discovered the system worked so well there was no need to use a modified form of water jacket for the cylinders, which

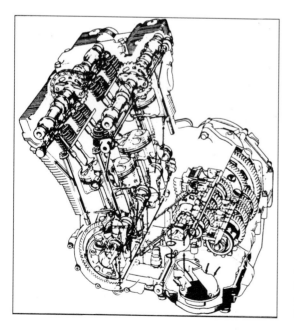

Suzuki engineers came up with a wet-sump engine design for the new GSX-R750 in 1985.
Lubricating oil was also used to cool the engine, helping to keep weight down.

14

the engineers had initially thought would be required.

What the development team found difficult to comprehend was that this was such an effective way of cooling an engine. Why had no other manufacturers discovered this? Maybe they had and found a blind alley reason for abandoning the concept.

According to Suzuki *Tech News*, what confirmed their engineers' findings was: 'intuition, which becomes honed by victory after victory', within the racing department, that is, 'a sense of what is the right direction'. It concluded: 'And perhaps, as in life, the simplest things are the hardest to discover but are most worth while.'

It certainly began to look that way, especially when all the benefits of oil-cooling were weighed up. The use of oil as the coolant and a lubricant meant a saving in weight (no water-cooling jackets or radiator), lower engine oil temperature, engine component longevity, and that oil life – specifically, a constant viscosity – was extended.

It also meant higher engine revs were possible because of the lower oil temperatures. Components, such as the crankshaft, con-rods and pistons, could be made lighter owing to the lower operating temperatures.

Oil-cooling also aided the search for extra horsepower. With engine internals being lighter there was an immediate gain in power-to-weight ratio – but the engine would be able to spin more easily thanks to a reduction in reciprocating weight.

The company called their oil-assisted, air-cooling system Suzuki Advanced Cooling System (SACS) and it was this single discovery that proved to be the most important element in the design of the GSX-R750 Hyper Sports.

So how did SACS work? The system utilized two oil pumps, one primarily for cooling, one for lubrication. The lubrication pump was responsible primarily for minimizing friction of the crankshaft bearings. This pump had a peak flow rate of 50 litres per minute.

The second, cooling pump sent oil to a gallery inside the magnesium cylinder head cover. To make the system work efficiently the size of the cylinder head had to be increased and the floor of the camshaft/valve-train cavity had to be wide and flat.

Oil entered from two openings in the rear of the cylinder head and was channelled into eight main routes, four on each side of the cylinder head. The oil then passed over the exterior surface of the combustion chambers, where it absorbed the heat.

There were two other tubes that delivered oil to portions of the gallery closest to the right and left engine sides, but cooling requirements there were minimal since these areas were closest to the external cooling fins of the cylinder head.

The cycle was completed when the heated oil was delivered via two drop tunnels to the 5.5-litre oil sump. Oil was prevented from being thrown around within the camshaft/valve-train cavity (and thus incurring frictional losses and reducing foaming should it strike the inside of the cam-chain tunnel) by a simple device Suzuki called the 'oil chamber plate'. This achieved minimum oil seepage and was an integral part of the gallery design.

This cooling pump had a peak flow rate of 40 litres per minute – a safe rate

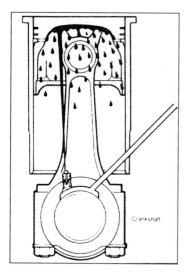

Oil jets were directed to spray lubricant into the underside of the piston crown to aid cooling.

which Suzuki dubbed SOL-AIR (Suzuki Oil-Cooler Airflow Control). The cooler had a capacity of 8,000 kilocalories per hour – which compared to a normal oil cooler of average capacity of 1,500 to 2,000kcal/h.

Even during extensive destruction testing engine oil temperature never exceeded 135°C. Suzuki claimed standard air-cooled production engines ran at 150°, and further claimed that under normal running conditions, their GSX-R750 engine ran at 100°.

above the SACS target flow rate of 20 litres per minute delivered to the cylinder head gallery. SACS did not rely on high pressure, but the overall design to guarantee efficiency.

Furthermore, the oil in the cooling system did not actually go through an oil cooler while in the system. The oil drained to the sump like the crank lubricating oil. The oil was then routed via a specially designed, large-capacity cooler,

Weight Saving

As already mentioned, the lower engine operating temperatures allowed for lighter internal components. The lower temperature allowed metal in the engine's components to resist stress to a greater degree, so less metal was required. The crankshaft main journal was reduced from 36mm (in the GSX750S engine) to 32mm in the GSX-R750. The maximum diameter of the

The original 1985 GSX-R750F Suzuki. (Beaulieu Archive)

1985 Suzuki factory TTF1 bike.
(Glenn Bayly Collection)

crankshaft was also reduced from 36mm to 34mm.

The reduced crankshaft weight, in turn meant lighter pistons, gudgeons, pins and con-rods could be used. Suzuki's design team employed a computer stress-analysis programme – Infinite Element Calculus – to determine this and ensure that the engine maintained optimum balance.

But even with the main internal assembly reduced dramatically in weight, the team could not stop there when working to Yokouchi's 97lb (44kg) weight-saving target. The bottom camshaft sprocket's teeth were reduced in number from 17 to 15, while the upper camshaft sprocket went from 34 to 30 teeth. This not only reduced weight, but also achieved another goal: reduction in the overall engine height.

The cylinder head weight was reduced by a further kilo thanks to using a magnesium casting – the first time such a material had ever been used on a production motorcycle cylinder head. The

magnesium also offered great heat dissipation qualities – and looked great!

Suzuki resisted an inclination to save further weight by using magnesium engine side covers, preferring to err on the side of safety. Magnesium case covers would not have been sufficiently resistant to abrasion in the event of a crash.

Suzuki *Tech News* provided an impressive list of component weight reductions, in terms of percentages, compared to the previous GSX750 model: piston 11 per cent reduction; con-rod 25 per cent reduction; crankshaft 19 per cent; cylinder head 22 per cent; cylinder head cover 39 per cent; cylinder 17 per cent.

The SACS breakthrough gave Suzuki engineers a healthier safety margin of high rpm, so the engine dimensions comprised a large bore size of 70mm and a shorter stroke of 48.7mm for a displacement of 749cc. This compared favourably to the previous year's GSX750S (67mm x 53mm) displacement of 747cc. And, to maintain cam-chain tension at high

Suzuki sold the GSX-R750 on the company's racetrack reputation, hence the customer sales brochure for the 1985 GSX-R750F showing the new bike against the backdrop of the Paul Ricard pits straight with their factory endurance racer in the background. The literature was printed in Japan and issued in February 1985. (Glenn Bayly Collection)

tension at high rpm, a cam-chain idler sprocket was incorporated.

Suzuki opted for a four-valve-per-cylinder head design after looking at other three-, five– and six-valve options. They decided that the engine's efficiency would be determined not by the number of valves per cylinder but by the effective opening area of the valves (the valve lift volume). As Suzuki *Tech News* put it: 'Why have a large mouth but a tight throat passage?'

Suzuki's Twin Swirl Combustion Chamber (TSCC), first seen in a four-valve engine back in 1980 when the GS1100 was launched, was redesigned. Essentially, TSCC took advantage of the turbulence caused by the incoming charge of fuel into the cylinder to increase air flow and improve flame propagation. Basically, early TSCC machining produced two shallow hemispheres with a ridge between them, the ridge being intersected by a spark plug located in the centre of the chamber.

The shape of the chamber directed fuel into two separate parallel swirls rotating forward from the valves and up the cylinder wall, with two V-shaped squish areas located between each set of valves to accelerate the swirl during compression. The combustion chamber was small and shallow, so a higher compression ratio was possible, allowing the use of a flat-top piston with small cutaways for the valves. It is interesting to note how much the cylinder head design had in common with that of the Formula One

GSX-R750F (1985)

Four-cylinder, four-stroke, oil-cooled, DOHC, TSCC, four valves per cylinder

Engine
Bore and stroke	70mm x 48.7mm
Cubic Capacity	749cc
Compression ratio	9.8:1
Carburettors	4 Mikuni VM29SS
Ignition	Transistorized
Starter system	Electric
Lubrication system	Wet sump

Transmission
Clutch	Wet, multi-plate type
Gearbox	Six-speed, constant mesh

Suspension
Front suspension	Posi Damp Fork System, 41mm telescopic, coil spring, oil-dampened, spring, four-way adjustable
Rear suspension	Full Floater, spring preload fully adjustable, damping force, four-way adjustable

Brakes and Tyres
Front brake	Twin 300mm disc, hydraulically operated twin Deca piston
Rear brake	Single 220mm disc, hydraulically operated
Front tyre	110/80V-18
Rear tyre	140/70V-18

Dimensions (in/mm)
Overall length	82.8/2,105mm
Overall width	29.3/745mm
Overall height	47.4/1,205mm
Wheelbase	56.5/1,435mm
Ground clearance	4.7/120mm
Seat height	30.1/765mm
Dry weight	387lb (176kg)

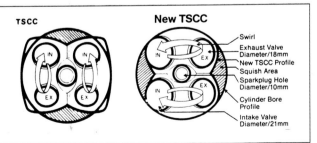

The new TSCC (Twin Swirl Combustion Chamber) design of the 1985 GSX-R750 was totally within the cylinder bore. Pictured left is the old-style TSCC.

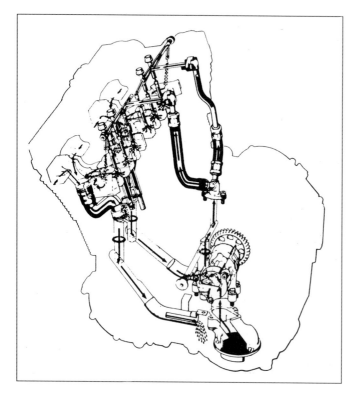

With the oil-cooling system of the GSX-R750 some 21 quarts of oil were pumped into the camshaft/valve train area every minute.

car-racing Ford Cosworth DFV of the period!

With improved charging, smaller valves could be used, so a narrower valve angle was needed to fit the valves into the bore. The smaller valves also meant they were less masked by the combustion chamber walls.

However, the old TSCC system, while effective, was not as efficient as it could be – as John Ulrich pointed out in *Cycle News* when reviewing the new GSX-R750 in 1985:

The combustion chamber edges overlapped the cylinder bore. Some race tuners seeking more power cut chamfers into the top of the cylinder – located at the four corners of the combustion chamber – thinking it would improve flame propagation and discourage detonation.

Suzuki thought so too. The new GSX-R750 did not have the TSCC quenching

Cutaway of the original GSX-R750 engine.

Life was tough for Yoshimura in the USA. They were forced to run the ageing GS750 in Superbike competition during 1985. This shot shows the 1984 bike with Graeme Crosby during practice at Daytona. (Alan Cathcart Archive)

zones overlapping the cylinder bores. The new TSCC was more compact with larger valves compared with the previous GS750 (26mm inlets and 24mm exhaust) with an included angle of 21 degrees. Valve-timing had the intake opening at 38 degrees and closing at 66 degrees while the exhaust opened at 63 degrees and closed at 37 degrees. Intake lift was 8.2mm and exhaust lift 7.5mm.

The intake size was matched with the Direct Air Intake System (DAIS) while the exhaust was matched to the capabilities of the 4-1 Vortex exhaust headers. DAIS incorporated a huge, eight-litre airbox, located under and inside the gas tank – positioned where the rider gripped the tank with his knees. The aim was to allow a clean air flow into the new, flat-slide Mikuni VM29SS carburettors, which offered improved fuel metering and very quick throttle response over the previous round-slide carbs. Use of Theremetel-treated metal, as used on jet engine turbine blades, allowed Suzuki to reduce weight of the system by 39 per cent compared to the previous year's GSX750.

Finally, a six-speed transmission was incorporated to enable the rider to take full advantage of the engine's high-revving characteristics. Suzuki also fitted a hydraulic clutch.

CHASSIS DESIGN

It was not enough, however, simply to produce a powerplant to deliver new-world sportsbike performance figures. Suzuki also needed to come up with a chassis to harness the horses – keeping within Yokouchi's strict targets but every bit as strong and dependable as conventional tubular steel chassis.

A very significant portion of the 97lb (44kg) weight reduction came from the design of the frame. Takayoshi Suzuki (no relation to the corporation!), who was in charge of frame design, revealed:

The primary method used by the team was to reduce the aggregate number of components in the frame. By doing this the number of welds reduced correspondingly. Fewer welds mean lower weight and offer the additional advantage of shrinking labour costs.

Suzuki's GSX750 frame – the first aluminium alloy frame to go into large-scale production for a road bike – used no fewer than ninety-six components. Takayoshi Suzuki's target was to reduce this to thirty-two. What his design team

actually achieved was a frame fabricated from twenty-six components! They designated it MR-ALBOX, for Multi-Rib Aluminium Alloy Box Section. It weighed just 17.8lb (8.1kg).

It incorporated five cold-cast special aluminium alloy components and twenty-one pieces of extruded aluminium alloy box section. Weight was further reduced by using aircraft-type rivets in some areas instead of welds, even though it had previously been thought that cast and extruded components should not be joined.

The GSX-R750 had a relatively low seat height (in road bike terms) of 765mm. This compared to the norm of the era's conventional sportsbikes of between 790mm to 810mm. The figure was not arrived at by accident.

Suzuki drew on their endurance racing experience with the GS1000R to come up with the ergonomics of the machine – and seat design was borrowed from the racer. They figured that the 'functional unity' of rider/machine was the fundamental element in endurance racing, the aim being to minimize fatigue to ensure the rider's maximum concentration.

Agility was another key factor in chassis design and the Suzuki achieved a potential banking angle of 55 degrees –

The original GSX-R750F introduced in 1985. (Glenn Bayly Collection)

far in excess of the FIM's minimum requirement. Reducing the overall engine width achieved this by allowing the generator to be relocated from the end of the crankshaft to the top of the crankcase behind the cylinders, and be driven by gears.

Suspension uprating was also part of the overall package. Up front, the inner tubes of the conventional cartridge forks were increased to 41mm. This compared with the skinny 37mm forks fitted to the GSX750S. The triple clamps were beefier – and made of aluminium – incorporating a fork brace. This construction meant increased strength and rigidity plus a substantial weight reduction over previous forks.

Internally the new forks had a revised version of what Suzuki called their Positive Damping Fork (PDF), which offered four-way adjustment. Still at the front end, there were new four-piston calipers (DOP – Dual Opposed Piston) gripping dual, 300mm diameter, spirally drilled disc rotors.

Suzuki knew that the low seat height could not be achieved with their conventional Full Floater rear suspension, so came up with a new system incorporating an eccentric cam to deliver comfort at full extension and firmness at maximum compression. In short, it offered comfort when touring but retained sports capability.

The overall size of the new Full Floater was substantially reduced in comparison to the previous Full Floater suspension with the number of parts reduced by 35 per cent. There was also a new aluminium alloy box-section swing-arm and a two-piston rear disc brake with floating rear caliper and parallel rear torque link.

Suzuki's endurance racers used 18in rims back and front, so the new GSX-R750 used the same-dimension, six-spoke alloy wheels, matched to ultra-low-profile, V-rated, new rubber tyres from Bridgestone: 110/80 front, 140/70 rear. Hollow front and rear axles were also used, made from high-quality chrome molybdenum.

And with its sleek racer-style bodywork and clip-ons the bike looked dressed for action – much more aggressive than Yamaha's sit-up-and-beg, half-faired FZ750 rival.

Suzuki spared no effort in creating the GSX-R750, producing bristling new technologies in engine design and a new framework in which to house its awesome potential. And the targets were achieved: a claimed 104.5bhp at 10,500rpm; redline, 11,000rpm; engine weight, 161lb (73kg); overall weight, 388lb (176.4kg).

The figures compared favourably to the previous GS750 engine launched in 1993: 86bhp at 9,500rpm with an engine weight of 176lb (80kg). No wonder Suzuki *Tech News* pondered:

Try to imagine the polite but rather intense discussions between Engine Design Team Chief, Mr Kiryu and the Frame Design Team Chief, Mr Suzuki, concerning exactly where to shave 44kg [97lb] off the overall weight of the GSX-R750 with Mr Yokouchi looking over both their shoulders.

Fujio Yoshimura and the Japanese Titles

When Hideo 'Pops' Yoshimura died in March 1995, his son, Fujio, succeeded him as President of Yoshimura Japan. A former racer himself on a Honda CB72, Fujio junior had already built up the American-based Yoshimura R & D and has been involved in racing development of the GSX-R750 from the very start. He recalls:

In States now we run whatever Suzuki send us. We do special tuning here: some parts, carburation etc. But back in 1986 Yoshimura did all the development: special camshafts, valve springs and retainers, pistons, con-rods, carburation. So much. The rest of the parts we used were kit parts: transmission, crankshaft, dry clutch – all from the Suzuki factory.

Fujio remembers problems during the early days of the GSX-R:

We had lots of connecting rod bolts splitting off. Lots of bottom end problems. Mid-season in '86 we changed to Carillo rods and that helped us. Then in 1987 we developed a 'Stage III' Yoshimura-tuned engine. It was all new stuff: new piston design, new cam profile, higher compression ratio, a new carburettor up to 40mm from 38mm. It made quite a lot more horsepower. Around 140bhp, I seem to remember.

In 1988 Suzuki unveiled the short-stroke but Yoshimura R & D continued to race the old long-stroke engine. Schwantz, though, raced at Daytona with a factory short-stroke motor. Even Yoshimura was surprised at Suzuki's decision to go for a revvy motor.

We didn't expect the new engine to be that way. But we had to race with it. Schwantz wanted to race Daytona. Winning the 200-miler was a great confidence boost for him before going to the GPs. But it was not expected to be a race-winning machine. We spent a lot of time in winter developing the 88 model but experienced a lack of the torque that was needed. An engine with short-stroke means you lose the torque – it's as simple as that.

We could get the high rpm so we tried to spin more and more rpm but then ran into cooling problems. The oil cooling system was okay but the high rpm caused heat build up. We had to run bigger oil-coolers. It was a big circle for us.

But this is a fact: The bike that won Daytona in 1988 won because of Kevin Schwantz's riding ability. Down the straights the old Suzukis were much faster than Kevin's bike!

Up to 1988 Fujio was concentrating on development work back in Japan for Yoshimura R & D but from 1989 Don Sakakura was in charge at R & D's base in Chino, California, with Suzuki factory-supplied equipment.

During 1988 in Japan, Yoshimura were running the older long-stroke engines. Fujio recalls: 'Doug Polen started riding for me in Suzuka 1988 then rode for us in 1989 and won the F1 Japanese Championship with the long-stroke engine.'

Polen's arrival in Japan brought a revival of fortunes to the Yoshimura camp after a dismal (by their standards) 1998 season. Yoshimura had, after all, dominated the All Japan F1 Championship since the GSX-R750 launch in 1985. Fujio remembers:

The bike had been introduced at Cologne the year before and my father and the designer Mr Yokouchi were both there. They said at the press conference, 'This bike is going to be a race winner.' Suzuki had not won the All Japan F1 Championship (which began the previous year).

Pops Yoshimura fell ill in 1985 and spent much time in hospital so Fujio was effectively in control of company matters. The pair had a stormy father/son relationship – like in many families. In the book Yoshimura Racing History it says:

Pops was a real craftsman, tuning of the engine was a sixth sense for him. Fujio came from a new generation (with different ideas and methods) and there were many arguments between them – as constructors, as engine tuners and as father and son ...

Fujio continues the story:

In 1985 we won the championship with Satoshi Tsujimoto. My father was alive then and I didn't know it but he told Tsujimoto that if he won the All Japan Championship he would take him to Daytona. Tsujimoto remembered it!

In 1985 we had eight races and he won five or six. That year Yamaha came out with the five-valve engine. Honda had the VFR. Kawasaki had the GPX. It was a competitive season although I must say that apart from Yamaha, direct factory involvement wasn't so deep as it is now.

The general consensus was that while Honda had good horsepower, they came up short in the chassis department. Moriwaki (with Kawasaki) lacked horsepower and Yamaha were not really competitive at all. Yoshimura, with the GSX-R, had an unbeatable all-round package.

Yoshimura also won the All Japan F1 title in 1986 with Tsujimoto, who was dubbed 'Kamikaze Boy' by the American Yoshimura crew, and in 1987 with Yukiya Ohshima. But in 1988, with the growing tide of factory intervention from all four manufacturers, Ohshima – noted for his steady, safe riding – lost the championship and Polen – who had run some end-of-season races for Yoshimura in Japan – was signed for the 1989 season, which he duly won.

Overall, 1989 was a pivotal year in terms of development for the Yosh F1 effort. For the first time the exhaust headers sported the now trademark Yosh canisters welded onto the exhaust headers. Fujio explains:

They gave us a better power curve. More torque low down. I looked at the two-stroke expansion chamber, big volume – and asked how come it has that? Pressure is very important and how come it had to have that big volume? It was my first question. I thought maybe we should pinch some ideas from the two-stroke guys. The design is patented in Japan and we've applied for the patent in the States too. It's really difficult to make those things. You have to make them right otherwise they can break.

Also in 1989 the F1 frame was different with much more bracing. Chassis development was carried out by Suzuki. Not only was the main frame different, it also had a different linkage. Fujio adds:

Also new radial tyres came on the scene. Tyres, suspension, frame – we saw so many advances. We had a good rider and a good package – so far ahead of everyone. It's impossible to pinpoint one thing that stood out. It was also our fourth season with GSX-R so we had lots of experience.

Polen won F1 and F3 titles, the first rider to ever achieve this. However, the team was unable to capitalize on the success. Early in the 1990 season, Polen crashed hard at Willow Springs, California testing his Yosh superbike before Daytona. He caught his foot in the rear wheel and severed four of his toes. He missed the season opener and though he battled gamely back into action for round two at Suzuka, another DNF during the year killed his back-to-back title chances.

That same year, Suzuki delivered a new chassis with much more bracing around the headstock area – effectively boxing in the top end of the motor. Fujio says this was the beginning of the end for the oil-cooled motor:

We always knew temperature problems would affect us. Then Suzuki also came out with a totally new frame – full box section. It was a good chassis (in terms of handling and steering qualities) but the combination with the air-oil-cooled engine boxed in the heat! At least the previous frame allowed the air to circulate. But now we had more problems than before. Of course you can't tell those things on a dyno but when you get to the track they show up.

Polen dropped to third in the championship and there was not one win in the All Japan series for Yoshimura. The following year, 1991, saw the gap between Suzuki and the opposition increase further but the water-cooled motor in 1992 brought a new lease of life, with Masano Aoki and Kenjii Ohsaka the riders. But the axeing of the F3 series brought even more competition to the F1 class with the redundant stars of F3 all eager to impress in the big class. Fujio takes up the tale:

We qualified second in the Suzuka Eight-Hour and got 145bhp out of the engine but the Suzuki factory was also directly involved in the four-stroke project (with their own race effort in Japan) so we were in competition – and have been ever since … We still work together but at the track we're competitors. At Daytona we are still as one team but in Japan we are rivals.

In 1992 Aoki didn't win the championship (Kawasaki's Keichi Kitagawa did) but won some races. Once again the engine was new and we struggled for a couple of years to develop the engine – develop the team.

Aoki went fast but crashed and burned through 1993; Kitagawa was champion again. From now on it would get even tougher for Yoshimura. There were to be no more titles with the old generation of GSX-R750. Japan adopted the Superbike rules, scrapping the old F1 class, which did not help Yosh either.

Fujio wants to agree that the more liberal F1 rules helped keep Suzuki in the ballpark – but stops short of publicly announcing such. Did the switch to Superbike affect Suzuki more that its rivals? 'I can't say that … Maybe … But I can't say,' is his reply!

And 1996 brought the new GSX-R – and yet another learning curve to overcome. Fujio says:

It was mostly chassis problems but also the engine. The engine did not give enough acceleration – but you have to remember it is just the start of the programme for the new bike. But now there is no F1 class, it is all Superbike with heavy factory involvement so all the factory takes three or four riders each. There are no good riders left for teams like ours.

Now to win Superbike you have to have good rider, good engine, good tyres, good suspension, good chassis. Every part has to be dialled in. Has to be perfect to win races now.

But Yoshimura will continue to develop Suzuki's bikes – the GSX-R750 in particular – and Fujio has a soft spot for the marque that has brought the Yoshimura name so much exposure:

I think it's been an excellent motorbike. Very unique. As Suzuki said with the GSX-R logo, it's a racing bike. The concept has always been speed and race. Race-ready motorcycle! A lot of people can enjoy the performance with the standard motorcycle.

You can't buy stuff for RC45s, YZF750s. But you can get parts for the GSX-R. All the aftermarket people like us: Vance and Hines, companies all over the world, have done so many aftermarket parts for this model – it's just so popular.

2 Making its Mark – Launch of the GSX-R

Clothed in a race-style, full fairing racing seat with the option of a single-seat cowl, the GSX-R750 looked every inch a racer for the road. And that is exactly how the bike was perceived by the press.

Mat Oxley, testing the new 'R' in the 5 February 1985 issue of *Motor Cycle News* proclaimed:

The Japanese have finally realised that compromise needn't dictate sportsbike design. Suzuki's new GSX-R750 is closer to a four-stroke racer on the road than anything else before. It is to the F1 racer as the RD500LC is to the GP machine.

Oxley tested the bike at Suzuki's Ryuyo four-mile-long test track near their Hamamatsu factory and saw 140mph (225km/h) at 10,600rpm running into a strong head wind and said

the bike should be good for 145mph (233km/h).

Superbike magazine rode a GSX-R during TT week and tester Graham Scott commented: 'According to Suzuki the GSX-R is a "Professional Power Sports Bike". According to some people it is, essentially, the most remarkable achievement since splitting the atom …'

Scott did not actually swing a leg over a Suzuki press fleet machine but used Mark Bullen's TT entry, a stock GSX-R only with Metzeler Sport tyres, Goodridge braided brake lines and a Kawasaki steering damper. And this was raced not only in the Production TT, but also in the TTF1 six-lapper!

Lean and lithe: the original Suzuki GSX-R750 TTF1 bike at Ruyuo circuit, Japan, in 1985. Note the narrow-waisted frame, single oil-cooler, unbraced swing-arm, Brembo brakes and Campagnolo wheels. (Rex White Collection)

Scott observed: 'That oil-cooled motor is light and very powerful. It'll pull from the 3,000rpm base line, is fairly flat until 6,000; it picks up from there to 7,000rpm and then charges hard to the 11,000rpm redline.'

Even though Suzuki had opted for 18in wheels, the steering (with a head angle of 26 degrees) also got the thumbs up. Scott added: 'The forks are obviously set pretty steeply and this combines with the 18in front wheel to give a lovely neutral feeling to the steering ... It feels safe and stable until a twist of the throttle brings you smoothly upright again. Lovely.'

Oxley also said: 'By going for fairly radical geometry Suzuki have managed to make the GSX-R steer as quick as a bike with a 16in front wheel ... the bike has the super sensitive feel of a real racer.'

SUPERSTOCK

It was to prove to be just that thanks to a new race series starting in England, the MCN Superstock Championship. This series was conceived by road-racing entrepreneur Bruce Cox to be for modified road bikes, with the emphasis on keeping costs down to a minimum so that privateers had a reasonable chance to remain competitive. It was estimated that a fully prepared Superstocker could be had for around £4,000 – with little work required on the motor during the season.

Superstock permitted unlimited suspension modifications, racing exhausts and slick tyres but the frame had to remain stock and engine modifications were limited to 'polishing and lightening' – terminology that was to bring some serious controversy in subsequent years.

Canadian dealerships took delivery of the new GSX-R750 in 1985, while the US had to wait until 1986. Michel Mercier won the Canadian Superbike National title in 1985. You can just tell this guy was an ex-flat-track champion! (Colin Fraser)

Superstock was enthusiastically embraced by three of the main UK importers: Honda, Yamaha, and Suzuki, with some bitterly fought racing during the eleven-round series to thrill the crowds, although the championship battle came down to just two marques. Honda's three-year-old VF750 design was simply too slow in a straight line against the new Suzuki and Yamaha's latest five-valve-per-cylinder FZ750.

Mick Grant won the 1985 championship, riding a works-entered GSX-R750. At forty-one, Grant showed there was still life in the ageing war horse as he sped to five race victories.

He dominated the first four races. The series opened on Good Friday, 5 April, at Brands in the wet. Roger Marshall initially led on the VF750 but Grant took over mid-distance and cleared off to win the ten-lap, 26.14-mile (16.25km) race at a canter from Marshall with Ray Swann third on an FZ750 Yamaha, making it three different manufacturers on the podium – exactly what Superstock was meant to be about!

But Grant was on a roll. Donington was next, and two days later he won again, this time with the GSX-R750

clearly faster than its opposition. However, Yamaha rider Steve Parrish made a fight of it, and the Suzuki was adjudged to have crossed the line first by a scant one-hundredth of a second!

On Easter Monday it was a different story, with Grant winning from start to finish – a performance he duplicated in the fourth round at Mallory on 21 April. Grant's advantage was that his Suzuki had arrived a little earlier than his rivals' bikes and given the team a little edge in race development.

The bike arrived at the Heron Suzuki headquarters in Crawley in March, giving the team just one month to race-prep ready for the opener. Nigel Everett and Paul Bolton were the two team mechanics, with Rex White team manager. Privateers who had put their money down before the festive break had to wait until after the season had kicked off to get their machines!

Modifications

The factory literature had claimed 100bhp from the new GSX-R750 but when the motor went on the dyno it

Mercier leads Reuben McMurter's Yamaha FZ750 – another new superbike model. Note the differences in riding styles determined by the stock machine set-ups: the GSX-R with traditional clip-ons, the FZ with its high-mounted, superbike-style bars. (Colin Fraser)

Frenchman Herve Moineau, teamed with Jean-Pierre Oudin and Richard Hubin, won the Spa 24-Hours on the Dominique Meliand-entered, factory GSX-R750. (Kel Edge)

recorded just 83bhp at the gearbox after running in. Everett admitted to Alan Cathcart during a track test at the end of the year:

Progressively modifying it within the rules brought it up to scratch. We fitted a racing exhaust from the TTF1 bike, the airbox was removed and the carb main jet size upped from 97.5 to 130. That gave us exactly 100bhp at 11,500rpm, though Mick doesn't usually rev it over 11,000rpm.

Compression was also upped from the stock 9.8:1 to 10.7:1.

This was relatively moderate tuning compared to some of the North American (Canadian) tuners who were whacking compression up to 14.5 or 15:1. The consensus was that this oil-cooled GSX-R responded well to high compression!

While Grant's Superstock engine, owing to the demands of the rule book, had to remain relatively stock, the rolling chassis came in for some major modifications.

With the offset provided by the standard yokes and an 18in front wheel the front end was not stable enough for rac-

ing. The team also wanted to run a 16in front end to standardize the tyres they were running with their other bikes. Grant, of course, had a good handle on the range of Michelin compounds available. Finally the team settled for a 12/60 16in at the front, while at the rear was an 18/67 16in.

The result was a transplant of the entire front end from the 1984 GSX-750R TTF1 bike: Kayaba 40mm forks with hydraulic anti-dive, 16in front wheel, 310mm Brembo brake rotors gripped by Tokiko four-piston calipers. The team also fitted a White Power rear unit but kept the stock linkage to offer 4in (100mm) of travel.

This was all well within Superstock rules but perhaps not within the spirit of the competition, which had been devised as a low-cost formula. After all, how many privateers could source such equipment?

The rules also permitted removal of all the street bike paraphernalia: twin headlights, speedo, rear light, indicators, starter motor and generator, though the

Suzuki still had a battery fitted to power the total-loss Kokusan-Denki CDI system. This divesting of surplus equipment meant weight came down from 388lb (176kg) in dry street trim to 350lb (159kg) with oil.

By the fifth round of the contest at Donington the opposition had caught up, and Grant was carrying an injury sustained at the TT. Parrish won from Marshall, and Grant finished third.

Yamaha dominated Snetterton with privateer Keith Huewen leading home Parrish; Honda and Suzuki protested against both results after the race and Parrish was disqualified when it was discovered that his carbs had been smooth-bored.

Another privateer, Trevor Nation on a Suzuki, won the next round on the tricky Woodland circuit at Cadwell with Grant relegated to fifth behind his own team-mate, Australian Graeme McGregor.

The last four rounds were all Suzuki's. Grant won at Oulton, then Nation took Scarborough and the final round at Brands while Mark Salle won the penul-timate Thruxton event. Nation's Brands victory was a last gasp lunge for the line to beat GP returnee Rob McElnea, who was riding a Heron Suzuki. Grant was placed second, fourth and seventh in those races to secure the title with 127 points to the 98 of his nearest rival, Marshall.

Superstock was the class to get all the publicity in England during 1985, being perceived as a vibrant new concept with full support of the factory-backed importer teams. And Suzuki took the major honours in a series where Joe Public could identify the winning bikes with what they had out in the parking lot.

PRODUCTION RACING

However, the ACU Metzeler Production Championship offered an even closer tie to the street – bikes raced here had to be box-stock with the only mods permitted being ones for safety reasons!

Mick Grant finished second in the World TTF1 series riding for Heron Suzuki. This shot was taken at Montjuic Park where Grant finished third in a race marred by a multi-bike crash that left Tony Rutter seriously injured. (Kel Edge)

Suzuki took an early delivery of their Superstock machine and transplanted a TTF1 front end. Apart from discovering that the threads on the spin-on oil filter were too fine, the bike ran faultlessly all year. (Alan Cathcart Archive)

Suzuki dominated this championship too – not only in the final championship standings but in the numbers game as well. Of the six rounds, Trevor Nation won three and Phil Mellor won three. Nation took the title with 57 points to Mellor's 45, while Vince Field was third overall.

The season began at Thruxton on 17 March 1985 but the 750 entry (there was also a 751-1,500cc class race on the programme) was seriously reduced owing to the late delivery of the Suzukis to their customers. Nation won the race on a Honda, but by the second round at Donington the GSX-Rs had arrived and started to make their presence felt.

Mellor won from Vince Field and Paul Iddon – producing an all-Suzuki podium. Mellor won the next two races but Nation's wins (since switching to Suzuki) in the final two races while Mellor was out injured gave him the title.

Mick Grant and Suzuki also won the reintroduced Production TT, ahead of Canadian Kevin Wilson, Tony Rutter and New Zealander Glenn Williams – all of them on GSX-R750s. To underline the Suzuki's supremacy, eleven of the first fifteen riders home were Suzuki-mounted.

WINNING EVERYWHERE

GSX-Rs were winning all over the world. Juan Garriga dominated both F1 Silhouette and Prototype racing in Spain on the new bike, while Rob Phillis consistently beat the bigger GPZ900 Kawasakis and Honda VF1000s in Australian production racing on an 'R' and Michel Mercier took the Canadian Superbike crown on a Superbike-spec GSX-R.

Mercier's crown was the final championship year in Canada for the Canadian

The TTF1 motor delivered 107bhp at 12,700rpm. The Superstocker (right) gave 100bhp at 11,500rpm. TTF1 had Brembo four-piston calipers, the Superstocker had Tokico. Both employed twin 310mm floating discs. (Alan Cathcart Archive)

Motorcycle Association (CMA) and there were only two point-paying races, one in the east, one in the west. The following year would see a season-long national series promoted by a new organization curiously tagged Racing Associates Canada Events – better known as RACE. (It is worth noting also that the Canadian 750 Production championship also went to a Suzuki rider, Mario Duhamel, son of the legendary Yvon, elder brother of the now legendary Miguel!)

Mercier's title was significant since his was the first for the GSX-R750 championship title in North America. American Suzuki opted not to import the exciting new machine until the following year (1986), although a youngster by the name of John Kocinski teamed up with ageing hero David Aldana to race a GSX-R in Western Eastern Roadracers' Association (WERA) endurance races!

Yoshimura Suzuki, however, was forced to run a tricked-out version of the air-cooled GS700 in the 1985 AMA Superbike Championship (the street

bike reduced by 50cc because of import restrictions). Cooley left and Yoshimura employed a twenty-year-old fiery hot-shoe from Texas called Kevin Schwantz.

The bike was unreliable – it broke a clutch hub leaving the grid at Daytona – and Schwantz crashed a few times, but he still scored three race wins and wound up seventh in the final standings. The GSX-R days would come in 1986!

TTF1

In the world's premier four-stroke road racing category of the era, TTF1, the British-based Heron Suzuki team did not enjoy the same degree of success the GSX-R750 had elsewhere. Once again the engines were developed by Yoshimura for Suzuki, and, just as in 1984, they came up short in the horse-power stakes.

It was not just the works team that suffered. There were ten similar Yoshimura race-kitted engines sold to dealers at subsidized prices in a bold

Dealer Team Suzuki marketing bid to swamp the TTF1 grid with a horde of look-alike GSX-Rs. Rex White recalls:

Denys Rohan, the top man at Heron Suzuki, came up with the idea of having up to fifteen 'dealer team' riders on the grid to support our 'works' team. The engines, which would normally have cost around £5,200 were sold to these teams at around £3,000 for them to fit into their own chassis. In return for the subsidized purchase price, the bikes had to look like ours but could still carry the dealer team's own logos. People like Tony Rutter and Andy McGladdery had the engines.

But the plan did not work out. Not only were the engines lacking in horsepower, allowing Honda to dominate the racing, but the TTF1 racing GSX-Rs earned a woeful reputation for breaking main bearings and con-rods.

At the TT Grant had all but given up. After a week of wrecked engines, he hinted to journalists that the TTF1 bike would not make the distance. He was right – it blew up again. On the other hand Tony Rutter had no such problems, finishing second on his GSX-R. He was quoted in *Motocourse* thus: 'one of the best racing machines I've ever ridden ...'

Grant's team mate McGregor suffered a near-worse fate. His flat-out tank-slapper at Greeba Castle during the opening lap was so violent he suffered a broken collar-bone, without even crashing! Rex White recalls the team's trail of broken engines:

We had terrible trouble with reliability. We finally discovered it was a lubrication problem caused by over-tuning. Shell tried so hard to develop special oil and we modified the oiling system internally to get more lubricant to the big ends. We even tried using Motul oil, which was supplied to us by the importer, Tom Walkinshaw [now a leading figure in the car racing industry and owner of the Arrows TTF1 car team]. It was better but didn't overcome the problems.

With the British season starting early, on 17 March 1955 at Thruxton, Grant was forced to use his old air-cooled bike to claim third place behind Honda duo Marshall and Burnett.

The official Heron Suzuki bike arrived in kit form on Thursday at the Shell Oils Transatlantic Trophy meeting over Easter at Donington and were built up overnight and then raced in the Transatlantic rounds during the weekend. With everyone else mounted on 500GP bikes, Grant was always going to struggle but it was only when the motor was dyno'd straight after the meeting that it was discovered how much of a struggled he had actually had.

On successive dyno runs, it produced just 107bhp at the gearbox, at 12,700rpm, roughly translating to 120–122 at the crank – a far cry from the '130–137 depending on specification' White claimed Yoshimura had quoted! And just to ensure it was not simply a duff motor, the team's spare was also run up and produced a similar figure. To put it in perspective, the TTF1 engine produced only 7bhp more than the stock Superstock engine, and only 1bhp more than the previous year's air-cooled GSX-750R.

This meant that Suzuki were effectively running 10–15bhp down on the RVF Hondas raced by Marshall, Burnett and Joey Dunlop. In addition, the Suzuki power delivery was very peaky, with a usable power-band of around 600–800rpm, whereas the V4 Honda offered a wide spread of torquey horsepower. Alan Cathcart, who tested both bikes at Snetterton, discovered that a typical lap required twenty gear changes per 1.92 miles (3.09km) on the Suzuki, compared to just nine on the Honda!

The motor was based closely on the stock GSX-R unit, even running a stock crank that was lightened and polished. Polished steel con-rods arrived mid-season from Japan, and were fitted after the early failures. Forged, three-ring pistons were used, stock steel 26mm inlet/22mm exhaust valves, stock oil pumps, racing camshafts (hollow like the road bike's but with more duration and lift) plus a flowed and polished cylinder head. The Heron crew also fitted larger oil pipes (20 per cent larger than stock) to the large oil radiator.

Carbs were stock flatslide 29mm alloy-bodied Mikunis bored to 33.6mm – although the team did have one set of trick Mikunis. Carburation glitches dogged the team. White admits:

I think that not having the best carburettors was the biggest contributing factor to our lack of horsepower. We picked up a set from Yoshimura in the States. They cost us £3,000 – half the price they would have cost in the UK. The management would not allow me to buy any more. Mick had the trick carbs.

The same CDI ignited the race bike as was used on the Superstocker, but with a

The TTF1 GSX-R breathed through four 33.6mm flatslide Mikunis. Note the factory dry clutch. (Alan Cathcart Archive)

rev-limiter of 13,000rpm, although Grant never used to spin the motor beyond 11,500rpm. The hydraulically operated wet clutch was replaced with a cable-operated dry clutch.

The TTF1 bike, with its extruded, light alloy, square-tubed frame, was much more compact than the Superstocker with a much shorter wheelbase (54.25in/1,380mm for the TTF1 versus 56.75in/1,440mm). The riding position was much more cramped, the chassis geometry being more like that of the

Mk8 RG500 Suzuki square-four, two-stroke production GP bike.

The bike came equipped with 18in wheels but the team switched to 16in ones front and rear, steepened the head angle to 25 degrees by fitting different steering-head inserts, and fitted it with the same suspension as the Superstock bike, including a White Power rear shock fitted to a beefed-up rear suspension pivot and a braced-up swing-arm. Only after the bike had bottomed out all around the TT course and proved virtu-

The Superstocker used four 29mm flatslide Mikunis and stock wet clutch. (Alan Cathcart Archive)

ally unridable did the team discover than it offered only the same 4in (100mm) of travel that the Superstock bike had, and not 7in (175mm) as they had thought. The problem was then rectified by fitting a Kayaba shock. The dry weight was 312lb (142kg). But White recalls:

The chassis featured some castings in the frame fabrication where previously the frame was entirely fabricated. The rear shock pivot (a casting) used to flex. It was overloaded and eventually would crack. We had to reinforce that. It was a pain. You get a brand new bike and expect to just get out there and blitz everyone but it didn't happen that way …

The 16in wheels and tyres gave us a headache too. There were ground clearance problems but the real worry was the quality of the tyre. The idea was to give a bigger footprint of rubber on the road but the compounds were not always good. Sometimes they were super-grippy and would be destroyed before the end of a race. Other times they lacked grip. And the tyres didn't like being heated up, cooled and then heated again. Even a four-lap practice session was enough to alter the grip factor in the tyre when it came to using it for the race.

Of the seven British TTF1 rounds, Suzuki won only one – at Scarborough, when Honda were absent at the *Bol d'Or* in Southern France. Graeme McGregor headed an all-Suzuki rostrum ahead of Trevor Nation and Grant, who had lost second gear.

The Dealer Team Suzuki effort collapsed. Dave Morris's fourth place in the second round at Donington was arguably the best result for a Suzuki privateer all year – and the engine preparation was down to him: the 'special' customer-kit engines had not even arrived then. In Honda's absence Trevor Nation did, however, finish second at the Scarborough round when Grant was hindered by that missing second gear.

Grant (62 points) still finished second in the final points standings to Honda's Marshall (90 points) while McGregor (45 points) was fourth overall behind Burnett (58 points).

Motocourse illustrated Grant's frustration at battling against the V4 Hondas in the TTF1 arena by repeating something he said at Cadwell: 'Honda have stolen a jump on us but the Suzuki factory haven't put much emphasis on F1 – I'm sure they could build something competitive if they wanted.'

Grant also finished second in the World TTF1 Championship. McGregor finished third but the Suzukis were again defeated by Honda – specifically, Joey Dunlop's awesome RVF750. Grant's best ride was a second place at Assen on 29 June; McGregor and Grant also finished second and third in the stifling heat of Vila Real on 7 July. Both times Dunlop was the winner. In the final round on the 7.4-mile (11.9km) Dundrod course in Northern Ireland it was the same story: Grant had to battle with McGregor to claim yet another runner-up spot to Dunlop. White recalls:

I think Mick became paranoid towards the end of the year. He knew he could win the Superstock title and I'm sure he stopped sticking his neck out in the other races. You could tell by the lap times. He never said he was planning to retire but his attitude changed towards the end of the year – like the danger side of the sport was getting to him. I think he decided enough was enough and it was time to get out – and getting out with the Superstock title was a great way to end his career.

World Endurance

Honda also took the World Endurance honours but Suzuki had their moments of glory in the six-race series. Dominique

Meliand's SERT (Suzuki Endurance Racing Team) outfit had factory bikes very similar to those of the British Heron Suzuki team. They weighed just 346lb (152kg) with oil but no fuel, including the lights and generator. SERT retained the 18in wheels but had an option to switch to 17in later in the year when new Michelin radials were ready. Different camshafts, pistons, exhaust system, lightened crank and a close ratio gearbox helped push power output up to 132bhp at 13,000rpm.

Le Mans in April, a non-championship round in 1985, was still considered a major event – and a prelude to the World Championship. It attracted no fewer than twenty-two GSX-R-equipped entries, including the two SERT bikes. There were ten bikes with the full race kit, including special frames and so on.

Strangely, SERT entered only two riders per bike (three were permitted) and both crews hit problems. Moineau, who qualified on pole, crashed in the morning warm-up, 'racing' Honda's Gerard Coudray. He took part in the 24-Hour event, and, heavily bandaged and part-nered by Richard Hubin, managed to finish second.

Patrick de Radigues crashed the other bike. He pushed back but, with two broken ribs and a fractured ankle, left only Jean-Pierre Oudin to ride so the team had to be withdrawn. With a third rider the team could have continued.

Suzuki were still able to celebrate a victory, however. A privateer team, funded by a consortium of Marseilles dealers, won the race when GP250 star Guy Bertin, Phillipe Gouchon and Bernard Millet took the lead after both Rothmans Honda RVFs were sidelined with broken frames.

Swedish privateers Anders Andersson and Per Jansson won the Six-Hour at the Österreichring, Austria, beating the works Honda! Kevin Schwantz and Graeme Crosby finished third. Meanwhile Shosuke Kita/Satoshi Tsujimoto were fifth in the Suzuka Eight-Hour on Yoshimura GSX-R750s. Suzuki may have not won the prestigious race (Honda did with Wayne Gardner and Masaki Tokuno) but GSX-Rs ridden by Patrick de Radigues/Jean

After winning the Austrian 1,000km and becoming the main challenger to Honda in the series, Anders Andersson's team was invited to the Suzuka Eight-Hour. When they arrived at the factory team workshop they discovered a bike specially for them (number 19). Here the bikes are loaded up on the team transporter ready to go to the track! (Anders Andersson Collection)

Phillipe Oudin and Herve Moineau/ Richard Hubin finished fifth and seventh respectively ahead of eighth-placed Andersson/Jansson – and the Swedes continued to lead the points chase.

Two weeks later the French-entered SERT Suzuki took the Spa 24-Hours – where eight of the first ten qualifiers were Suzuki-mounted – with Jean-Pierre Oudin/Richard Hubin/Herve Moineau in the saddle. Oudin finished third overall in the series behind Honda's winners, Gerard Coudray and Patrick Igoa.

Maybe Suzuki did not sweep the board with their GSX-R750 in 1985 but the achievements in winning the production and Superstock classes showed just how competitive the bike was in relatively stock trim. In open class four-stroke competition it was certainly not disgraced either, and lessons learned from the season would be put to good use for 1986.

3   America On-Line

A year after its 'world' launch, Suzuki's GSX-R750 hit the American market. Following the ballyhoo of the 1985 model launch the 1986 base machine received only minor updates. The G model, first imported into the UK in May 1986, came with a 20mm-longer swing-arm to take the wheelbase to 57.3in (1,455mm). Cosmetically the exhaust system now had a slotted heat shield on the muffler instead of the perforated one. And there was a new one-piece dual seat.

The fairing had a taller belly-pan shape, which pointed forwards. Air ducts in the fairing side panels were revised. Flatter mirror housings were used instead of mirrors set in pods. Full Floater graphics moved from the side panels to the tailpiece, under the GSX-R750 logo. *Superbike* magazine said in its July 1986 issue:

They've added three quarters of an inch to the swing-arm to improve top end stability ... But for some new big end bolts, differently finished con-rods and a slightly revised silencer, the motor is unchanged – 100bhp of cammy, humpy brute power ... The '86 GSX-R reinforces what you already knew, it's a hard rider's machine – lean, light and functional. It wasn't developed from the racetrack, it was built for the racetrack.

The Limited Edition Suzuki launched in 1986 was a great hit with the racers – for those who could buy one! (Alan Cathcart Archive)

GSX-R750 Limited Edition (1986)

Four-cylinder, four-stroke, oil-cooled, DOHC, TSCC, four valves per cylinder

Engine
Bore and stroke	70mm x 48.7mm
Cubic capacity	749cc
Compression ratio	10.6:1
Carburettors	4 Mikuni VM29SS
Ignition	Transistorized
Starter system	Electric
Lubrication system	Wet sump

Transmission
Clutch	Dry, multi-plate type
Gearbox	Six-speed, constant mesh

Suspension
Front suspension	Posi Damp Fork System, 41mm telescopic, coil spring, oil-dampened, spring, four-way adjustable
Rear suspension	Full Floater, spring preload fully adjustable, damping force, four-way adjustable

Brakes and Tyres
Front brake	310mm floating Twin disc, hydraulically operated twin Deca piston
Rear brake	Single 220mm disc, hydraulically operated
Front tyre	110/80V-18 V250 radial
Rear tyre	140/70V-18 V250 radial

Dimensions (in/mm)
Overall length	83.2in/2,115mm
Overall width	29.3/745mm
Overall height	47.8/1,215mm
Wheelbase	57.3/1,455mm
Ground clearance	5/125mm
Seat height	31.3/795mm
Dry weight	387lb (176kg)

The LTD in action – Gary Goodfellow won the 1986 Canadian 750cc Production Championship with this machine. Note the dry clutch. (Colin Fraser)

Michel Mercier raced a tricked-out version of the LTD to victory in the Canadian Superbike Championship. (Colin Fraser)

THE LIMITED EDITION

While the UK market GSX-R remained virtually unchanged, in the US a new model was launched: the Suzuki GSX-R750 LTD – Limited Edition. American-based Cycle magazine did not pull any punches with its introduction of its test: 'The LTD is more than flashy paint, flawless fibreglass and trick parts. It's a true factory-built special, a limited edition in every sense, designed for the racetrack, sold for the street, and priced somewhere in between.'

It sold for $6,499 in the States – $2,000 more than the base model – and was bought mainly by racers. The bike never reached the UK showrooms. According to Martyn Ogborne, formerly with Suzuki's GP team but now working in Suzuki's marketing department: 'Heron Suzuki had plenty of stock without importing the expensive Limited.'

What made the LTD so special? Mostly changes to the chassis. For a start there were fully floating 310mm front brake rotors, four-piston calipers and master cylinder all from the GSX-R1100.

Also up front were beefy 41mm front forks with NEAS (New Electrically Activated Suspension) anti-dive – also from the 1100 but with spring and damping rates to suit the lighter 750 model. As *Cycle* pointed out: 'these changes would enable the rider to exploit the traction limit of racing slicks.'

There were also a three-point steering damper, wider clip-on handlebars, and a special aluminium-bodied rear shock with a remote, gas-oil charged reservoir to overcome the stock steel unit's reputation for overheating. Cutaway sides to the solo seat also allowed cool air to pass through the Full Floater suspension cavity behind the motor where heat build-up on the standard model obviously caused the stock suspension to overheat and fade.

The LTD motor featured a lightened countershaft sprocket cover – and most exciting of all, a cable-actuated dry clutch as seen on the works racers in

Contingency Cash Breeds Success

Doug Polen – in at the start of the GSX-R750 year in 1985 and back in the saddle of the works Suzuki in 1996 with the all-new GSX-R750T. (Kel Edge)

Suzuki's GSX-R750 and the later GSX-R1100 formed the backbone of club racing in the United States thanks to a generous contingency bonus scheme posted for a mono-marque race series by American Suzuki – the GSX-R Cup with classes for the 750 and 1100 machines.

The series offered racers the chance to compete on equal machinery – and earn good money. Doug Polen made more than $90,000 racing a GSX-R750 during the 1986 season.

What the success of the series did was to ensure that the GSX-R series of motorcycles became the big success story of the eighties. And the series continues even into 1997 – extended back to three classes with the introduction of the all-new GSX-R600 (a three-class format was also run in 1989, 1992 and 1993).

From 1986–96 Suzuki paid out $2,785,000 in series contingency money. The highest annual purse was in 1992 when Suzuki paid $350,000 covering three classes. Kurt Hall won all three classes in 1992. The Cup Final purse during the same eleven-year period equalled $530,000. The highest Cup Final purse was paid in 1993, with $70,000 posted for three classes plus the Can-Am Cup.

Polen had retired from racing in 1983, unable to secure the backing to break out of the Texan club scene even though he was breaking lap records and wining races regularly. His interest in racing was rekindled by the announcement of the GSX-R National Cup series for the 1986 season – thanks to its impressive contingency prize fund.

Being effectively club-level racing, entering the series meant Polen went racing every weekend all over the US, learned new tracks and earned a living from Suzuki cash. He was not the only rider to adopt this approach, but he was by far the most successful!

The initial idea behind the series – established by Suzuki Japan official, Hank Ohta, who is now the President of Suzuki Philippines – was that American Suzuki wanted a contingency programme to support the people who were going racing with the GSX-R750.

Ohta established links with local club organizations across the US to develop a contingency bonus scheme for finishers in various classes of races who were Suzuki mounted. Cup points have always been allotted to the races with the lowest spec classes, be it production in the early days of the series, through Superstock, to Supersport in recent years. The aim has been to ensure minimum modifications to machinery.

The Cup currently runs in ten different geographical regions with the top five point scorers in each class being invited to Road Atlanta for the Cup Finals during October (the only time the Finals raced elsewhere was in 1987 at Riverside – the circuit has since been bulldozed and is now a shopping mall!).

Bill Syfan, American Suzuki's Sports Promotion Supervisor, whose job description includes management of the Suzuki GSX-R Cup remarks:

We've always tried to pay (contingency money) in the class with the least mods to let the public see that these bikes are very close to what people can go and buy.

We never ran completely stock because the classes evolved. Back when the Cup started there were clubs running 'production' with stock pipes etc but now only one club in all of the States is running a true production class with stock exhausts. The rules across the country are much closer now – most run very similar Supersport rules.

While there are the minimum of mods at club events, the Finals are strictly policed and run to one set of rules – identical to the Supersport 750 rules employed by the hosting club, WERA (Western Eastern Roadracers' Association). Syfan adds:

The guys know this beforehand. I send out a WERA rule book with the invitation to every rider. All the rules are very close now anyway [between various clubs]. It's been far easier in the last five years than it was in the eighties.

We've not had too many 'incidents' either [when discussing the controversy one might expect to erupt with a spec-bike class]. Sure, we had some guys disqualified for illegal engine mods but only one since I've been involved. One year Kurt Hall ran a different master cylinder on his bike than was allowed. He wasn't disqualified but he was fined heavily. It's been pretty straight forward the past few years.

In addition to cash, points are accrued on a local level, and then the top GSX-R riders from each club are invited to compete in the Suzuki Cup Final – a prestigious event at the end of the year at Road Atlanta held during WERA's Grand Finals.

A major marketing ploy at the outset was to ensure the Suzuki Cup Final races were televised, even if none of the other local Cup races were. So come the end of the year all the top racers from ten different regions arrived in Georgia for the final shootout – a major event. Syfan recalls:

In the first year when Doug Polen came out of semi-retirement he got a 750 and an 1100 Suzuki and went out and won some $90,000. He travelled all over, hitting something like sixty club events. It was a crazy travel schedule but it kind of put him back on the map.

Syfan has been with Suzuki for five years and was initially hired to run Suzuki's contingency programme:

It's still my main mission there. I had worked on the other side, from the club's side, sending results to the company. But since then my job has evolved into running support teams.

However, contingency is still very important. We had a big push last year [1996] with the new bike. But we've always had a strong contingency programme and the most consistent. We've seen other manufacturers set up similar programmes but we're the only ones who have stuck with it.

We've been pretty consistent with the amount of money we pay, the number of events we pay. Since I've been at Suzuki we've paid seventy-five club events every year. That's a lot of money.

Canada has also had its own GSX-R Cup series, on a smaller scale than the US version. In 1993 there was a Can-Am Cup Final during the Road Atlanta meeting. Syfan again: 'We fielded our top five guys from the 750 race from earlier in the day against the top five Canadians from their series. It was fun and Mario Duhamel managed to get on the box (in third place) for the Canadians.' Canadians still compete in the GSX-R Cup Finals but are now integrated into the regular programme rather than racing in a Match Race format.

Despite the strong Cup series at home, and America's reputation for laying waste to almost any race series their riders compete in abroad, there was never any regular representation of the stars and stripes in the Suzuki World Cup. Even when Polen raced in the F1 class it was a 'Japanese' effort. Syfan explains:

I think Suzuki wanted to build the series here rather than send Americans to Europe. There were too many costs involved to send our winners over there. Also the scheduling didn't help. Our event traditionally is in mid-to-late October – and we have always had qualifying races right up to within two weeks of the finals.

For all that, the American series roll of honour reads like a who's who of Stateside stars. Doug Polen won four titles, two in the 750 class; he went on to the Yoshimura factory ride and later won back-to-back World Superbike titles with Ducati. Scott Russell won two 750 GSX-R Cup titles. He then joined the Yoshimura team and later won the World Superbike crown with Kawasaki. Britt Turkington won the 1991 750 class and then joined Yosh to win the AMA Supersport 750 title. Aaron Yates won the 1995 750 class Cup. The following year he joined the Yoshimura team, won his first AMA Superbike race, and clinched the AMA Supersport 750 title – all in his first year as a factory rider! Of the American GSX-R Cup, Syfan concludes:

If you look at the winners over the years it reads like a who's who of American factory riders. There's no doubt Suzuki Cup success looks good on the resumé. We don't allow factory riders to compete in the series: it's for the 'privateer'. Most of the guys get some sort of help but the series didn't ever develop any kind of dealer involvement.

Back in 1986 it was $1,300 per race win. But for past eight years it's been $500. That's still decent money if you win all three classes (750, 1100 and 600) and travel but there are not the people earning a living now like back when it started. Roadracing has become so professional here now that people realize they have to go out and do the AMA Pro races to get noticed.

We'll continue though. The series helps sell a lot of GSX-Rs; that's great for Suzuki and a fantastic tradition built over the past eleven years.

Suzuki Cup Final winners (750 class only):

1986	Doug Polen	
1987	Doug Polen	
1988	Scott Russell	
1989	Scott Russell	
1990	Tommy Lynch	
1991	Britt Turkington	
1992	Kurt Hall	
1993	Gerald Rothman	
	Can-Am Cup	Gerald Rothman
1994	James Randolph	
1995	Aaron Yates	
1996	Mark Miller	

All finals raced at Road Atlanta except 1987, raced at Riverside.

Kevin Schwantz finished second to Eddie Lawson on the Yoshimura Suzuki – the first time the GSX-R750 raced in AMA Superbike competition. Note the trick Kayaba forks with brake-operated anti-dive from a GP500 machine. (Alan Cathcart Archive)

A Yoshimura Suzuki at Daytona in 1986 – this is Tsujimoto's machine. (Alan Cathcart Archive)

1985. It gave the street GSX-R that distinctively rattly 'works bike' noise!

The LTD fairing had additional ducting – one on the lower left and one on the lower right to direct cool air towards the dry clutch – and there was a new solo seat. The LTD weighed 458lb (208kg) – 6lb (2.7kg) lighter than the stock model.

After testing the LTD, *Cycle* magazine concluded:

The LTD is wasted if it never turns a wheel on the racetrack. The $2,000 premium that turns a GSX-R into an LTD will be too stiff for most riders anyway but for the racer, who would pay much more to duplicate the LTD's racing components, two grand is a pittance.

The LTD is the real thing, the ultimate factory-prepared, finish-it-yourself racer. They simply don't come off the showroom floor any closer to the race track than this. Or any better.

AMA RACING

Arrival of the GSX-R in US showrooms also meant that the model was now eligible for AMA Superbike racing, and Suzuki equalled their best-ever result in the 200 when Kevin Schwantz took his Yoshimura GSX-R750 to second place behind the factory-prepared Yamaha FZ750 of Eddie Lawson. With Honda-mounted Fred Merkel third on a V4 Honda VFR Interceptor, there were three different manufacturers in the top three – the first time this had happened at the 200 since 1976, thus underlining the growing appeal of Superbike racing.

Suzuki's previous best visit to the Victory Lane podium had been way back in 1969, when expatriate Briton Ron Grant also finished runner-up to Harley's Cal Rayborn on a TR500, two-stroke twin.

Yoshimura fielded four 'factory' bikes at the 1986 Daytona for Schwantz and Japanese TTF1 Champion, Satoshi Tsujimoto. The British Heron Suzuki team also had out-of-retirement Kork Ballington on their Skoal Bandit-liveried machine (more on the British team later). Ballington stayed in the States after Daytona, signing to race an RS500 Honda triple for Bob MacLean.

Revvin' Kevin

Kevin Schwantz rode for Yoshimura R & D for three full seasons. He never won the AMA Superbike crown, and only ever won the Daytona 200 once – but by then he had been groomed for stardom and was on his way to race full-time in the GPs for Lucky Strike Suzuki.

But the Yoshimura years shaped Schwantz's career and during those three seasons he became known as the fastest and most spectacular superbike rider in the United States.

Schwantz was signed by Yoshimura for the 1985 season after John Ulrich, currently the owner and editor of *Roadracing World* but back then editor of *American Roadracing,* had persuaded Yoshimura team boss Suehiro Watanabe to give the young charger a test.

In Peter Clifford's outstanding book, *Kevin Schwantz – the World's Champion,* Ulrich recalls how the Yosh team was low on budget and needed a hot talent to put its GS700 on the pace in AMA Superbike competition against the works Hondas.

Schwantz won three races during 1985 and eventually finished second in the series, even though the Yoshimura team had not planned on doing the full schedule. In fact Ulrich recalls in Clifford's book that American Suzuki actually came up with some run budget for two races that Yoshimura had not planned on doing.

For 1986 Yoshimura's Stateside effort escalated to coincide with the appearance of the new GSX-R750. Schwantz finished second to Lawson at Daytona but the bike was beset by problems and Schwantz recalled the year in Clifford's book by saying; "'86 is probably best forgotten, one of those seasons that started off good and just went downhill from there _ It was a humbling year. The best you could say is that it was character building.'

The following year started differently. Schwantz crashed at Daytona while leading but he won five of the last six rounds. However, another crash, in the second race of the two-leg Laguna Seca round, proved a crucial error and Wayne Rainey won the title.

After several trips to Europe during 1987, Schwantz signed to ride for a full Lucky Strike GP500 team in 1988, so his only Stateside Superbike race was Daytona. After an early scrap with Doug Polen, who was riding his 1987 bike, Schwantz, on a special bike from Japan based on Suzuki's new long-stroke engine, won the 200. The motor was not quick, however, and even today Fujio Yoshimura attributes the victory to the riding skill of Kevin Schwantz.

There are no Superbike titles in the record books, but lots of race wins – and some memories of races lost through crashes. But everyone remembers the Superbike years of Schwantz and the Yoshimura Suzuki GSX-R750 and perhaps Watanabe's comments in Clifford's book best sum up Schwantz's attitude to racing:

He was always impressive when he rode for us. He never gave up. Some people talked about the fact that he fell down, that he made a mistake. I didn't feel that. I wouldn't call them mistakes, he was just trying very hard.

It took Schwantz a long time to lose his youthful enthusiasm for riding on, and sometimes beyond, the ragged edge – way beyond the Yosh years that helped shape his future. But the world's racing fans benefited by being treated to the antics of this spectacular racer. And the World 500GP title finally came for the people's champion in 1993.

Left: Tsujimoto's bike featured a different front end to Schwantz's with internal anti-dive in the hand-crafted Kayabas. (Alan Cathcart Archive)

Below: Former 250/350 World Champion Kork Ballington had a run out on a Skoal Bandit-backed GSX-R750 at Daytona in 1986. Compared to the Yosh bikes, Ballington's was relatively stock. (Alan Cathcart Archive)

The Yosh and Heron bikes differed in that the American team ran 18in wheels with Dunlop tyres while the Britons continued to use Michelins with a 16in front wheel (the SERT endurance bike ran 17in wheels!).

The Heron bike had a stock-looking GSXR-R750 frame but the Yoshimura team had heavily braced theirs with plating and gusseting. All the bikes were under the AMA's 390lb (177kg) weight limit and had to be ballasted. This was achieved by adding lead shot in the lower alloy frame rails, alternator and starter-motor cavities; Rex White still has the alternator with the lead shot in his home workshop. Ballington's bike had the most lead added – some 8lb (18kg)!

The Yosh bikes all looked similar except that Schwantz's bike had RG500-type Kayaba forks with brake-operated anti-dive. Tsujimoto's machine, however, featured special hand-crafted Kayabas with Forcelli Italia-type internal hydraulic anti-dive.

At the time, AMA rules permitted a 1mm overbore, hence the Yosh bikes' bore and stroke of 71mm x 48.7mm displacing 771cc. Internals featured the usual Yosh-developed package of trick camshafts, pistons, valve springs, rods, crank, ported cylinder head. The bikes also had their own special exhaust system (incorporating cylindrical balance chambers linking each pair of header pipes to improve low down power delivery of the otherwise peaky engine performance), 36mm flatslide Mikunis, 12.5:1 compression and claimed 131bhp at 12,000rpm. The motors also had dry clutches like the new LTD street rod.

Roland Brown raced this stock-looking GSX-R in the British Superstock series. Brown was one of many competitors to embrace the low-cost formula. (Kel Edge)

At the end of March Schwantz travelled to England and borrowed an ex-Tony Rutter Kidderminster Motorcycle Mart Suzuki to top the scorers in the eight-race Shell Oils Transatlantic Challenge at Donington Park over the Easter period.

A season that started so well soon turned sour, however, with Schwantz often being the fastest qualifier in AMA Superbike but then finding his efforts blunted by bikes that kept blowing up or crashes. Honda's Fred Merkel won the title, which was determined by a strange aggregate score of Superbike and Formula One points. Schwantz did not record one race win all year and finished way down the point standings in tenth place. Canadian Gary Goodfellow – expatriate New Zealander, GP motocross competitor and AMA rookie road racer – was the top Suzuki Superbike rider of the year in seventh place overall with an impressive third at Brainerd behind Honda factory duo, Wayne Rainey and Merkel.

Moineau on the 1986 endurance bike, now with underslung brace on swing-arm, and Lockheed single pot front brake caliper. Note the bracing on the top frame rails – this was to be adopted as a styling feature on subsequent GSX-Rs. (Kel Edge)

SKOAL BANDIT

For the Heron Suzuki team the season promised much, started slowly, picked up pace mid-season then ended in tragedy with the death of their rider, Neil Robinson.

The team won backing from Skoal Bandit, producers of a smokeless tobacco that came in small pouches, popular in the United States and marketed heavily in Europe. Skoal, owned by US Tobacco, had backed the Suzuki GP team of Rob McElnea and Paul Lewis in 1985 and that deal continued into 1986. However, the budget was limited and by 1987 all the funds would go to the F1 team leaving the 500 crew to chase new backers. They got Pepsi on board for 1988.

Mick Grant had retired at the end of 1985 so Paul Iddon, who had finished

runner-up in the European 500cc Championship the previous year, and up-and-coming Chris Martin were signed for the World and British championships. The bikes were essentially the same as the 1985s – with revised cylinder heads.

But after two rounds of the World Championship, it was Anders Andersson, the thinking man's racer from Sweden, who led the championship on his Suzuki Sweden GSX-R750 – a works bike very similar in specification to the Heron team bikes, but with more emphasis placed on technical development.

Marc Lucchinelli had won the opening round at Misano with a new eight-valve, desmo V-twin Ducati. Andersson was second, followed by another Suzuki, ridden by Australian Rob Phillis, who was

Above: Skoal Bandit team boss Rex White with Neil 'Smutty' Robinson (left) and Paul Iddon. (Rex White Collection)

Left: Chris Martin at Brands with the Skoal Bandit Superstocker. (Rex White Collection)

Skoal Bandit F1 bike at Misano – not a great weekend for the team. (Alan Cathcart Archive)

making his European debut aboard Roberto Gallina's Yoshimura Suzuki.

For the Skoal team it was a disaster. Both bikes blew up and Neil Robinson's private Suzuki went out with sheared sprocket bolts. Meanwhile Iddon's crank failure also spelled disaster for privateer Andy McGladdery, who crashed on the subsequent oil slick and broke his collarbone.

Neither Lucchinelli nor Phillis appeared in the eight-round series again but Andersson grabbed the points lead after a third place finish behind winner Dunlop and Iddon at Hockenheim.

Yet Andersson's lead was not destined to last. Dunlop predictably won the TT and the Assen round but the trip to Holland brought significant changes to the ailing Skoal Bandit team fortunes.

Trevor Nation finished fourth in a 750 Production TT dominated by GSX-Rs. He also won the 1100 event on the Island. (Kel Edge)

The Skoal Bandit is in the foreground but on the far side of the grid at the Assen TTF1 round is that man Schwantz, this time racing a 500 Suzuki based on the Gamma roadster.

In the British championship, Iddon had scored a solitary second place in the Mallory second round but otherwise the season had been a disaster with broken valves, pistons, rods and bearings littering the pit garage floors!

Irish rider Neil Robinson also had problems with his privateer Suzuki. After finishing fourth in the British Championship TTF1 round at Donington the previous week, he needed some parts before he could join the grid at Assen. He knocked on the Skoal Bandit Suzuki coach door to ask Rex White if he could borrow some spares and ended up being offered a ride with the team, who were a man short after Martin had crocked his elbow in a crash at the very same Donington race.

Martin's form had been a disappointment. Rex White reflects:

Chris moaned a lot about vibration from the engine but Paul never complained. We discovered Chris was always under-geared compared with Paul's set-up, and consequently buzzing the engine. Chris was making the transition from racing a 500 two-stroke and it seemed he was trying to ride the F1 bike the same way. He never lived up to the potential he had shown the previous year on his own 500.

Robinson took up White's offer and very nearly won the race. He was leading with three laps to run when a knackered rear drive chain jammed up the rear wheel. Robinson's consolation was a new lap record of 2m 19.63s. Iddon, however, came third, just behind Kevin Schwantz, who was riding the same RG500 road bike John Weeden had raced at the TT. Martin would later race the bike when he recovered from injury.

Iddon won the Spanish round in the 100-degree heat of the brand new Jerez

The 1986 Suzuki GSX-R. (Genn Bayly Collection)

circuit to get within 14 points of series leader Dunlop who had been involved in a car crash en route home from Assen and was still suffering from five broken ribs. Robinson was third in the race behind Graeme McGregor who was on Steve Wynne's Ducati.

Iddon's Jerez success was Suzuki's first World TTF1 victory since the class regulations had limited engines to 750cc. The previous Suzuki winner had been Rob McElnea in 1983 at the Dutch round!

Dunlop and the RVF bounced back to win the Vila Real race in Portgual but Suzukis filled the next six places with Iddon and Andersson both on the rostrum. Much of the reliability shown by the Skoal Bandit team was brought about by using a larger selection of stock road bike internals rather than the tricked-out race kit equipment they had started the year with.

Dunlop, however, wrapped up the title by winning the penultimate round at Imatra in Finland. Iddon, Robinson, Andersson completed the top four – Robinson having led until he was slowed down by a puncture. Again, White recalls Robinson's plucky nature:

Smutty [Robinson] had a clear lead with three laps to go then came into the pits with a flat rear tyre. Nigel checked it over and said there was no chance the tyre would come off the rim and sent Neil back out into the race. Smutty knew exactly what the problem was and just did enough to finish.

The final round was at Dundrod, where the fast-emerging Robinson finally took a well-deserved victory, defeating the local hero in his own backyard. Dunlop had made the wrong choice of tyres for the wet conditions. Sadly, less than one month later, Robinson was killed in a crash at Oliver's Mount, Scarborough, during the British TTF1 round. White recalls:

Smutty was a nice bloke – one of the nicest I ever worked with. He was very determined on the track but so easy going and fun-loving off it. And he was just coming good.

I always left Scarborough to the riders. If they wanted to ride it was their choice. It was the same for the TT. If they didn't go there was no animosity from the company, no lost wages etc. All our riders always wanted to do the North West and the Ulster anyway but we tended to sign one rider who was keen to do the TT [and Scarborough] anyway – success there [the TT] still got a lot of publicity. Smutty was an all-rounder and wanted to race at Scarborough – but it turned out to be a terrible weekend.

In the final championship analysis, Iddon finished the series runner-up to Dunlop, with Andersson third and Robinson fourth. Iddon also won a round of the British championship at Silverstone in late September and finished fifth in the final championship table despite not contesting the full series.

The title was won by Mark Phillips, riding a Padgetts Suzuki RG500 (a 500 Gamma road bike engine in a Mk10 race chassis!) but GSX-R750s in the hands of Ray Swann and Andy McGladdery also won races in the six-round series.

SUZUKI FORTUNES ELSEWHERE

GSX-Rs dominated the 750cc Metzeler Production Championship for the second successive season, with Phil Mellor edging two points ahead of Trevor Nation to clinch the title – even though Mellor raced the final Cadwell round in agony with a broken wrist. Seven of the eight races were won by Mellor (three) and Nation (four).

But in Superstock the honours this time went to Yamaha and Kenny Irons. Nation and Huewen won two races apiece on Suzukis but Irons won the other five to clinch the series with 118 points to Honda's consistent Richard Scott's 105. Huewen finished third overall.

Suzuki's promise shown at the tail end of the 1985 World Endurance Championship sadly did not come to fruition in 1986. Honda steam-rollered all six races in the series – and the non-championship *Bol d'Or*. Herve Moineau and Bruno Le Bihan finished fourth overall on Meliand's SERT entry.

Rob Phillis made a sensational European debut, finishing third at Misano on a Yosh Suzuki sporting the decals of his Australian Suzuki backer, Mick Hone. He took no further part in the series, however. (Kel Edge)

The SERT works bike was said to produce 132bhp, breathing through four Mikuni 34mm flatslides with the motor boasting 12:1 compression. Showa suspension was used front (40mm forks with adjustable spring pre-load and compression damping) and rear. Wheels were 17in Campagnolos front (3.5in) and rear (5.5in) shod with Michelin rubber. Front brakes were twin floating discs with Lockheed twin-piston calipers. Weight, with all the lighting and associated electrical gear in place, was 156kg.

In the Suzuka Eight-Hour, Schwantz teamed up with Tsujimoto – who won the All Japan series for a second successive season – and finished third behind Honda winners Wayne Gardner and Dominique Sarron and the Yamaha of Australians Michael Dowson and Kevin Magee. Yoshimura's other entry, Yukiya Ohshima and Shoji Miyazaki – Tsujimoto's team mate in the All Japan series – finished tenth.

In Canada Gary Goodfellow won the 750cc Production title riding a Limited Edition model, and even in the southern hemisphere GSX-Rs were doing the winning. Four-time Australian Champion Rob Phillis had lost his crown to the strong Australian Honda effort in 1985 but Mick Hone imported one of the special Yoshimura GSX-R engines for 1986 and Phillis took the title by winning the last race of the year against Malcolm Campbell's tricked-out VFR750, which had a works engine similar to that used by Wayne Gardner at Suzuka. And in South Africa the national production racing series was dominated by Suzukis, with Wayne Heasman taking the title in a last-round decider from New Zealander Dave Hiscock.

4 Suzuki – Enduring World Champions

The GSX-R750H arrived in England early in February 1987 with only minor changes to the previous year's model. There was a revised front mudguard – painted white – and a larger-diameter front wheel spindle. This may not sound very exciting, but the fatter wheel spindle acted as a fork brace, reducing front-end flex; compare similar, but more obvious, thinking on the much later Britten V-twin race bike front-end. Engineer John Britten actually incorporated a huge cast wheel spindle to aid fork bracing.

The GSX-R fairing lower was now dark blue instead of white and the seat came in a darker blue hue. Mirror pods returned on the 1987 model in place of the flatter ones tried in 1986.

A red/black/white version joined the traditional blue/white Suzuki livery in the showrooms, while the side panels sported new Full Floater graphics.

There was also a limited edition, single-seat version of the H in black and gold livery. Basically this was a makeweight model, with more startling changes due a year down the road.

ENDURANCE SUCCESSES

On the racetrack, however, another year of development put the GSX-R750 in a strong position. Herve Moineau and Bruno Le Bihan dominated the World Endurance series with an impressive string of podium finishes – including

Schwantz fought a bitter, season-long struggle with Honda's Wayne Rainey for the AMA Superbike title. (Alan Cathcart Archive)

Schwantz's Yosh engine incorporated Carillo rods to overcome weaknesses shown in the 1986 motors. Note the 'boost' bottles welded to the exhaust headers. (Alan Cathcart Archive)

three outright victories in the eight-round series.

Since Moineau and Hubin had won the title in 1983 Honda had pretty much dominated the following three years, and no one complained, least of all Meliand's crew, when the big H opted to contest only three major long-distance events in 1987 – the non-championship Le Mans 24-Hours, Suzuka Eight-Hour and the *Bol*.

SERT claimed that horsepower on the 1987 bike was up to 135bhp at 12,000rpm. There was an extra oil-cooler in the fairing nose compared with the 1986 bike. The bike still had 41mm Showa front forks but there were now Nissin four-pot brakes fitted behind the fork legs, replacing the old Lockheed twin-piston calipers. There was also a Showa rear shock but the swing-arm now had bracing atop the arm instead of the old underslung bridge. Three-spoke Marvic 17in wheels replaced the 1986 five-spoke Campagnolo wheels of the same diameter.

Honda's 155bhp oval-piston NR750 was debuted at Le Mans, ridden by Australian hero Mal Campbell plus two journalists, Gilbert Roy of the French magazine *Moto Revue* and Japanese Ken Nemoto of Riders Club. But it was the Rothmans RVF Honda team, consisting of Dominique Sarron, Jean-Louis Battistini and Michel Mattioli, that made the pace. They beat the Moineau/Le Bihan/Jean-Louis Tournadre-ridden Suzuki by two laps even though Honda lost time in the early hours repairing a rear brake problem.

The next round in Estoril lacked the razzmatazz of the hugely popular French race. It also lacked competition for Suzuki, who romped home with a seven-lap winning margin. Endurance racing returned to England in May with the Donington Eight-Hour. The works Suzuki of Moineau and Le Bihan won yet again, but this time came under intense pressure from the British Team MCN Yamaha ridden by Geoff Fowler and Mat Oxley. For the second race in succession, however, the Britons ran short of fuel and lost time as Fowler was forced to push in.

Bimota entered the fray at Monza and won the Six-Hour race with Virginio Ferrari and Davide Tardozzi on their new FZ750 Yamaha-powered YB4, which they were also using to good effect in the World TTF1 Championship. Suzuki finished second to secure a 15-point series lead and then won the Zeltweg Eight-Hour the following week – leading from start to finish.

Suzuka was a different prospect. Moineau had not scored a point there in three years in a race that traditionally not only attracted the very latest trick machinery out of the Japanese manufacturer's R & D workshops, but also boasted the finest line-up of riders imaginable with the top 500GP and four-stroke runners in the world. It was an event that the Japanese used to launch their following year's racing machinery – and to

this day remains the most prestigious event in motorcycle racing.

Therefore in 1987 Suzuka saw the debut of Suzuki's latest factory bike – sporting a new-style chassis with massive aluminium castings, the steering head and swing-arm pivot areas being connected by aluminium extrusions.

The race was an odds-makers nightmare, with all four manufacturers highly competitive. The early battle was between Honda's Wayne Gardner, Kevin Schwantz and Ohshima on a Yoshimura Suzuki and Kork Ballington/Rob Phillis's Kawasaki GPX750.

The Tech 21 Yamaha YZF750 of Kevin Magee and Martin Wimmer was also in contention and took the lead after four hours, when Gardner's partner, Dominique Sarron, crashed. Schwantz had already crashed out and the Suzuki torch was carried very effectively by rising Canadian-based New Zealand hero Gary Goodfellow, and Japanese rider

The frames were beefed up by welding secondary frame rails on the outside of the originals! Note the asbestos sheeting around the carbs – and the very basic attempt at ducting air to the carbs. (Alan Cathcart Archive)

Katsuro Takayoshi on a second Yoshimura entry, sporting Olio Fiat backing.

As dusk descended during the final hour, Takayoshi, holding a narrow lead, crashed after colliding with a backmarker whilst under pressure from Magee, allowing Yamaha to break a three-year dominance of the event by Honda. Even more significantly, Moineau and Le Bihan brought the works Suzuki home in fourth place – a tremendous result considering the competition.

Belgians dominated the Spa 24-Hours with Richard Hubin, back in the SERT line-up and teamed with Michel Simeon and Mark Simul, finishing eight laps in front of fellow countrymen, Johan Van Vaerenberg, Eric de Donker and Paul Ramon. Moineau, Le Bihan and Tournadre had brought back the latest specification GSX-R750 factory bike from Suzuka and finished third, having hauled themselves back into contention

after three crashes! This meant that the Suzuki crew now had a 30-point lead over Van Vaerenberg with two rounds left; they then went on to increase that lead with another easy win, at Jerez.

The big guns were back on the grid for the final round, the *Bol d'Or* at Paul Ricard in Southern France, with all four Japanese manufacturers aiming for a slice of glory in the French classic. The race for the lead went down to a Honda versus Yamaha scrap, and when Patrick Igoa crashed the leading Yamaha just before midday on Sunday, he left Sarron, Battistini and Mattioli to pick up their second French 24-Hour win of the year.

Moineau's team finished third, a long way behind, but the title was theirs – and Suzuki's. Mat Oxley, writing the season review in *Motocourse*, commented: 'Suzuki took third, a massive 12 laps behind the leaders, which proved to all that they'd only won the World title because there was no real competition.'

Kevin Schwantz's front end – 43mm Showas with external spring preload adjusters and independently adjustable high and low-speed compression and rebound damping. Nissin four-pots grip 310mm rotors. (Alan Cathcart Archive)

Doug Polen raced a Kosar Suzuki in 1987. Here he flicks through the Daytona chicane in front of FZR750 Yamaha-mounted Reuben McMurter, and the Suzukis of Anders Andersson and Roger Marshall. (Colin Fraser)

WORLD TTF1

In the other major international four-stroke series, the World TTF1 Championship, Bimota took the honours thanks to a certain Virginio Ferrari, the World 500cc runner-up to Kenny Roberts in 1979. Bimota, like other manufacturers, were using the season to develop a machine ready for the new World Superbike Championship that was mooted for a 1988 green light.

It was the most competitive season of TTF1 ever, with Fred Merkel entering the short circuit races on an Italian-entered Rumi Honda VFR750, prepared by ex-Suzuki factory rider (from the 1970s Formula 750 era), Ron Grant. And there was a top German Hein Gericke-backed team, consisting of Peter Rubatto and Klaus Klein – also on Bimotas.

Skoal Bandit lined up with Paul Iddon again, but only after much political manoevring in the background. Initially, Iddon had been dropped by Rohan – even after an impressive first season with the team in 1986. 'I don't know why Iddon was dropped,' says Rex White. 'I was never consulted. Instead, Kenny

Irons had agreed terms to join us and we had signed Roger Marshall, who had been released from the Honda team.'

But it was the GP500 Suzuki team who eventually secured the services of Irons, the 1986 UK Superstock Champion. Team Manager Martyn Ogborne takes up the story:

First of all Niall Mackenzie had signed a letter of intent to join us but then went elsewhere [to join the HB Honda 500GP team]. Then we tried Raymond Roche but he went to Ducati. Mike Baldwin was the next in line but nothing materialized so we signed Irons.

So Iddon it was, with thirty-five-year-old ex-Honda man Roger Marshall on the Skoal Bandits plus Anders Andersson from Sweden, who made up the main Suzuki threat, while the German importer-backed team of Ernst Gschwender and Bernd Caspers contested the short-circuit races with Kurt Stuckle-prepared machinery. Leading privateers also relied on Suzukis: Briton Andy McGladdery on his home-built GSX-R750-based special and British-based New Zealander Glenn Williams also entered one of the oil-cooled machines.

Does it rate a ten? Schwantz throws away the Daytona 200 lead and arch-rival Rainey wins the race. It would be a crucial result when totting up final points. (Colin Fraser)

And, of course, there was Joey Dunlop on a Honda. Not the all-conquering RVF of 1986 but a VFR750, based more on the roadbike so that Honda too could concentrate on developing the machine in readiness for 1988.

Iddon proved a point when he won the first round in Misano but the big shock was Merkel's second place – ahead of Dunlop, who had lots of suspension problems. Marshall had been following in Iddon's wheeltracks when his GSX-R sprang an oil leak and lubricant began finding its way onto the rear tyre. Andersson ran off the track and head-butted a steel barrier, compressing a vertebra, an injury that was to plague him all year.

The Skoal bikes looked fast, and Iddon proved they were now reliable. White says: 'We got much better equipment in 1987 but the biggest single thing that helped us was using Carillo con-rods. They gave us the reliability we needed.'

Bimota, after problems in Misano, enjoyed a one-two at the Hungagoring, with Ferrari beating Tardozzi. Andersson was third with a split oil-cooler. For the second meeting in succession, Roger Marshall posted the fastest race lap but crashed out – as did Iddon who had a 12-second lead at the time. 'I eased

off then suddenly lost the front end. It cocked me up for the championship,' admitted Iddon is his usual forthright manner in an end of season interview.

Perhaps predictably, Dunlop won at the TT. Phil Mellor, riding a Heron Suzuki, was placed second and Marshall – having been plagued with carburation problems – came in fourth behind Yamaha's Geoff Johnson. Iddon retired when the chain started to rip the sprocket apart.

Back on the short circuits, Ferrari won the Assen race with Tadozzi again second. Then came the two Skoal Bandits, Marshall ahead of Iddon. The fourth round of the championship was abandoned after Klaus Klein crashed going into the second lap of the rain-lashed Ulster GP and was killed.

There was a round in Japan for the first time, at Sugo – again in preparation for the up-coming World Superbike series. Kevin Magee, riding a Yamaha, won the race but Suzuki rider Yukiya Ohshima finished second. The best-placed TTF1 regular was Andersson, who finished seventh. Marshall had been dicing with Magee until a spectacular crash eliminated the Skoal Bandit star, while Iddon went out with a broken exhaust bracket.

Back in Europe Bimota dominated again, this time at Hockenheim, when Ferrari again beat Tardozzi. Gschwender finished third on the Suzuki with Dunlop fourth and Iddon sixth. Marshall was absent, racing in a British televised race at Silverstone. Andersson went out with a split oil-cooler again.

Going into the final Donington round, Ferrari had 45 points to the 36 of Dunlop and Tardozzi. Iddon was in fourth place with 28. Dunlop needed a 10-point cushion over his Italian rival to retain the title but Ferrari cruised to seventh place while Dunlop could do nothing to close down the two leading Suzukis in the forty-lap, 100-mile (160km) race and wound up third. The title was Ferrari's by three points.

Iddon finished the season as he had started – winning. In a Skoal Bandit shoot-out Iddon came out ahead of 'team mate' Marshall after running the entire race without stopping, while Marshall had pitted to take on fuel.

It was all down to Andersson's methodical approach to racing. He had realized that the Donington track was not such a high-speed course and opted to run 36mm carbs instead of his 38 or 39s. The smaller carbs would offer better fuel consumption in the long race. Iddon and his mechanic, Paul Boulton, somehow found out and, without the knowledge of the rest of the Skoal Bandit team, asked to borrow a set from Andersson's spare bike. Team mate Marshall had no idea of this until he had to pit in the race for fuel and realized that Iddon was going the full distance without a stop – effectively winning the race.

After the race there was acrimony between the Suzuki 'team mates', and Andersson, although the innocent party, caught some of the flak (see p. 78). Marshall was really upset, but comments he made after the race suggested he knew about the carbs before the race began. In the post-season interview in *Road Racing Monthly* he said:

We didn't know Paul and his mechanic had borrowed the carbs and tried them in practice until they told us on Sunday they were going to use them. I was told I would have to stop and Paul wouldn't. Obviously I questioned why and was told about the carbs. I asked for a set but there were none available. I was disgruntled to say the least. I didn't say anything to the press after the race because I don't like bitching, but in my opinion, if you run a works team both riders would be treated as equal.

Roger Marshall on the Skoal Bandit at Daytona. (Rex White Collection)

Happier times for Schwantz, here celebrating his Mid Ohio win.
He won the final three AMA nationals but still could not prevent
Rainey and Honda claiming the Superbike title. (Colin Fraser)

White says: 'The whole thing happened behind my back. It was a case of mechanics talking amongst each other. Paul ended up with an advantage and it caused sour grapes in the team – a bit of aggravation…'

AMERICAN SUPERBIKE

In America, Superbike had taken a hold. Formula One, the American version encompassing 500cc GP bikes, ageing F750 dinosaurs and exotic four-strokes, was beset with falling entries, and finally led the AMA to condemn the class.

Superbike, which had been running alongside Formula One as a separate class since 1976, finally came of age. Suzuki lost out in the AMA Superbike wars against Honda but a bitter battle developed between eventual champion Wayne Rainey and Suzuki's Kevin Schwantz. Rainey won the first three rounds, Schwantz won five of the last six with only Honda's Bubba Shobert man-aging to break the Texan's Suzuki stranglehold in the latter half of the series.

Yoshimura Japan built four factory bikes for the American Yoshimura team for the new season reportedly at a cost of $60,000 per machine. The bikes were based on Yoshimura's $8,100 128bhp Stage III engine, using the same longer-duration, higher-lift camshafts, valve springs, oversize 71mm pistons (taking advantage of AMA Superbike rules to bump displacement from 747cc to 768cc), close-ratio six-speed gearbox, dry clutch, Carillo rods and a black box set to limit revs at 12,750 instead of 12,000.

The Carillos overcame the fragile con-rod problems of the previous year. The consensus at the time was that many teams, including Yoshimura, were over-tuning their engines, but the 1987 version was still putting out a very competitive 138bhp at 12,000rpm – at the gearbox!

Internally the new bike had special cylinder porting, using 27mm intake valves instead of 26mm but retaining stock exhaust valves. The biggest gain in horsepower, however, came from trick magnesium 37mm Mikuni flatslides (with throttle slides that rode on needle bearings and thus reduced the need for super-stiff return springs) instead of the 36mm kit carbs. The carbs did not come cheap at $5,000!

New asbestos-lined ducting from the fairing nose directed cool air to the air-box. The air temperature was said to drop by 40–50°F at the velocity stacks. A separate oil-cooler for the SACS system also helped lower temperatures in the 13.6:1 compression motor. A lot of attention was paid to reducing engine temperatures. In 1986 Yoshimura motors had run an oil temperature above 100°C, which inevitably meant a loss of power and that less cool air was reaching the carburettors.

The titanium exhaust (weighing just under a kilo (2lb), less the aluminium silencer!) was Yoshimura's 'duplex' system (selling to privateers at $1,700) with small canisters between cylinders 1 and 2, and 3 and 4. The theory was that exhaust gases would flow through the small canisters at low rpm, increasing the exhaust header volume for improved mid-range power. Then at high engine speeds the exhaust gases would bypass the canisters, effectively decreasing header volume to aid peak power.

Even if the expensive parts had been available to customers, the trick ported heads, bigger valves, and one-off airbox might not have been.

The Yoshimura dyno showed the stock GSX-R to deliver 86bhp, compared with the Stage III-kitted engine's 128bhp and the factory engine's 133bhp; it had an advantage over the Stage III motor from 7,000rpm upwards.

Chassis uprates in the catalogue included Nissin four-piston calipers (the fronts and a rear Nissin sold for $1,175 – as did the 310mm floating front rotors). The rear 210mm disc was a factory special item. The suspension was special too – 43mm Showas with external spring-preload adjusters and independently adjustable high- and low-speed compression and rebound damping. These replaced the previous year's forks, robbed from an RG500 GP bike.

The hand-built special frames had massive welded-on aluminium sections

Gary Goodfellow, shown here winning a Mosport Canadian National race, also used his near-stock GSX-R750 to take third place overall in the Laguna Seca AMA National. (Colin Fraser)

Michel Mercier stands his GSX-R LTD on its nose on the way to the Canadian Production national title. (Colin Fraser)

'doubled' around the standard frame loop to reduce flex. Anders Andersson's bike had the same, but with a much neater finish. The British entry for Roger Marshall had a diagonal frame brace inserted under the seat. The Yosh bike also had a heavily bridged aluminium swing-arm.

Even with the additional metal, the Yosh bike was under the 390lb (177kg) AMA limit and had to have strips of lead strapped to the bottom frame members. Andersson's bike had molten lead poured into the frame tubes.

The Swede's bike was full of neat touches, such as hand-carved ISR brake calipers, Ohlins inverted front forks and rear shock.

Yoshimura, like most of the other teams, were using radial tyres on the banking for the first time, but with 17in Michelins at the front while the rear was shod on 3.5in and 0.5in Technomagnesio wheels. Honda had switched to Dunlop.

During the winter these two major teams had swapped tyre companies. Rainey, after problems in 1986 with Michelins, had switched to Dunlop 18in radials. Schwantz had used Dunlops in the US during 1986 but after riding a Michelin-shod GP500 Heron Suzuki at the end of the year was impressed by the French tyres. When Suzuki wanted Yoshimura USA to switch to Michelins because Schwantz's Dunlop association conflicted with company policy, Schwantz found himself on 17in Michelin radials in 1987.

When it came down to it, even though Michelin had a supply problem during the season, most people considered the Michelins to be the best tyre combination during the year. Rainey began complaining about his bike's handling but, according to John Ulrich's account of the season in his *Motocourse* review, it was more a case of Schwantz becoming more switched on:

The idea that Schwantz's Suzuki had been changed and improved throughout the year turned out not to be the case. What changed was Schwantz's approach to riding, which was the direct result of what he had learned whilst riding the RG500 in Grands Prix.

Schwantz had crashed out of the Daytona opener whilst leading on the

34th of 57 laps – allegedly catching his brake lever on a hay bale whilst passing a back-marker. He badly broke a finger. Rainey, despite tyre problems, won the race. Suzuki completed the podium with Schwantz's team mate Satoshi Tsujimoto second and a fast-emerging Doug Polen third on a kitted GSX-R750 entered by Texan millionaire Richard Kosar. Polen also won the Supersport 600 race riding a Honda and would go on to win eight of the nine rounds during the year on his way to that title.

At Road Atlanta there was controversy when the Suzuki came up light on the scale during technical inspection, and it was only a question mark over the accuracy of the scales that allowed Schwantz to race. Tsujimoto did not make the cut, however. According to Yoshimura sources, his mechanic removed the ballast during maintenance and forgot to replace it. Schwantz battled with Rainey but a fairing bracket broke, causing him to run off the track. He faded away to third place.

Brainerd was next; this is a high-speed circuit and both Schwantz and Tsujimoto crashed in the same turn at around 160mph (255km/h) in practice. The Japanese rider had broken a bone in his neck and would not race again during the year. Battered and bruised Schwantz was beaten by Rainey again in the race but only by five seconds and, despite his obvious discomfort, looked a lot happier on the GSX-R.

Then came the wins at Loudon and Elkhart Lake – even though Schwantz's bike was obviously slower than Rainey's VFR on the long straights of the Road America track. Schwantz also won the red-flagged first race of the two-leg Laguna Seca round; Rainey stopped with a blistered rear tyre. Polen came second. Polen crashed in the second leg, however, as did Schwantz after high-siding. Shobert won the race and with his first-race third had done enough to win overall.

Schwantz was back to his winning ways at Mid Ohio and Memphis, but, going into the final Sears Point race, all Rainey needed was one point (fourteenth place) to clinch the title. Schwantz won again – even after a red-flag for a

Bruno Le Bihan pitches the Works Suzuki into a Le Mans hairpin during the early-season non-championship 24-Hour race. Teamed with Herve Moineau the French outfit claimed the World Endurance title. (Kel Edge)

Paul Iddon poses with the factory TTF1 bike, which was very similar to the French team's long-distance runner. Iddon was drafted back into the team alongside Roger Marshall after initial signing Kenny Irons was snapped up by the GP500 squad. (Rex White Collection)

Shobert crash – but Rainey finished sixth to claim the crown.

One title Suzuki did earn in the USA was the Formula USA Championship, with Scott Gray taking a Yoshimura GSX-R to victory in the anything-goes class of racing.

MATCH RACES

Earlier in the year, the Schwantz and Rainey contest spilled across the Atlantic to the Match Races at Donington Park, where it was painfully obvious that the pair did not get on. Clearly head and shoulders above the rest of the field, both in terms of riding skills and machinery, the duo waged war and at no time during the Easter weekend was their battle more physical – or more public – than in the last lap of the second race at Brands Hatch.

Schwantz had already won the opening encounter and was leading the second when Rainey stuffed his Honda inside at Druids on the final lap. Rainey held on into Clearways, only to have the Suzuki charge under him at Clearways,

and the bikes exchanged paint. Rainey had the line and held on to the flag while Schwantz fought a wild slide on the exit and lost by a split second. Roland Brown in *Motocourse* commented:

It's awe-inspiring stuff, and the crowd love it, even if Rainey doesn't: what he did was dangerous – nobody needs to ride like that.

This battle had nothing to do with any Anglo-American match race. This was Texan against Californian, Suzuki versus Honda, Michelin against Dunlop... American against American. 'We have pretty well the opposite in everything and we both have a point to prove,' said Schwantz, defending his tactics by pointing to an equally violent Rainey-instigated fairing-bashing incident in the first leg. The fact that this was a team race appeared not to have occurred to either man.

The Shell Oils Transatlantic Challenge, which moved to Donington on the Sunday for the final six races over two days following the first three at Brands, was a walkover for the Americans. Schwantz, having won four of the races to Rainey's five, still came out on top in the overall point standings – 165 to 161.5 – and thus picked up a £5,000 prize!

It was no surprise the Britons struggled since the majority of the team was running mildly tuned Superstock machines rather than all-out Superbikes the Americans had at their disposal. And the World TTF1-chasing Britons like Iddon, Marshall and Dunlop were off chasing points in Misano the same weekend!

Third overall in the points was another of the USA team, Gary Goodfellow, a New Zealand-born Canadian resident who was fast emerging as a hot talent from the AMA series.

Goodfellow had been a motocrosser in New Zealand from 1974 to 1980, won National titles, and scored points in the World Championship. He then moved to Vancouver in Canada to set up his own motorcycle shop, sponsored a couple of riders and got hooked on road-racing himself.

After some impressive results in 1985 and 1986 in Canada he picked up backing from the Suzuki importer for the 1987 season and starred in the Match races in England with his Peter Wiley-fettled machine. Later in the year Goodfellow sustained multiple injuries

in a Canadian national, at his home circuit of Westwood, British Columbia, after being hit from behind on the start line when his bike stalled.

The other Canadian-based rider to come to the fore was Michel Mercier. With three years of experience with the GSX-R (as opposed to the two of the Stateside crews) Mercier (thirty-two) was fiercely competitive with his Mike Crompton-prepared Suzuki Canada GSX-R Limited. Crompton had a good pedigree, having worked with American Honda during the Spencer years. Mercier claimed his second straight, RACE-sanctioned, Canadian National Superbike crown riding a Sunoco-backed Suzuki in the seven-round series.

Another name for the British to note was twenty-seven-year-old Doug Polen. Riding the Kosar Suzuki, he finished fifth overall with some rather stylish riding compared to the wilder antics that Schwantz and Rainey had displayed most of the weekend. For 1987 Polen had joined Ottis Lance in the Kosar Suzuki team, owned by twenty-

The works Suzuki with crude air intakes and no real airbox! The swing-arm now has bracing atop the arm unlike in the previous year. Brakes are by Lockheed. (Kel Edge)

two-year-old millionaire, Richard Kosar. But Polen continued production racing and when interviewed during the Match races reckoned that he would be running some twenty-five different tracks during the season ahead.

SUPER ONE

In England there had been the usual round of championship format changes but for 1987 the scene had undergone more radical changes than usual. Gone was the TTF1 series, replaced by Super One – a kind of formula libre series that pitted up to 750cc two-strokes against up to 1,300cc four-strokes.

It was dominated by Roger Marshall on a tricked-out Suzuki, which had a GSX-R1100 engine slotted into a GSX-R TTF1 chassis. This 135bhp rocket-ship was dubbed 'the Beast' and

provided thirty-six-year-old Marshall with a most competitive mount.

When Mark Phillips started putting in some good rides on a 500 Suzuki, Marshall even tried the carbon-fibre-framed factory Suzuki GP500 but ultimately went back to the Beast and continued his winning ways. He won five out of the eight races in Super One – and three out of four in the end of year Motoprix (which had similar class regulations).

Suzuki continued to dominate the Metzeler 750 Production series, with Phil Mellor named Champion (he had won both 750 and 1100 titles the previous year on Suzuki) ahead of Ray Stringer and Brian Morrison – all on Suzukis. In Superstock, though, the tide had changed and Yamaha's FZ750 was the bike to beat. Keith Huewen won the championship but the GSX-Rs rallied late, Phil Mellor winning at Thruxton and James Whitham taking two of the last three rounds.

Iddon proved his worth by winning the first round of the World TTF1 championship at Misano. The season ended in acrimony, however, when he borrowed some smaller carbs from Anders Andersson to run the Donington race non-stop. (Rex White Collection)

THE SWEDISH CONNECTION

When Suzuki announced the new GSX-R750 they did so with a major presentation to coincide with the launch. They also produced factory race bikes for importers to buy – in ready-to-race format for Endurance and TT Formula One.

Heron Suzuki, Suzuki Germany, Suzuki Sweden and the French Endurance team were allocated these machines, which were designated XR51.

Swede Anders Andersson was racing for the Swedish Suzuki importer and recalls the new bike arriving very late:

We only got it in '85 at Le Mans. We picked it up at the airport on the way. The engine was not so special to start with. It was good enough, with lots of involvement by Yoshimura and we were the fastest at the time – but the frame was really nice.

The frame didn't have so much in common with the 1000R because the new engine was so much smaller. But the new frame was so much narrower than the road frame. You had to open the front half of the frame to get the engine out. It was bolted together on one side. It was really low and narrow and a lot stronger than the roadbike which was quite good when it (the roadbike) was not that stable. The roadbike was nice and light but not so stiff.

The 1985 Season

Andersson says that Suzuki developed the bike through 1985 and 1986 with second– and third-generation frames, and that Suzuki had personnel at major meetings to offer technical support: 'They were easy to work with. They listened a lot when you had problems and would come up with solutions.'

That first Le Mans 24-Hours was not a championship race. Andersson's team had a big crash on oil at night and more or less destroyed the bike. Yet within two weeks they had been supplied with all the required parts, including some updated equipment. Andersson recalls:

Then we went to Italy and finished second to the works Honda. In Austria the Honda crashed in front of us. The Meliand Suzukis were not as fast as ours and they broke down sometimes and we didn't!

We had Motospeed (run by internationally acclaimed drag racer/tuner Thomas Klarkner) preparing our engines so we didn't actually do much work. We just maintained them a little better on our rivals. We were never down on speed – and usually a bit faster. Maybe that's why we got such help from Suzuki Japan? They could see our organization was good, even though we only had a very small budget compared to the French team. We were running on maybe 10 per cent of the budget the French team had!

The third round of the series was the Suzuka Eight-Hour. It was the only race Andersson's team had planned not to do simply because of the limited budget. But by now they were leading the championship and suddenly there was a letter from Suzuki Japan:

They were inviting Suzuki Sweden to the Suzuka Eight-Hour. We didn't have a clue about this race. The invite was only for two riders plus two mechanics. But we said ours was a private effort with a lot of helping friends so we said, 'Thank you for the invitation but either we all go or none of us will.' They said, 'OK, you can all come.' They paid for all seven people in our team!

We arrived two weeks before the race at Hammamatsu. It was the first time in Japan for all of us. We managed to pick up a race programme and saw we were number 19 for the race. So we got to the factory and were taken to the race shop. It was very small workshop, no fancy big facilities. A few guys were working away and there were three bikes almost finished – all brand new. One with number 3, number 4 and one with number 19. They had built a bike specially for us. We didn't know anything about this.

It was built specifically for Suzuka. Right down to the right gearbox ratios and gearing for the track. We updated our bike in the factory during the next week as well and then went to the test track. It's an awesome place, there's a straight of over 3km (1.8 miles) alone. They were a little bit scared because only a couple of years before a French guy was killed testing there. So the straight had all these chicanes marked with cones to slow the bikes down.

Our bike was the fastest of all of them! The Jap test rider was so impressed. But we thought they would kill us! But while our engine was fast, our chassis development was way behind so we used their bike. The gearbox was specially made with ratios to suit the track. Uphill straightaway the ratio between fourth and fifth was just perfect.

Later on we moved the entire workshop to the track. But the event was just a little bit too big for us. We were a little over-awed. Next pit to us was the Tech 21 Yamaha Genesis of Taira and Roberts. It sounded like a duck farm next door. All week it never stopped with these American accents, 'whack, whack ,whack' – all week going on about tyres, suspension, motor. It never stopped!

Also in the race were Wayne Gardner and Kevin Schwantz, who was teamed with Graeme Crosby. It was Schwantz's first time in Japan. His bike was nearly the same as Andersson's but run by Yoshimura. Andersson says:

We struggled a little with the politics. We weren't used to that level so we struggled a bit with tyres. But I remember very well how huge the event was – 251,000 paying spectators. That was before they had restriction on the number of people. And there was over 3,000 press!

In qualifying I couldn't relax. We were twenty-fifth the first day but I went back to the hotel and thought about it all and eventually qualified twelfth. I got a flying start and in the first hour of the race I was battling with Schwantz in eighth or ninth. And we weren't even in the top grading list for tyres.

Anders Andersson contested the Swann series with his TTF1 bike. (Anders Andersson Collection)

Schwantz was exciting. He had his feet off the pegs in almost every turn but somehow managed to stay on. Crosby, though, was so good at the time in Japan. They finished third.

(Tadahiko) Taira and Roberts were battling with Gardner and Dominique Sarron but with less than hour to go the Yamaha shit itself. Gardner (with Masaki Tokuno) won the race. We had a really good fight for fourth to ninth with Phillis, one of the French Suzukis, Coudray/Igoa. They were our rivals in the championship but crashed out.

We finished eighth; it should have been a little better but our problem was lack of experience. It was 38°C and so humid. We didn't know what Suzuki had to help us out. They had sports drinks. I'd never tried that before and took some on the morning of the race and it sent my stomach crazy so I couldn't take any fluids after that. I lost 4kg [9lb] in the day – I did little bit longer shifts than my team mate. In the last hour I lost two places, which I shouldn't have done. It literally took me six months to recover!

But we had an ever bigger lead in the championship after that – with the Honda crashing out. Only the top ten scored those days. After the race we had a big meeting with Suzuki because we had a good chance of the championship. They told us to list anything we needed! So we made lists of parts.

Funny thing was I had my wife with me (she was my girlfriend at the time) and she had her eyes on the Suzuki Swift cars. In the list with the footrest parts, triple clamps, we added, 'black Swift for Mieka'. It was just a joke but this was read out in an open meeting with a translator in front of all the Japanese technical people. The management was there too. Mr Itoh was the boss in those days. He was a great guy. He liked to go out for a beer with the boys in the evening. When they read out the black Suzuki Swift the room erupted! It was so funny.

Nürburgring was next and the Swedes started to feel the pressure. On race day it was snowing in the morning – Swedish conditions. At the start of the race it had turned to rain. Andersson was second after the first hour but his team mate, Per Jonsson, was the acknowledged racing master – a maniac in the wet, as Andersson once described him! When he finished his stint they had two laps lead over the Honda. Then it stopped raining and started to dry up.

Just when he was due in, Igoa went out on cut slicks and wobbled around out of the pit lane to get some heat into the tyres and Jonsson had to go wide to avoid running into him. Andersson recalls:

Maybe Igoa thought he was alone on the racetrack? Whatever, out there in the dust there was oil and Per had a big crash. The bike caught fire and Honda won the race.

But we could still win the championship with only the *Bol* left so we drafted in Rob McElnea as our third rider. When we arrived the French were panicking. I remember that just to put a little extra pressure on them, we fitted a dummy engine (just with shells on the generator, we took the starter motor off). We rode it up to scrutineering and it was 8kg (17½lb) lighter than the other factory bikes. They were spewing!

Our bike was fast – as fast as any of the other bikes. Rob Mac did real good but he crashed on oil, and I crashed on petrol. We tried to win the race but if we had tried to be a bit more sensible maybe we could have finished second in the championship. Honda won the title. The French Suzuki team didn't like the competition – after all they were considered to be the factory team.

To finish his season, Andersson took the endurance race bike to the Hockenheim TTF1 World round:

I just took the lights off and finished second – easily. I was in front of Grant, and McGregor. My bike was really quick. As a private team to do endurance is such a hard thing – such a workload. We were not able to pay mechanics. We just took along friends who had a big interest in the sport.

So I decided after Hockenheim to concentrate on F1 in 1986. It was so easy [in terms of preparation compared to long distance racing]. We just filled the bike up with petrol, took one spare set of tyres and raced.

F1 at the time was 'lazy English operation'. Nobody bothered to measure fuel and so on. Joey [Dunlop] had his RVF and he was winning everything. We checked our fuel consumption in that German race and realized we didn't even have to stop for fuel in the race. All the others were refuelling. After that, everyone had to check their fuel. It made more work for them. I guess they hated me for that!

1986

When Andersson asked Suzuki for continued help for Endurance in 1986 they said they could not give the same level of support as previously because their main effort was with the French. Meliand's team was given full support. Still, Andersson was positive:

But Suzuki said we could keep the bikes we had and they would also give us more parts. That was good – good enough for F1 for sure. In 1986 we had a very good bike. I carried on doing F1, including the Isle of Man. There was also the Heron Suzuki team but that was an importer team like us. They had a factory machine – more or less the same as ours.

It was during the 1986 season that Swedish suspension specialist, Ohlins, escalated their involvement in road racing – through Andersson:

They had actually started road-racing with (Kenny) Roberts in 1982, but in 1986 we did the first prototype with an upside-down Ohlins front fork. I started to develop that with the Ohlins guys on the F1 bike around mid-season.

Anders Andersson with his Suzuki Sweden TTF1 bike. Note the heavily braced frame and triangulated swing arm. Andersson's Suzuki was one of the first TTF1 machines to sport upside-down forks – by Ohlins. Another Swedish company, ISR, provided the four-piston calipers. Note also the ISR front brake lever/master cylinder assembly. (Alan Cathcart Archive)

By running a TTF1 programme, Andersson was forced to race on road courses as well as the short circuits:

When I went to the TT I got a lot of help from the English guys – especially from Mick Grant. Everyone tried to help out that year. There was a lot of road circuits that year. I didn't have much experience on the roads – only Imatra and some small tracks back home.

I really enjoyed the roads. But sure the safety was a different level. I had so many friends in those years: Sammy McClements, Phil Mellor, Klaus Klein (all three ultimately died on road courses). I used to travel with Klaus. When he got killed that was the end for me. I was in front of him at the time, Phil Mellor was leading and I was second (at the 1987 Ulster GP). He just aquaplaned. The race should never have been started. He knew, we all knew, you either cheated off the start line and got away or you got killed. That spray was so bad – the water on the road was incredible.

But back in 1986 Andersson did the full World TTF1 series – actually leading the points for a while – but ultimately finished third:

I was happy with that. The GSX-R was very reliable. Very early in 1985 they had connecting rod problems and a few other things. But we never ran that high mileages so we never had problems. Gearboxes were maybe a bit suspect too. But in endurance trim, horsepower was only 125-128bhp. For F1 in 1986 we had a bit over 130 at the countershaft. Then by late 1986 we had 138 on the sprocket!

The 1986 TTF1 series had a nice atmosphere but the competition was quite stiff – especially at places like Donington, the normal type of circuits! At the TT I struggled with stupid things. I didn't have a generator and the race was a lot longer than any other. On the last lap we had a flat battery and a misfire. I was seventh going into the last lap and finished eleventh. No points!

We used the upside-down forks for the first time at Assen. I was the first one to use them and we had no real problems. The engineer in charge was Matts Larsson. He's now head of the race department. He was not that experienced at the time, coming from a motocross background, so it took a while to get the new forks sorted. The first ones we used were chopped-down motocross '83 forks – when they worked with (Hakan) Carlqvist and (Jacky) Vimond at Yamaha!

1987

By 1987 Suzuki's support was dwindling. The big push promoting the new GSX-R in 1985 had slowed down. However, Andersson continued to race a GSX-R and was comfortable with the company:

I always felt it was easy to work with Suzuki. They are not such a big company, not so many middle men, so you deal direct with the engineers. Mr Itoh was also very enthusiastic and a very strong character inside the company. You could trust if he said something that that would be the way it was going to be. I still see him and he's still the same guy. They have been lucky to have a guy like that.

Andersson's bike was still competitive in 1987 at World TTF1 level:

As I said we had 138bhp at sprocket. That was the best and it was fast enough. Only the RVF was faster.

I finished fifth in the championship but I struggled a bit. The new Bimota was really quick that year with Ferrari and Tardozzi. I think I did a better job in '86 than I did in '87. I had the equipment but I didn't really do the business.

Andersson's methodical approach to racing got him into hot water with the Skoal Bandit team, even though he was an innocent party:

In '87 most teams were still lazy in some areas. I worked on fuel efficiency a lot. Many races I could go without fuel stop. I thought about how to approach each race. At Donington I could easily go full distance. I didn't use the biggest carbs I could have. It's not a high-speed track so I used 36mm, I think. Some of them had 38–39s.

Iddon came and asked if he could borrow my spare set from my spare bike so I said, 'yeah no problem'. He did that without asking anyone in his team. He ran the smaller carbs so he could finish the race without a stop but his team mate, Roger Marshall, had to. Iddon pissed everyone in the team off. Everyone in their team thought I was the bastard giving away equipment but if Roger had asked first he could have had them!

I was leading the race in the first third of it. I had my bike well set up – suspension etc – and I had the six-piston ISRs that no one else had. My brakes were awesome. Even though Marshall and some of the other boys were good around Donington my bike was just fast enough down the straights so they couldn't catch me – I could out-brake anyone. But after ten to fifteen laps my arm pumped up solid [a common problem for riders during a long race on the Donington GP circuits with its three dead-stop turns] and I dropped back.

It was the first year of the ISRs. I used them all season. The guy who made them had previously supported someone in the GPs. But this year was the one to publicize them for sale. We did a lot of testing. They were good brakes.

This was part of the main reason why, even with a very small budget, I could compete with the bigger teams. In Sweden we had Motospeed, ISR (for brakes and technical equipment) and Ohlins.

SUPERBIKE 1988

By 1988 Andersson's plan was to go Superbike racing. 'Those accidents didn't help the cause of F1 in '87. Superbike – that's what I wanted to do: four-stroke racing on permanent circuits. When Klaus got killed the road circuits were not so attractive anymore.'

And with the advent of World Superbike came the launch of the new short-stroke Suzuki, complete with CV carbs:

The main problem was that you had to use the bike as it was homologated. The carbs were a major problem. Small carbs, vacuum carbs, are very difficult to get to work with a short-stroke engine. There was not enough air speed in the intakes.

For F1 in Japan it was not so bad (thanks to different, more liberal rules) and the road bike was not so bad. But the race bike… The only one that worked good early was the one Schwantz rode at Daytona. He was right there. What did they do to make that one go? We don't know!

We didn't get ours to work until around half-way through the season and it was never quick enough for Superbike. I had some decent finishes, maybe seventh I think, but we had to increase the air speed so much before it really started to work.

I really liked the series with the organization with McLaughlin running things. I put a lot into the series as a rider's rep as well. Some track organizers were not treating us so good. There were still some poor tracks and organizers with bad attitudes. Safety was not an issue at that time so we had a lot of work in that area.

I lost interest a little bit because I knew the Suzuki was not going to get any better in the immediate future. I knew it would be the bike for '89 and '90 as well but it wasn't competitive and we couldn't make it competitive.

We got a little bit of help from the factory still because they were good people. They always replied to our faxes straight away and said how they could help us – or if they couldn't help. We couldn't expect more, especially as they were making a big effort with the 500 at that time.

Andersson actually ran some F1 races using a different carburation set-up and proved a point:

With flatslide 38mm carbs and the mods we needed to do to heads and so on the bike was really good. I did the Kuovola F1 race but I used the good '86 F1 bike which I still had at home!'

He also finished fourth in the Donington Park final round to wind up fifth in the points:

[The bike] was 152kg [334lb] in running condition and the geometry made it really nice and easy to ride!

In 1988 I ran that bike in the [Eurolantic] Match Races. I had a bit of an argument with the Swedish importer about support so just before going to England I took a can of black spray to my bike and painted it. No stickers, nothing else.

Andersson scored a couple of fifth places but ended the series with a broken collar bone after the bike blew a countershaft sprocket seal, and oil on the rear tyre pitched him off at Goddard in spectacular fashion.

I planned to stop racing after the end '88. I had done twelve years by then. I was thinking about family and so on and didn't see anything coming (in terms of racing opportunities). But the Swedish Yamaha importer suddenly offered me a new OWO1 for World Superbike and some Swedish races on production bikes. I said 'yeah!'

5 Slingshot into Second Generation

At the end of 1987 *Cycle World* gave riding impressions of two Yoshimura Tornados – 750cc and 1,100cc street bikes, based on GSX-Rs, built in limited quantities (thirty of each). The 1100s were produced by Yoshimura US and then shipped for sale by Yoshimura in Japan as an imported motorcycle to evade Japan's 750cc displacement limit.

The 1100 Tornado, incidentally, was curiously dubbed the 'Bonneville' for the Japanese market only!

In Japan the Tornados could be bought complete, while in the USA Yoshimura US could supply all the parts to build either machine. The 750 Tornado F1, to give it its full name, had 1mm-larger pistons, bigger valves and special

The original Yoshimura GSX-R750 Tornado F1 street bike brochure.

GSX-R750J Slingshot (1988)

Four-cylinder, four-stroke, air/oil-cooled with SACS, DOHC, TSCC, four valves per cylinder

Engine
Bore and stroke	73.0mm x 44.7mm
Cubic capacity	748cc
Compression ratio	10.9:1
Carburettors	4 Mikuni BST36SS
Ignition	Transistorized
Starter system	Electric
Lubrication system	Wet sump

Transmission
Clutch	Wet, multi-plate type
Gearbox	Six-speed, constant mesh

Suspension
Front suspension	43mm telescopic, spring preload, fully adjustable
Rear suspension	Full Floater

Brakes and Tyres
Front brake	Twin disc, hydraulically operated Nissin four-piston
Rear brake	Single disc, hydraulically operated
Front tyre size	120/70VR-17 V250
Rear tyre size	160/60VR-17 V250

Dimensions (in/mm)
Overall length	81.1/2,060mm
Overall width	30.3/770mm
Overall height	44.5/1,130mm
Wheelbase	55.5/1,410mm
Ground clearance	4.7/120mm
Seat height	30.9/785mm
Dry weight	429lb (195kg)

The 1988 Slingshot GSX-R750J with short-stroke motor and revised frame looked similar to the braced-up factory bikes of the previous year. (Colin Fraser Archive)

camshafts, 36mm flatslide Mikunis and either a USA-made Yosh pipe, or a Yosh Japan Cyclone pipe – depending on the market it was destined for. The 1100 was given similar upgrading treatment.

The changes offered wider spread of power, improved carburation and better top end. *Cycle World* said the 750 delivered 'performance similar to a one-litre sportsbike.'

Stock bodywork, forks, rear shock, wheels, front brake calipers and rotors were all junked in favour of uprated aftermarket components: low-line gas tank, single seat and louvered fairing plus low clip-ons and rearsets. Showa forks, Yoshimura/KYB shock, Nissin calipers, and Yosh discs completed the race-bike-for-the-road package.

The Tornado brochure offered four stages of engine tuning and a bodywork kit that included some curious-looking six-hole aluminium disc wheels bearing the Spour logo. There were also four performance kits: a complete engine assembly kit; a dry clutch assembly; a top

engine power-up kit including ported head, gear clusters, carbs and pipe; and a chassis kit including different-rate fork springs, rear shock and a range of sprockets, brake pads and hoses and fittings.

SECOND-GENERATION REVAMP

But Suzuki had bigger plans. They completely revamped the GSX-R for 1988 – the second generation was about to begin. It had to. Honda had just introduced the technically exotic, V4, gear drive-DOHC RC30, upping the ante in the Superbike stakes.

To say that many of the changes made to the new GSX-R750 launched in 1988 evolved from what was learned on the race track would be an understatement.

The 1988 GSX-R750J Slingshot featured a completely new frame, new carburettors and revised engine internals

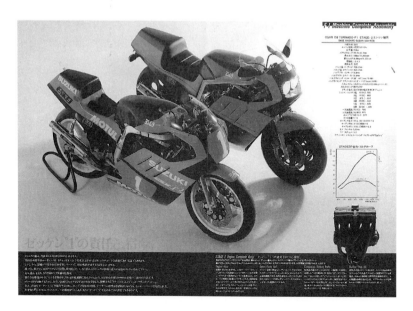

Yoshimura sold the Tornado on images of their TTF1 race bike.

The brand-new Slingshot on test in Japan. The styling resembled the World title-winning endurance racer. (Colin Fraser)

to offer a revvy, short-stroke format in a much smaller, more compact motorcycle.

Production racing had shown that the previous box-section alloy GSX-R frame was prone to flex. The new frame followed the same principles as the one seen the previous year during the Suzuka Eight-Hour: it had beefy aluminium castings for the steering head (at 80mm, some 20mm bigger than before) and swing-arm pivot areas – connected by 2.75in (700mm) wide aluminium extrusions, which formed the frame main spars – some 14in (356mm) apart at their widest point above the engine.

Suzuki claimed that this construction was more rigid and more compact. But it was also heavier than before. The new frame was fabricated from thirty-eight different parts and weighed 33lb (15kg) – 15lb (7kg) more than the previous GSX-R frame.

The new swing-arm also had more torsional rigidity and featured a larger-section, forged cross-member to which the revamped Full Floater rear suspension

Doug Polen raced the ex-Schwantz 1987 bike in AMA nationals for Yoshimura throughout 1988. He finished runner-up to Honda's Bubba Shobert. (Colin Fraser)

In 1988 Kevin Schwantz had signed a GP500 deal with Suzuki but did Daytona as a one-off on a specially prepared Yoshimura GSX-R750 – based on the new short-stroke engine. It was slow but Schwantz won the 200-Miler. (Alan Cathcart Archive)

attached. The distance between the swing-arm pivot and the suspension attachment cross-member was also increased. Suzuki claimed that the suspension, thanks to redesigned lever linkages, provided a smoother, more consistent rear wheel movement through the suspension stroke.

The non-reservoir, steel-bodied rear shock, like the front fork, was by Showa. Suzuki had previously usually used Kayaba suspension front and rear.

Up front the new 43mm Showa forks were the same make and size that Schwantz's Yosh bike sported in 1987 but were obviously very different

Sakakura has his head in the front brakes while Schwantz checks out how many bugs he has zapped! In the background is Honda's Doug Chandler sporting Freddie Spencer backing on his leathers. (Alan Cathcart Archive)

Polen Powers to Cup Glory

Doug Polen dominated the first two years of the Suzuki GSX-R Cup. He joined Yoshimura R & D in the US, then moved to race for Yoshimura in Japan for two years, where he won the F1 and F3 All Japan titles. Then he went on to become a two-time World Superbike Champion with Ducati. And the wheels turned full circle in 1996 when Polen chose the brand-new GSX-R750 for his privateer racing effort.

A pensive Schwantz during practice for the 1988 Daytona 200. (Alan Cathcart Archive)

1986

Polen had actually pulled out of racing after the 1983 season and it was the lure of Suzuki Cup cash that sparked his attention in 1986. Polen points out:

The Suzuki Cup was not a new thing in terms of contingency prizes – Honda and Yamaha had done it in previous years – but never in the magnitude Suzuki did in '86.

It was good to promote their totally new GSX-R. I looked at it [the Suzuki Cup programme] and thought 'This could be really good.' When I left racing in 1983 I was ripping up track records. I was stomping everyone in Texas. And they had, what, six or eight GSX-R races in my region! And there's $1,000 to win the thing. I figured I could make six to eight thousand bucks. Cool.

Polen's enforced 'retirement' had been for financial reasons. Finding sponsors to go motorcycle road racing was not easy in Texas. 'It wasn't as if I didn't have the speed, my big problem was not getting any coverage because the magazines weren't covering what was happening in Texas.'

A local dealer in Polen's home town of Denton offered him a bike for the Suzuki Cup – in fact it was from the bike shop that the initial idea of Polen chasing the Suzuki Cup developed:

Yeah, they were the ones who asked me if I wanted to do it in the first place and got me interested. I said, 'Look, we'll run the races and depending on what results we get will dictate if we go to the next race on the nation-wide schedule.' I thought I'd do all the races I could afford. I first started with a GSX-R750 and won the inaugural race at li'l ol' Talladega, Alabama. Hadn't been on a bike in three years. Compared to what I used to race on, man, this bike was neat. This thing was a race bike! You ran this bike stock. There was no pipe for it. There was no such thing as Supersport. It was stock production, stock pipe. You could change jetting, tyres, rear shock, front suspension but that was it.

Polen alleges that other competitors were running tricked-out engines but he still came on top with his 'stocker':

Of course, everyone was leaning on engines as hard as they could. Zillion angle valve jobs. They crank down on it a lot harder now that they did then. But mine was pretty stock. I just ran it. After the first two rounds I picked up an 1100 so then I was making $2,000 per round!

Polen used the contingency cash for expenses to do the next race. 'I just kept going to races, because I kept winning. When I totalled it up, out of 51 races, including the National finals, I won 45. That's a 90 per cent win ratio – not bad, huh!'

Polen won the 750 class but finished second to Dan Chivington in the 1100 category. Magazine stories of the time suggest Polen netted over $90,000 in that hectic first season. The man himself reckons it was more:

I won around $100,000. That's not sponsorship. I didn't have any. That's all contingency money. I picked up a Honda Interceptor 500 ride – they paid $700 a win. And $2,700 later (after a weekend's work) I'd be off to the next race. They paid $5,000 for winning a Suzuki Cup Final race.

1987

Polen's name was up in lights so it was no surprise that he soon had a front-line Superbike seat – even if it was on a privateer team. For 1987 Polen raced for Richard Kosar, a young Texan millionaire with a passion for bike racing. Polen explains:

Kosar needed someone – a fast guy. They had run Yamahas but Yamaha didn't want to help them in '87. I had the ability to come in and say, 'Look, Suzuki are really keen to help me.' Hank Ohta, the guy who came up with the idea for the whole Suzuki Cup deal, helped me to a situation where I could get bikes, kit parts, and spares from American Suzuki. I could put that into the Kosar deal. They didn't have bikes, Yamaha had said, 'Sorry can't help.' So they were going to have buy bikes. I said, 'Hey, look what I've got.'

The Kosar bikes, though, were kit bikes, nothing like the Yoshimura R & D machinery. Polen recalls:

The differences? Night and day. Not even close. We ported the head, did this, did that – but it was no Yosh motor. There was no factory Suzuki at that time anyway – it was Yosh doing all the development at that time. We just made do with what we had. There were some races where I was stuffing it up them [giving the Yosh riders a hard time on the track].

But the reason why I did it [raced for Kosar] was that I wanted some track time and I wanted some Superbike seat time. The more seat time you can get, the more polished you get.

Polen was still racing every single weekend, either with the Kosar Superbike or in the GSX-R Cup – or both!

Kosar paid me a salary. Plus I got the contingency money. I also got free tyres [Dunlops – after using Michelins the previous year] in '87 and started developing the 591 with David Buck in the US. He and I worked on that.

That season, Polen finished fourth in the AMA Superbike series behind Rainey, Schwantz and Shobert – all three of whom were factory-supported riders. Polen also won both classes of the Suzuki Cup Finals at Riverside – the only time the Finals have been run outside of Road Atlanta in the twelve-year history of the series.

1988

The next year Schwantz went to the GPs, and Polen went to Yoshimura. But, as Polen recalls, Schwantz did race Daytona with a factory bike, based on the new short-stroke machine. Polen raced the 1987 ex-Schwantz bike:

Schwantz had the trick stuff – short stroke, big-bore. I didn't care. I wanted to run what I could get. I was happy with that. I zipped him at the line (after five laps) and got my Camel Challenge $10,000. I got more money than he did for winning the race! Today I'd rather trade him the win for the cash. Daytona is the only thing I haven't won!

Polen wound up second in the season points behind Honda's Bubba Shobert:

A crash at Mid Ohio was the difference. I was leading [the race]. The bike did something real unexpected over the brow of a hill. I lost the front. It never happened all race, then it did it and maybe you look at it later and think, 'Maybe we should have adjusted it a little different to this.' But it never cropped up till the last lap of the race. More or less, it was a mistake on my part.

At Sears in the last race of the year I had to win and he had to finish third, or worse, for me to get the title. I won. He was second, 36 secs behind. I laid the place on fire. But where was Scott Gray [Polen's team mate]? He was supposed to be there. He was fast enough to do it. But we had the Camel Challenge earlier and he wanted to win the ten grand. He unloaded in Turn Nine and ended up destroying the thing, knocked himself out and didn't race.

1989

From America, Polen moved to Japan to race full time for the Yoshimura team:

Yosh were having problems in Japan. They didn't have anyone [capable of winning races]. Ohshima was not getting the results so Yosh asked me to go over and stay there to race. It was a really good experience, living in Japan, but the bike wasn't that good to start with. We developed it through the season and I was on the box (podium) all year long. It was a good consistent year – and I won the F3 title as well riding a little gem of a 400.

Polen says there was no comparison between the Yoshimura R & D AMA Superbike of 1988 and the Yoshimura Japan bike of 1989. 'They [the Japanese] had Formula One rules', he states. 'It was a four-stroke Grand Prix bike. One-off this, one-off that. And we could adjust everything.'

Yet, in comparison with what the other manufacturers were running, the Yosh Suzuki was still up against it:

Well, we were racing against an RVF. You could kick an RVF around Suzuka – it would roll around that place on its own. Those bikes were really fast. My Suzuki was quick but not that quick. I was quicker than all the Japanese riders – they were not the force they are now. I made up the difference the bike didn't have. It was a good combination. It put Yosh in a good situation.

Polen won four races out of eight and was second twice. He also won five or eight F3 races on a GSX-R400, and still recalls the little bike with enthusiasm:

It was a gas to ride. I mean that thing was cool. 250 slicks. Rail city. I had two different bikes – one [the 400] was like riding a 250GP and then I had to get on the Superbike – on the same day. Like it was grip city with the 250 then have to battle the Superbike. I was more than happy to get on the 400 – any time!

Polen also did the Daytona 200 in 1989 and recalls:

Fujio and I came over. Twenty-three laps into the race, Number 23 [Polen's race number] went out with an oil leak. The radiator vibrated, spread and leaked. After that they welded seals top to bottom to keeping them from separating. I was leading by 37 secs – 24 laps into a 57-lap race. I would have lapped them all, man. Lapped them all! I was like, 'Man this is cool.' I qualified two seconds faster than anyone else.

1990

The 1990 season started badly for Polen. Testing the Daytona Suzuki a month before the 200-Miler at Willow Springs, California, he crashed hard and got his foot caught in the tumbling bike. Four toes of his left foot were sliced off.
Yet only two months later Polen was on the pole at Suzuka:

I missed the first race of the season but got back for Suzuka – to everyone's surprise. We tried some different shift pattern deals. Heel and toe. We pulled that off pretty quick – like I'd go into corners and the thing would back-shift. But I was on the pole – all the Japanese thought that was cool!

Polen finished fourth in the comeback race, and third in the series. He did a one-off US race mid-season at Road Atlanta, when the Yoshimura R & D's riders Duhamel and Crevier were both injured. Polen scored his one and only win of the year there, beating eventual champion Doug Chandler.

So what tyres did Polen run, given that Yosh were on Michelin at the time and Polen was contracted to Dunlop? Polen says: 'Michelins, of course. Dunlop said, "Hey, we're not going to hold you back for a single race – just don't do anything stupid like wearing a Michelin hat!"' Yoshimura R & D boss Don Sakakura has a different recollection (see page 92).

THE EARLY 1990s

After 1990 Polen went to Europe and smashed record after record on Fast By Ferracci Ducatis to win the World Superbike crown in the most convincing manner, snatching 17 races in 24 starts. He repeated the title win in 1992.

After a season back home in the US with Ducati (he won the AMA Superbike title), and then a one-and-a-half-year rollercoaster ride with Honda in World Superbike, Polen returned to race in the US with backing from The People's Network – a specialist cable TV station offering self-improvement programmes.

In 1996 Polen was one of the first privateers to buy Suzuki's new-generation GSX-R750 to race – and he picked up a deal to ride for SERT in World Endurance. The wheels had come full circle. So what does Polen have to say about the GSX-R?

Basically the GSX-R750 put me where I'm at. And I'm back on a GSX-R again. It was good going back to the Suzuki last year – so much fun to ride. After the Honda, trying to get that thing to steer, stuff like that, the Suzuki was so much easier and a lot more fun. We had development work to do but by the end of the year [1996] I was up people's butts again. The old GSX-R was, and the new one still is, a blast to ride!

Polen leads team mate Scott Gray at Daytona. (Colin Fraser)

internally (and there was no external adjuster as on the race bike!). The stanchion tubes were gripped by forged aluminium-alloy triple clamps, giving a GP-style rake of 24.83 degrees with 3.9in (99mm) of trail. Despite being bigger, the new forks weighed less than the 1987 units.

The front brakes were now 310mm floating rotors, gripped by race-developed Nissin four-piston calipers with 30mm leading and 34mm trailing pistons to provide even pad pressure and wear. These were only available as limited-edition kit brakes the previous year but now were street stock! Pad material was now new-compound sintered metal for longer life and more consistent braking.

There were new cast-alloy, hollow three-spoke 17in wheels front and rear – exactly as Yoshimura Suzuki had run in 1987. These were shod with low-profile Michelin radials as original equipment.

Compared with the 1987 bike, the latest model was shorter in wheelbase and overall length (with a 55.5in/1,410mm rather than 57.3in/1,455mm wheelbase and 81in/2060mm rather than 83.3in/2,115mm overall length) and the motor sat lower in the chassis than previously. Ground clearance was reduced by a quarter of an inch (now 4.7in/120mm as opposed to 4.9in/125mm). Seat height was up by three-quarters of an inch (30.9in/785mm compared to 30.1in/765mm) and overall weight was up from 387lb (176kg) to a rather porky 429lb (195kg) for the new J model, which was not so impressive compared with Honda's outstanding new V4 VFR750R – the bike everyone would come to know as the RC30 – which weighed 394lb (179kg).

The Suzuki bodywork, too, came in for a revamp, with a more slippery, aerodynamically efficient, V-shaped lower fairing for added ground clearance. Suzuki claimed that, compared to the 1987 GSX-R, the new fairing shape offered a 57 per cent reduction in frontal area while drag was reduced 11.2 per cent at 40mph (64km/h) and downforce was increased by 36 per cent at the same speed.

The seat section was also redesigned, and a new inner rear tyre-hugging fender was bolted to the swing-arm; both measures were designed to reduce turbulence. The fuel tank was resculpted and sat deeper in the frame rails to give a low, sleek look, yet still held 21 litres (4.5 gallons). Cycle magazine pointed out how similar the new J-model looked when compared with Yoshimura's Tornado 750, which itself was developed from their race bike. And to emphasize the racing pretensions of the bike, the 21-litre gas tank even came equipped with an indentation on top ready for the installation of a quick-fill race refuelling fitment!

The bore of the new short-stroke motor was increased from 70mm to 73mm, and stroke reduced from 48.7mm to 44.7mm to improve rpm and increase torque. Destroking the motor allowed Suzuki engineers to use the same-size valves as on the GSX-R1100 (28.5mm intake, 25mm exhaust) in the 3mm bigger bore. Pistons now featured short, slipper-style skirts with 0.8mm thick compression rings to reduce friction. They weighed less than half an ounce (12g) more than the previous model's slugs. The crankshaft journals were increased by 2mm to take the extra rpm loads, with a weight increase of 10oz (283g). Red line was

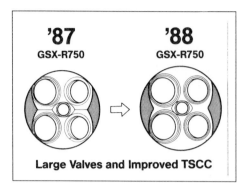

The 1988 also sported larger valves and an improved TSCC design.

now 13,000rpm, not only higher than on any other 750cc superbike on the market at the time – but higher, too, than Schwantz's 1987 Yosh superbike. Grant Leonard, commenting on the power delivery in *Superbike* magazine said:

It has lost its tight, buzzy feel and revs as freely as a GPX – but up to 13,000rpm. The real power lies between 7,000 and 12,000rpm, but there's stacks low down for hauling around too – The gearbox – with a foot-long dowel in the linkage – is slick and the clutch super-light.

Valve lift was increased for both intake and exhaust while flow at low valve lift

was improved thanks to the modification to the proven TSCC combustion chamber design. And, to aid its free-revving characteristics, Suzuki looked closely at reducing reciprocating weight of the internals whilst maintaining reliability.

The engines still relied on SACS oil/air-cooling, but like the Yoshimura race effort of 1987, Suzuki's engineers went in search of even more cooling efficiency, and increased the size of the oil-cooler of the new production machine (it was bigger than most radiators fitted to conventionally water-cooled machines)

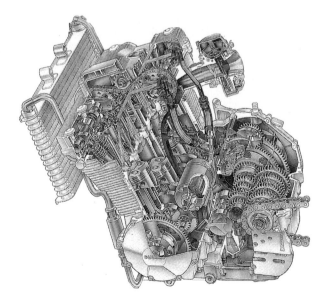

The 1988 GSX-R still featured oil-cooling but now had short-stroke configuration and Slingshot carbs.

and improved cylinder head oil-flow cooling capacity by 48 per cent.

The new road bike did not come equipped with hyper-expensive magnesium-bodied flatslides but it did sport new lightweight, aluminium die-cast bodied, larger 36mm flatslide Slingshot carbs, which featured vacuum-operated slides. These were claimed to be much thinner and lighter than conventional flatslides and had half-round indexing ridges on their faces. Suzuki claimed that the new shape provided a much smoother flow than straight-cut designs, thus reducing turbulence, eliminating dead air and increasing the flow in the carburettor throat. The slide's lighter weight also meant a softer return spring could be used, thus improving throttle action. The carb air intake had a smooth radius, without any ridges, to improve intake efficiency.

The engine also had digital electronic spark advance to control the precise movement of the ignition accurately. While the motor would scream its way to the red line, it also delivered good torque – not as good as the VFR Honda or Yamaha FZR750 bottom-end power, but better than previous GSX-Rs, according to *Cycle World* in their road test.

But what *Cycle World* discovered was the new lower-slung GSX-R had problems with ground clearance when ridden 'racetrack-hard':

When pushed fairly aggressively around the track the kickstand hits the ground on the left, and the fairing drags on both sides – even if the rider hangs off quite far. Worse yet, the new

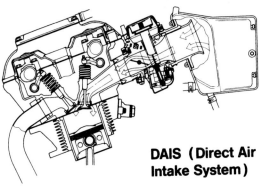

DAIS – the Suzuki Direct Air Intake System.

4-into-2 exhaust system bangs the pavement hard on both sides.

Basically, the GSX-R needed either a race shock or a kit ride-height adjuster! *Superbike* magazine noted:

Serious efforts have been made to lower the whole bike and the front end particularly. Suzuki may have gone too far here trying to give it the look of a pukka racebike. For the race boys it has created a serious ground clearance problem. The fairing touches down and the exhausts ground too. For racing the forks are dropped in the yokes as a matter of course on the new model as there's about half an inch of stanchion poking through.

It is worth noting that while Suzuki's engineers claimed the new exhaust system was more efficient than the old 4-into-1, the new pipework weighed almost 7lb (3kg) more! Remember, this was a time when manufacturers were becoming increasingly aware of government legislation to control noise pollution.

Winding up the preload on both ends meant that the risk of dragging hardware was reduced on the street but it obviously meant that road-racers – who Suzuki were hoping were going to want to put this bike on the track – would have to resort to some major suspension changes.

Leonard concluded his *Superbike* magazine test: 'As a racer it has no peers in the under-£5,000 market; on the road and for everyday use it's not the most practical, but is definitely the most fun.'

The same year, 1988, also brought the launch of the RC30 Honda – a V4 Superbike contender – in time for the new World Superbike Championship that was to kick off at Donington Park on 3 April. American Honda, however, did not import the bike, fearing government regulations restricting superbikes might be triggered by a bike that went beyond the standards set by Suzuki back in 1985. The RC30 was the lightest, fastest, most powerful, most expensive 750 to come out of Japan: the racetracks were to see a lot of the RC30 in 1988 and beyond.

With no RC30, American Honda was forced to race its VFR – now two years old. Rainey had gone GP racing so Bubba Shobert, Laguna Seca winner in 1987, became Honda's sole rider. And he was back on Michelins.

Roger Marshall, without a regular ride following the last-minute collapse of the sponsorship deal with the official Suzuki team, rode a stock-looking GSX-R750 supplied by dealer Padgetts during the traditional Easter Match races in 1988. He then starred at the Donington WSB opener, gaining fourth place. (Colin Fraser)

SECOND-GENERATION RACING

The Yoshimura R & D team had also lost Schwantz to Team Suzuki and the GP wars. Doug Polen, twenty-seven years old, was enlisted as his replacement, taking with him a Dunlop tyre contract. Polen was also contracted to race Supersport 600 and Supersport 750 for the Yoshimura team. After an abortive try-out with up-coming Thomas Stevens, Californian Scott Gray, the 1987 F-USA Champion riding a Yosh Suzuki, filled the second berth. He had a Michelin contract! There were also suggestions that both Polen and Gray had to take cash to the team, which had had its support budget slashed by Suzuki America – but these rumours were never substantiated.

Instead of concentrating their efforts on the new GSX-R750 – which was imported into the States – Yoshimura also opted to run their 1987 bike – officially unable to extract more horsepower from the new short-stroke motor than they had from the older long-stroke.

The season, as usual, kicked off at Daytona and Kevin Schwantz was entered in what was to be his only AMA Superbike ride of the year. He was supplied with a brand-new Yoshimura Japan Suzuki GSX-R750J, which proved slower on top speed than Polen's 1987 ex-Schwantz model and the similar 1987 bike ridden by Japanese TTF1 Champion, Yukiya Ohshima, who qualified fourth fastest.

Even so, Schwantz still managed to sneak pole position, after knocking himself about in an earlier practice crash in the chicane and injuring his left wrist. He also bruised his right foot.

Schwantz's bike featured an engine displacement of 770cc (73mm bore x 44.7mm stroke), taking into account the 1mm oversize bores AMA still permitted. It had a compression ratio of 13.2:1 with Yoshimura claiming 136bhp at 12,500rpm – at the gearbox – the same as for the 1987 bike but with improved acceleration. Power hit hard earlier (8,000rpm) thanks to Yoshimura cams – actually 1987 works profile.

There was also a curved alloy radiator, which would have been too costly to include in the privateer race kit! The exhaust headers continued to sport Yoshimura's 'mid-range-boosting' cylindrical balance canisters between cylinders 1 and 2, and 3 and 4.

The new, heavier frame meant that Yoshimura no longer had to ballast the machine to pass tech inspection, nor was there a need to brace up the frame spares to reduce flex as there had been with previous GSX-Rs. The weight was bang on the 380lb (173kg) AMA Superbike limit.

Up front there were trick prototype Showa forks with single-rate springing and no anti-dive. As in the previous year, the front end sported Nissin calipers and discs. The bracing on the swing-arm was now on top of the box-section arm; whereas previous year it had been underslung. Schwantz and Ohshima both ran Michelins.

The traditional Camel Challenge, a five-lap dash preceding AMA Superbike nationals of the era that paid $10,000 to the winner and $2,500 to second place, was rained off so was included as part of the 200-Miler – becoming the first five laps of the race!

Polen won the sprint but then Schwantz turned up the wick to win the

Man with the mike, Paul Fowler (second left), homes in on the 1991 World Cup winner, Michel Simeon. (Colin Fraser)

World Cup Glory

An innovation by Suzuki Japan for 1988 was the Suzuki World Cup Final held at the Jerez circuit in southern Spain during the weekend of 9, 10 and 11 December. The Finals, based loosely on the successful GSX-R Cup Series in America, brought together thirty-five top Suzuki riders from all over the world. They would compete in two races with the overall winner decided on points.

The total prize fund was (US)$24,000 with $5,000 going to the winner and money paid out right down to thirty-fifth place! Pole position was worth $500. Sponsorship came from Avello SA and the Suzuki Motor Co. Assistance came from the Spanish Tourist Board, the local Andalucian Tourist Council, Iberia Airlines and Michelin Tyres.

The bikes were based on production Spanish-market versions of the GSX-R750J with minor changes for the race track. Michelin Hi-Sport radial tyres replaced the original equipment rubber. The stock rear Showa units were replaced with remote reservoir shocks. Racing-quality brake pads were used. The 1989 model exhausts were polished aluminium instead of the stock black. Rear-view mirrors and turn signals were removed.

The machines, which riders were allocated by means of a lottery, were prepared with one simple objective in mind – to allow close competition under fair and equal terms using pure production machines with a minimum of alterations.

The entry list included; Tony Armstrong, Grant Hodgson, Trevor Adams from Australia; Toni Rechtberger from Austria; Belgian Patrick Orban; Mike Griffiths and Steve Dick from Canada; Gerard Jolivet, Phillipe Mouchet and Gerald Muteau from France; Mario Rubatto and Klaus Liegibel from Germany; Luis Carlos Maurel from Spain; Christer Lindholm from Sweden; and Britons Ray Stringer, Mark Linscott and Mike Hodges.

Grant Hodgson won the event from Swede Christer Lindholm and Frenchman Phillipe Mouchet. Incredibly there was no other racing during the weekend: the remainder of Sunday's race-day programme was filled with a rock concert and three Match races between Pepsi Suzuki GP stars Kevin Schwantz and Rob McElnea.

The second annual Suzuki GSX-R750 World Cup on 15-17 December took on a different format but was again held at Jerez. There was still a race for production GSX-Rs, but this time the entry was restricted to privateer riders. The new idea was to run a separate Superbike race for importer-backed riders, so Doug Polen lined up on a 1989 GSX-R750R in Kyoseki GP-X Oil-sponsored Yoshimura colours – the fairing actually coming from team mate Ohshima's F1 All Japan bike!

Unlike the production entry, which was forced to run new Michelin radials, the Superbike riders were allowed freedom of choice, so Polen was on his regular Dunlops.

Fifteen riders from nine countries contested the Superbike event and in the dry first leg Polen won by 17 secs from Frenchman Adrien Morillas and German Ernst Gschwender. In the wet second leg, Polen's Dunlops were not hooking up so well and his bike was sliding badly. He could only finish fifth so Gschwender's win over Ohshima and Morillas gave him overall victory.

A German – Klaus Liegibel – won the Production race, too, from a field representing eighteen nations. The prod bikes, thirty-two stock GSX-R750Ks supplied by Suzuki, were equipped with GSX-R750R-model Showa adjustable rear shocks and the Michelins. There was no steering damper fitted and neither gearing nor jetting could be altered. Each rider had five sets of tyres to use as he pleased.

After Grant Hodgson's win in 1988 it seemed that Australia was set to continue its domination of the series when Trevor Jordan qualified only sixth but won the first race by 8.84 secs, despite a mid-race rain shower.

Briton Ray Stringer – just back racing after recovering from breaking both wrists in a Mallory crash earlier in the year – finished second after battling with pole sitter, Liegibel, who had survived two mid-race tumbles! Stringer also raced in the Superbike event on a Durex Suzuki and was placed tenth overall.

The rain worsened for the second race and Liegibel cleared off from the start. Stringer and Canadian Steve Dick battled for second but both fell, Stringer remounting to stay second. Dick was credited with seventh. Jordan finished third to tie on points with Liegibel but the overall win went to the German because of his faster total elapsed time.

A total of forty-one riders crashed during the four GSX-R races. The European Suzuki importers came off worst: they had agreed to buy all the production bikes following the race, intending to sell them on!

With the Suzuki GSX-R750 World Cup entering its third year, the event moved to Paul Ricard in southern France, and was this time backed by Lucky Strike and Castrol. The races became a supporting event during the Bol d'Or World Endurance race weekend.

It also reverted to the original format of two races with all thirty riders from fifteen different countries on identically prepared production machines. Yet again an Australian was to the fore, this time Matt Blair, who qualified on pole and won both races. German Reinar Janisch finished second overall with Swede Tony Hogstrom third.

Germany hosted the 1991 World Cup at Hockenheim with Belgian Michel Simeon taking the overall victory but only after two of the closest-fought races in the event's history. James Whitham led first, but ran off course. Then Canadian Jeff Gaynor won the lead, only for his bike to blow up.

It was not the first. The German event brought controversy when several other engines failed. It was suggested that the new bikes had not been run in properly and had promptly seized on the flat-out Hockenheim course. It was also suggested the German riders had access to the machines prior to the event. All in all, it was not good PR for Suzuki.

For 1992 it was back to Paul Ricard with the new water-cooled GSX-R750W, Lucky Strike again being the title sponsors with Michelin, NGK, Castrol, Nissin and Showa also contributing sponsorship.

Frenchman Jean-Marc Deletang, a twenty-six-year-old from Blois, provided a home victory with the closest finish in the five-year history of the series. Just two-tenths of a second split Deletang from German runner-up Achim Penisch at the end of the decisive second race.

Twenty-six riders from fifteen different countries took part in the races in front of 100,000 fans for the richest-ever one-make series prize. A massive $32,600 fund was shared among the

GSX-R World Cup 1991 with James Whitham leading from Jeff Gaynor. Whitham ran off the track; Gaynor blew up. (Colin Fraser)

field with all the starters receiving $300. Deletang scooped $7,000 for his overall win, while pole position earned Penisch $700. Suzuki marketing service department manager, Mitsuo Itoh welcomed teams to the event and Italian Cristiano Migliorati, son of former 500GP racer Walter, won the first leg by four tenths of a second from Penisch. Deletang was third after his engine started to splutter short of fuel.

The second leg saw a repeat battle until Migliorati crashed out and Deletang outdrafted Penisch on the final lap to get the all-important win to take win the Cup with 32 points to 30 on aggregate.

The final GSX-R750 World Cup, again backed by Lucky Strike, was held in Italy at the Monza circuit in late September 1993. Italian Bruno Cirafici used his local circuit knowledge to dominate the event. He was fastest in each practice session and won both races in poor weather conditions on his way to collecting the $10,000 first prize.

Roberto Teneggi finished second overall while German Claus Ehrenberger was third. Frenchman Juan-Eric Gomez was the only rider to give Cirafici any real worries. Gomez finished second in race two after crashing at the chicane in the first leg whilst battling with the Italian.

Respected tuner Mike Crompton gives the thumbs-up after surveying Michel Mercier's crash damage

Gary Goodfellow raced with Japanese sponsors, Don Knit, in 1988. Here he leads fellow countryman Michel Mercier during the Donington World Superbike race. Both raced Suzukis. (Colin Fraser)

'real' race by 90 seconds from Polen. Schwantz was said to have told reporters: 'The $23,995 for the 200-Mile win was better to have than risk crashing out in the first five laps chasing $10,000!'

After twenty years of racing at Daytona, Suzuki had finally won the Daytona 200. But it was the last the series saw of Schwantz. Yoshimura's team leader, Polen, however, had another arch-rival to contend with – Bubba Shobert, who had crashed in his heat race at Daytona, missed the 200-Mile start due to a fuel vapour lock, but still pulled up to third place.

But while the pilot's names had changed from the previous term when Rainey and Schwantz had slugged it out, the race again became a war between the Honda and Suzuki factory number ones – Shobert and Polen respectively. And, for the second year running, it was Honda who came out on top. This was a disappointment for Polen, who had gone into the season hoping to lift six championship titles: AMA Superbike, AMA Supersport 750, AMA Supersport 600, 1100 Suzuki Cup, 750 Suzuki Cup and 600 Suzuki Cup!

Shobert won Road Atlanta ahead of Polen after Polen's Suzuki had faltered just after taking the lead from Shobert. It chimed back in but he ran off the track trying to repass the Honda. They reversed the result at Loudon. A week later Polen repeated at Elkhart Lake – as well as winning the Camel Challenge and both Supersport races – but then it was Shobert's turn at Laguna Seca, where the Michelins seemed to suit the course better.

Shobert also won at Mid Ohio, when Polen uncharacteristically slid off just after taking the lead. He remounted to finish sixth, blaming oil on the track from an earlier crash for his downfall.

While Polen picked up the final round, Shobert's safe second was enough to allow him to claim the title by five points. Doug Chandler was third, also on a Honda, and Scott Gray trailed in at fourth after several crashes.

Polen, however, won the 750 and 600 Supersport titles for Suzuki. The 750 class was an innovation at AMA Nationals and the new J model won every race. Polen took five races, including Daytona. David Sadowski won two. Scott Russell won at local track Road Atlanta and tied Sadowski on points for the runner-up slot, three points behind Polen. Cal Rayborn won the last race at Sonoma.

RACING IN BRITAIN

Polen also starred in the 1988 running of the traditional Easter match races. This time around the dire state of British racing was acknowledged and the event was renamed the Eurolantic Challenge – the competitors were a team of North Americans (four Americans, four Canadians), two UK teams and a European team that included an Australian!

Nonetheless the racing, with three rounds at Brands on Good Friday and three more at Donington the next day, was as exciting as ever, producing another Honda versus Suzuki scrap with Polen edging out Shobert by three points to be named top scorer. Polen won four of the six races and was placed second to Shobert in the other two.

Shobert – who had broken his wrist at Paddock Hill during practice the previous year – finished runner-up on three occasions but was beaten back to third in the second leg by Gary Goodfellow on a Suzuki. Scott Gray was third in overall points but never really shone as expected on the Yosh bike.

Ironically the Yosh bikes and Shobert's Honda were unable to run in the World Superbike race at Donington during the same weekend since their AMA-legal carbs did not comply with World Superbike regulations. Shobert started the race late.

In the British Match Race team was an all-new UK Suzuki line-up. This year there was no place for Roger Marshall, even though the team had let him take their bikes to race in the winter Swann series and Marshall had brought Suzuki two British titles the previous year.

There was no place for Iddon either, and Rex White was no longer involved in running the team. Instead Mick Grant was now team manager and had signed James Whitham and Phil Mellor on, it was claimed at the time, a meagre £5,000 annual salary! The Skoal Bandit Suzuki riders' salaries were more like £15,000 per year.

Rex White had asked for his duties to be reduced:

> I wanted to relieve the pressure a little. I didn't want to get out completely. I wanted to remain involved but more in the background. It was decided that Mick should take over as team manager and I'd help him as much as I could. It was still two full years of racing weekends before I stopped going to every meeting.

White's departure from the official position of team manager also led to the end of Marshall's involvement with the team. He had gone off racing in the Australian Swann series during the winter and came back to find himself without a ride. White recalls:

> Roger lost his place when Suzuki were unsure of their plans. There were no new bikes coming from Japan so the company (Heron Suzuki) decided on a low-key operation with Mick. But Mick didn't want to work at Crawley. All the equipment went to his workshops up north and he signed Jamie [Whitham] and Mez [Phil Mellor].

Suzuki pulled out of the World TTF1 Championship and there was seemingly no interest in the company pursuing glory in the exciting new World Superbike series either. White adds:

> I was the one who kept Suzuki's TTF1 campaign going. My only ally at Heron Suzuki was Denys Rohan. The company chairman, John Norman, never had the slightest interest in racing. Denys left, I quit and that was the end. I'll never understand why the company has not taken more interest in the sport.

Marshall, however, raced a near-stock Suzuki supplied by Padgetts during the Easter campaign and scored fifth and sixth places in the World Superbike, for fourth overall (the only time WSB featured an overall aggregate result of two-leg events), and he achieved tenth place in the Match Races, only two points adrift of Whitham.

Twenty-two-year-old Whitham, however, won the British Production title riding a 750J when the opposition was on 1000 Yamahas or 1100 Suzukis. Several other riders started on similar machinery but chucked in the towel early in the year. Whitham stuck with it and TX Michelin rubber gave an advantage, but the young charger still had to ride the wheels off the 750 at tighter circuits to score big points to balance out the tough meetings at fast tracks like Snetterton.

Whitham was also second in the TTF1 British Championship and Mellor third after Whitham, in particular, had given

eventual champion Darren Dixon a hard time. Dixon was riding an RG500 Suzuki for Padgetts – effectively a lightweight GP bike – against the heavier four-strokes. The 500 had advantages in horsepower, acceleration, braking and handling!

Suzuki did not contest the UK Superstock races after series organizer Bruce Cox introduced a control tyre rule and did a deal with Dunlop to supply rubber. Suzuki were contracted to Michelin but Grant says he withdrew from the series on a matter of principle, objecting to the idea of a control tyre rule for any national championship.

It was just as well that Suzuki did not take part: the series became virtually a mono-marque championship with the new Honda RC30s winning every single race and Brian Morrison taking the title. The potent new V4s also dominated the Supersport 750 TT with Whitham's fourth place being the best Suzuki result could have hoped for.

Ernst Gschwender on the Suzuki Deutschland GSX-R750 during 1988. Gschwender won the 1987 and 1988 German Superbike titles on Suzukis. (Kel Edge)

WORLD SUPERBIKE

New to the world stage in 1988 was the World Superbike Championship, yet instead of using this exciting new venture to promote the future of international four-stroke racing, the FIM also continued to run their ailing TTF1 series.

World Superbike, a concept created by former AMA National racer Steve McLaughlin and promoted by the New Zealand-based Sports Marketing Company, attracted a class line-up but sadly not many chose to race Suzukis. Anders Andersson was one who committed to a full season but the Swede struggled to make the new GSX-R750J competitive with the restrictive stock 36mm Slingshot CV Mikunis – as demanded by the series regulations. He eventually went back to racing in the TTF1 series, where flatslide carbs could be used. He won the Finnish round at

Kuovola and wound up fifth in the series.

Suzuki did have the occasional good result in World Superbike race, though. In addition to Roger Marshall's fourth in the first round at Donington, a Suzuki won at Sugo – the sole victory of the series – thanks to Gary Goodfellow. Riding a Yoshimura-supplied Suzuki he won the first leg and finished third in the second behind little-known Australian Michael Doohan on a Yamaha and local Honda works rider Kenichiro Iwahashi. Yoshimura's Ohshima finished third in the first race.

WORLD ENDURANCE

Suzuki claimed yet another World Endurance title in 1988 when Herve Moineau and Thierry Crine were crowned champions riding for Dominique Meliand's SERT outfit – the team's second straight title. Unlike

James Whitham finished runner-up in the Shell Oils British TTF1 series – Darren Dixon beating him with a square-four 500cc Suzuki two-stroke! (Terry Howe)

Trevor Nation was the runner-up in the MCN/EBC Superstock Championship. He raced this Suzuki at Brands Hatch in May and finished ninth, but, like most other title aspirants on GSX-Rs, he switched to an RC30 to remain competitive. (Terry Howe)

1987, when critics claimed it to be a hollow victory in the face of little opposition, the 1988 title came after tough competition from the rival factories.

The team finished third in the first of a very abbreviated series that now boasted only two 24-Hour races plus the Suzuka Eight-Hours. Moineau, Bruno Le Bihan and Crine finished third at Le Mans, fourth at Suzuka (without Le Bihan), and won Spa to beat Honda's Alex Vieira to the title by four points. Vieira, Christophe Bouheben and Dominique Sarron won the *Bol* while the Suzuki trio was second.

Suzuki also finished second at Suzuka with Schwantz and Polen a lap behind Yamaha's winners Kevin Magee and Wayne Rainey. The Yoshimura Suzuki was sponsored by Sietto GP1 oil and sported Michelin tyres. Polen, of course, ran Dunlops in his AMA campaign.

An innovation for 1988 was the Suzuki World Cup Final held at Jerez in southern Spain during the weekend of 9–11 December. The Finals brought together thirty-five top Suzuki riders from all over the world, with the overall winner decided on points from the two races.

Riding bikes based on production Spanish-market versions of the GSX-R750J, Australian Grant Hodgson won the race from Swede Christer Lindholm and Frenchman Phillip Mouchet.

6 RR for Real Race Bike

After the major revamp the previous year, there were no significant changes in store for the base-model 1989 GSX-R750K. Frame and engine were virtually the same and only the suspension was altered to eradicate the 1988 bike's propensity for dragging the pipes and fairing.

The non-adjustable shock top mount was lowered was lowered by 4mm and the fork tubes lengthened by 6mm. The fairing was also re-contoured around the lowers. The net result of the changes was no more ground clearance problems on the street.

For racing applications, however, there was a new, limited production, GSX-R750R – a street-legal race bike intended for World Superbike competition. Bore and stroke was 70mm x 48.7mm compared to the 73mm x 44.7mm of the street bike. It boasted reshaped intake ports, 10mm racing plugs (the road bike had 12mm plugs) and 40mm Slingshot carbs (compared to 36mm for the street). There were also racing valves and springs, a stronger crank, stronger rods and a magnesium valve cover.

The main oil-cooler was larger and there was an auxiliary cooler mounted low in the fairing. Crankcases and crankcase covers were chamfered for improved cornering clearance.

The RR came with a close-ratio six-speed gearbox, and a four-into-one stainless steel exhaust with aluminium muffler. The bodywork was fibreglass, with the fairing sporting quick fasteners and a lower screen. Fuel tank was aluminium alloy.

The RR Suzuki came up short in performance on the track compared to the rival Honda and Yamaha competition. On the road, the flatslide carbs made it hard to ride smoothly. (Rex White Collection)

Yoshimura's MJN Carburettor

Note: This text is edited from Yoshimura Japan's MJN Carburettor information sheets issued with an official Yoshimura 1990 catalogue by the Yoshimura UK distributor of the time during 1992.

MJN stands for Multiple Jet Nozzle Carburettor. According to Yoshimura's company history, Fujio Yoshimura invented the MJN in 1992. According to Yoshimura R & D race team manager, Don Sakakura, the Yosh Suzukis benefited from MJN in racing applications as early as 1989, when Jamie James won the AMA Superbike and Supersport 750 titles on GSX-Rs.

Fujio theorized, that according to flow mechanics, a fluid (air) that flows one way in a pipeline flows fastest at the centre and very slowly near the wall. This also means that the centre of the flow has the biggest negative pressure. Consequently an injection nozzle near the centre of the venturi part would help vaporize the fuel efficiently. This would help give a carburettor good vaporization and atomization – and improve throttle response.

And the differences between a conventional carb and the MJN carb? In a conventional carburettor the fuel comes from the lower part of the venturi bore (which is adjusted by the main jet, needle jet, and jet needle) to the exposed part of the tip of the needle and is then vaporizes and atomized.

With MJN, the fuel goes through the main jet, flows inside the hollow pipe of the multi-nozzle and then is sucked out by several small nozzle holes.

In a conventional carb, the difference in ratio between air and fuel against a sudden throttle opening gives time lag and gushes out big drops of fuel until the discharge flow stabilizes. This produces the effect of bad throttle responses or 'coughing'. There are also cases when fuel flows to the intake port as liquid because of bad vaporization. This could foul the plug.

In the MJN carb, the fuel vaporizes and atomizes well at any opening of the throttle making the correct mixture instantaneously. It thus offers a good throttle response.

Under braking, and with a closed throttle, fuel is being sucked out of the pilot jet of a conventional carb. And fuel that is not needed is not sucked out by strong negative pressure made by the clearance of the needle jet and the jet needle. This has a bad effect on the fuel consumption rate and can foul the spark plug. In the MJN, theoretically no fuel comes out when the throttle is closed.

In the MJN carb fuel is ideally diffused throughout the intake port and mixed with air at any opening of the throttle due to the fuel vaporization by a few holes of the nozzles. It also improves atomization of the fuel to give improved engine performance and quickens throttle response – on stock and race-tuned engines.

Yoshimura also claim that the MJN carb is less prone to sticking throttles and less affected by climatic or atmospheric changes. Finally they say that the system, owing to its increased efficiency, reduces CO and HC emissions.

Russell on the Yosh bike at Loudon in 1989. Note the new-style air intakes with a direct run into the dummy front section of the gas tank. Russell paid for the ride to make his name in Superbike circles – a few grand well spent! (Colin Fraser)

GSX-R750RR Slingshot (1989)

Four-cylinder, four-stroke, air/oil-cooled with SACS, DOHC, TSCC, four valves per cylinder

Engine

Bore and stroke	70mm x 48.7mm
Cubic capacity	749cc
Compression ratio	10.9:1
Carburettors	4 Mikuni 40mm Slingshot
Ignition	Transistorized
Starter system	Electric
Lubrication system	Wet sump

Transmission

Clutch	Wet, multi-plate type
Gearbox	Six-speed, constant mesh

Suspension

Front suspension	43mm telescopic, spring preload, fully adjustable
Rear suspension	Full Floater, spring preload, fully adjustable four-way rebound damping adjust

Brakes and Tyres

Front brake	Twin 310mm disc, hydraulically operated Nissin four-piston
Rear brake	Single 200mm disc, hydraulically operated
Front tyre	120/70VR-17 V250
Rear tyre	160/60VR-17 V250

Dimensions (in/mm)

Overall length	81.1/2,060mm
Overall width	28.7/730mm
Overall height	44.5/1,130mm
Wheelbase	55.5/1,410mm
Ground clearance	4.7/120mm
Seat height	31.3/795mm
Dry weight	411lb (187kg)

Two team mates: one ecstatic, one not so ecstatic. Scott Russell (right) has just won his first-ever AMA National Superbike round during 1989. Jamie James is the rider he edged out to win. The track is Road Atlanta, Russell's backyard. James, however, had the last laugh: he won the title and Russell was second. (Colin Fraser)

James Whitham did not fare too well at Daytona. His Suzuki was slug-slow compared with the American factory bikes. At home, though, he finished fourth in the MCN British TTF1 series. (Colin Fraser)

There was a 5.50 x 17in rear wheel. Rear suspension was a remote reservoir racing shock with adjustable rebound and compression damping.

An additional kit from Suzuki included forged pistons with high compression ratio, different cams, racing exhaust, different transmission gears to vary ratios, extra countershaft sprockets, racing spark plugs, dry clutch, racing cam-chain tensioner, black box ignition, starter motor and alternator plugs and a large sub oil-cooler – the sort of parts in the Yoshimura catalogue.

Kit chassis parts included a selection of rear sprockets from 38 to 45 teeth, adjustable swing-arm struts to change rear ride height, racing forks and springs, racing rear shock, adjustable steering damper, racing wiring harness with kill switch and small battery.

The claimed dry weight for the RR, as it was known, was 412lb (186.8kg). The price was £9,000 and only fifty were imported into the UK. They arrived late – after the Isle of Man TT in June!

When it did finally reach the showrooms – or riders' workshops – it was an expensive, dismal failure. On the race-track it still came up short on spec compared to the rival Hondas and Yamahas. And on the road the flatslide carbs messed up its usability as a road bike and the suspension changes made the bike over-sensitive on the road.

RACING THE RR

On track, Suzuki claimed major success in the States with Jamie James and Scott Russell finishing 1–2 respectively in the AMA Superbike Championship. The series was cut back to six races and produced five different winners on four different makes of motorcycle.

To join the Yoshimura team, both Russell and James paid a $25,000 deposit to race against winning and contingency money – a good deal to get a top Superbike seat. Russell said it was a sure-fire way to get the necessary top-class equipment to get noticed. It worked for both riders.

The season kicked off at Daytona and things looked good for Suzuki again. After qualifying, GSX-R750s filled the top six slots with Polen on pole by over a second from Russell, David Sadowski

Miguel Duhamel gave the RR a debut victory at the season-opening San Air, Quebec, Canadian national, edging out Honda Canada's John Ramsay in a dramatic last-lap battle. (Colin Fraser)

(Vance & Hines Suzuki), James, Gary Goodfellow (Don Knit) and German Martin Wimmer – on what was basically a street bike with a Yoshimura engine.

Russell was involved in a start-line crash that brought the red flag. He was unhurt and made the restart but his chain derailed, which lost him several laps.

Meanwhile oil caused Goodfellow to have a huge crash while he was leading after Sadowski had gone out with transmission problems.

Polen was leading when his bike developed an oil leak. Then James was in front on his way to victory with a huge lead and two laps to run when he thought his bike was running short of fuel. He pitted to refuel but it turned out to be an ignition fault. He finished the race second – to privateer John Ashmead, who raced a 1986 VFR750!

Russell won at Road Atlanta while Sadowski, with a slipping clutch, beat James for third. The second Yosh rider used a stock swing-arm after his trick one had broken in practice.

Russell was hurting at Loudon: he had crashed the Supersport bike and broken his collarbone. James won the Superbike race after battling with Sadowski until

the V & H bike broke. Russell finished an incredible third on the switchback 1.8-mile (2.9km) track after persuading a doctor to sign a medical release that said he was fit enough to ride!

At Elkhart Russell was leading on the last lap with James on the gas trying to close him down when the pair collided and crashed. Richard Arnaiz, riding a YZF Yamaha, picked up the win. At Mid Ohio Doug Chandler, on a Muzzy Kawasaki took the honours from Russell while James, thinking of the championship, finished a safe fifth.

It was all on the final race at Heartland Park, Topeka, Kansas – a new facility. James had severe brake chatter all race, which was later found to be a buckled front wheel. Nevertheless, he soldiered on, scrapping with Arnaiz, to finish fourth and wrap up the title by five points from his team mate, Russell. The latter finished second to winner Chandler to clinch the runner-up spot by four points from Arnaiz.

James also won the Supersport 750 class from Kawasaki's Chandler and Russell. Suzuki won nine of the ten races: James took three, Russell bagged four. Tommy Lynch and Sadowski scored one apiece – while Chandler scored

Kawasaki's only win of the year at Lexington.

POLEN'S SUCCESSES

Doug Polen, meanwhile, took the All Japan F1 and F3 championships riding for Yoshimura – the first rider to win both titles in the same season. He had raced the Suzuka Eight-Hour the previous year and won a couple of All Japan Superbike races. The exposure earned him the full-time slot. The outstanding performance in a dominant 1989 season was a win in the prestigious 200K Suzuki race. Polen also scored Suzuki's sole win in the World Superbike Championship when he won the miserably wet first leg at Sugo. He finished fourth in the second leg.

Polen also won a non-championship Superbike race in Mexico on 10 December riding one of the American Yoshimura bikes; he took full advantage of the AMA race regulations, which permitted 1mm-bore oversize engines and special works-based carbs. While Polen won in the stifling heat, he did not dominate as many expected and it was thought that the oil-cooled Suzuki had lost power in the heat – even though the bike sported two extra oil radiators mounted longways on the frame rails to supplement the huge curved radiator in front of the powerplant.

However, Polen was on a special Yoshimura Japan GSX-R750R for the second Suzuki World Cup in Jerez, which now had a different format. There was still a race for production GSX-Rs, but the entry was restricted to privateer riders. And now there was a separate Superbike race for importer-backed riders – where Polen lined up on a 1989 GSX-R750R.

In the dry, Polen won the first leg by 17 secs from Frenchman Adrien Morillas and German Ernst Gschwender but in the wet second leg he was unable to get any grip and finished fifth. Canadian Mercier – in his final race aboard a Suzuki – led but crashed and Gschwender won and took the overall

Ray Stringer set the pace in the Suzuki World Cup during 1991. (Colin Fraser)

title. Another German, Klaus Liegibel, won the Production race too. Mercier, whose name had sold many GSX-Rs in Canada, quit Suzuki to race Yamahas in 1990 and won the RACE national title for his new employer. He would quit racing for good at the end of 1990.

Elsewhere, as far as Suzuki racing was concerned, there was little to shout about in 1989. Apart from Polen's Sugo WSB win, Suzuki had little representation in the burgeoning World Superbike series. Anders Andersson had defected to Yamaha and Gschwender's German-importer team only contested selected races. The lanky Gschwender had won the German national title aboard a GSX-R750 in 1987 and 1988.

WORLD ENDURANCE

In World Endurance Moineau and Crine finished down in fifth place in a year when every race was won by Honda. The Suzuki threw a rod at Le Mans, finished third at Spa (with Michel Graziano) and in the *Bol* (with Adrien Morillas). Yakiya

Ohshima and Katsuro Takayoshi were placed fifth at Suzuka in the Eight-Hour; Schwantz and Polen were eighth, Moineau and Crine ninth. The Schwantz/Polen entry was half supported by Yoshimura and half by Suzuki Japan. The bike even had a split paint scheme: Yosh red and black on the left, Suzuki white and blue on the right!

In an effort to dissipate heat generated during racing, the machine had three oil radiators: one small rad actually sat behind a larger one across the frame in front of the motor and there was a third smaller rad in the fairing nose.

The traditional Suzuki GSX-R frame featured an adjustable steering head and a fully triangulated swing-arm. The previous year's Eight-Hour bike had the bracing under the swing-arm but Schwantz had ground through it. This year the bracing was on top of the arm but still managed to drag the bike in the turns! The bike had Kayaba forks, 17in wheels and GP rubber.

World TTF1 had also become the domain of the RC30, with the top five riders mounted on the V4s. Whitham's

Mick Grant took a huge contingent of bikes to the TT in 1989 with backing from Durex. It ended in tragedy with the death of team rider Phil Mellor in the 1300 Production TT. (Mick Grant Collection)

Doug Polen on the title-winning Yoshimura Japan GSX-R750 TTF1 bike he raced at the Jerez World Cup Finals. He won the first leg with ease but struggled for grip in the wet second race. (Colin Fraser)

ninth place in the series was won courtesy of his TT performance – and a fifth place at the Assen round later the same month. Other Suzuki scorers included Ohshima's third place in the Sugo opener. His Yoshimura team mate Polen finished sixth in the same event.

For Suzuki the British season had kicked off with a celebration. A new sponsor, Durex, the biggest manufacturer of condoms in Britain at the time, enabled the team to expand to four riders: Whitham, Phil Mellor, Jason Lodge and Paul Booler. Whitham and Mellor would race 600s, 750s and big production bikes while the two other young riders would represent Suzuki in the Supersport 400 class on RGV250s.

The team suffered a terrible loss during the 1300 Production TT when Phil Mellor was killed, but picked themselves up to continue the year. James Whitham finished sixth in the F1 TT and was fourth in the ACU British TTF1 series despite injuring his ankle in an Ulster GP crash. He was also joint third in the production class and fifth in the 600s even though his season was cut short. However, he did not break into the top ten overall standings in the televised, one-day Shell Oils Supercup in either the TTF1 or Superbike class.

Polen in Mexico on the Yoshimura R & D Suzuki. He won the non-championship race. (Kel Edge)

7   Return of the Long-Stroke

Suzuki continued to develop the GSX-R750 with a sporting application in mind. Race tuners found it difficult to extract winning horsepower out of the 1988 and 1989 short-stroke engines, so for 1990 Suzuki's engineers reverted to a longer stoke and smaller bore for the new GSX-R750L (70mm x 48.7mm – which was used previously in the 1986 and 1987 GSX-Rs compared to the last two years of 73mm x 44.7mm). This – plus altered valve angles – increased port velocity to allow more efficient cylinder charging and improved low– and mid-range torque.

The new engine also came with 38mm CV semi-flatslide Mikuni Slingshot carbs matched to reshaped inlet ports.

These incorporated a circuit that sprayed fuel into the venturis at full throttle to compensate for a leaner main jet. These had been revised for more mid-range response and improved throttle response.

Larger diameter intake valves (27mm – up by 1mm from the 1987 engine – and 24mm for the exhausts valves) left very little space for conventional spark plugs – hence the adoption of 10mm spark plugs to replace the 12mm plugs.

Other changes included a redesigned cylinder head, still fitted with SACS and working in conjunction with a new curved oil cooler.

The sporting pretensions were also helped by new cams, lighter yet stronger

The 1990 GSX-R750L reverted to a long-stroke format but styling remained basically the same. (Courtesy Superbike Magazine)

GSX-R750L Slingshot (1990)

Four-cylinder, four-stroke, air/oil-cooled with SACS, DOHC, TSCC, four valves per cylinder

Engine

Bore and stroke	70mm x 48.7mm
Cubic capacity	749cc
Compression ratio	10.9:1
Carburettors	4 Mikuni BST38SS
Ignition	Transistorized
Starter system	Electric
Lubrication system	Wet sump

Transmission

Clutch	Wet, multi-plate type
Gearbox	Six-speed, constant mesh

Suspension

Front suspension	Inverted 41mm telescopic, spring preload fully adjustable, rebound and compression damping adjustable
Rear suspension	Full Floater, rebound damping four-way, compression damping twelve-way adjustable

Brakes and Tyres

Front brake	Twin floating disc, hydraulically operated
Rear brake	Single disc, hydraulically operated
Front tyre	120/70ZR-17
Rear tyre	160/60ZR-17

Dimensions (in/mm)

Overall length	81.1/2,060mm
Overall width	28.7/730mm
Overall height	44.8/1,140mm
Wheelbase	55.7/1,415mm
Ground clearance	5/125mm
Seat height	31.3/795mm
Dry weight	425lb (193kg)

Miguel Duhamel represented Suzuki on three fronts in 1990 – in the US with Yoshimura R & D, in the world Endurance Championship with Suzuki France, and at home in Canada for Suzuki Canada. This is the Canadian effort, with Mike Crompton (right) overseeing bike preparation. (Colin Fraser)

con-rods with a bigger I-beam cross-section, short slipper pistons with crowns coated in Alumite (which Suzuki claimed improved surface hardness), and a new six-spring clutch to replace the old four-spring unit. The compression ratio remained unaltered at 10.9:1. Finally, the R once again sported a four-into-one exhaust race-style system – in corrosion-resistant stainless steel and based on the 1989 GSX-R750R system.

In fact, much of the spec of the bike was up to that of the previous year's RR limited edition race replica – at almost half the price!

ROAD TESTING THE NEW BIKE

Cycle World, in a launch test of the 1990 model, said the changes also smoothed out the power-band peaks and troughs to offer a linear power delivery all the way to the 13,000rpm red line (the same as the 1988 and 1989 motors despite the 1990 model's shorter stroke).

In stock form, during back-to-back dyno tests conducted by *American Roadracing*, the new motor was shown to produce 106bhp at 10,000rpm with 56.9ft/lb of torque at 9,250rpm. A small jetting change to the carbs saw that

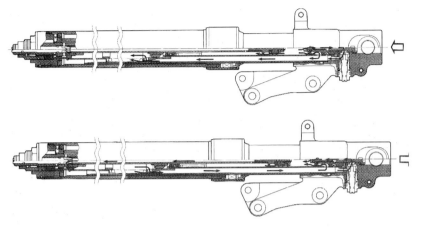

The 1990 GSX-R came with inverted forks; compression damping detail (top) and rebound (bottom).

increase to 119.1bhp at 11,250rpm and 58.9ft/lb of torque at 9,750rpm.

Chassis changes included a new 5.50 x 17in rear rim (1in wider than the previous year) to accommodate a wider section 170/60-17in Michelin radial – and to allow fitment of racing slicks! The stock rims were fine for racing use. At the front was a 120/70-17in Michelin with a more rounded profile than the previous year's.

There was also a reduction in rake to 25.3 degrees but the same trail of 3.9in was kept, which helped to slow down the steering a little. There was a 10mm longer swing-arm, which was also beefed up, though the *CW* test maintained that the GSX-R had lost none of its manoeuvrability.

So the Suzuki now handled better, had more stability and ground clearance and maintained its reputation as a lightweight, if maybe not as light as the original R back in 1985 (it had gained 37lb (17kg) in the six years!).

The 1989 bike had a reputation for having a duff rear shock (due to heat fade) with most serious sport riders running aftermarket units. For 1990 Suzuki upgraded the stock Showa shock by

Below: Improved Slingshot carbs for the 1990 machine featured diaphragm holes venting to the carb's own filter, separate from the intake tract to improve throttle response and smoothness.

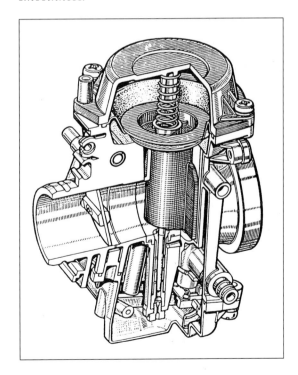

Duhamel won the penultimate AMA National of the year at Topeka, beating ultimate season champion, Doug Chandler. (Colin Fraser)

adding a remote reservoir, complete with compression-damping adjuster. The front 43mm Showa cartridge fork remained unchanged in the US but elsewhere the GSX-R750 sported a new inverted front fork.

The front brakes, previously with drilled rotors, were also upgraded to twin four-pot floating Nissin calipers, gripping 5mm thicker stainless steel rotors – no longer drilled, but slotted, to offer a greater heat-dissipating surface area.

In June 1990 *Motorcyclist* ran a shoot-out featuring the exotic RC30 Honda,

the heavy (512lb/233kg) Kawasaki ZX-7 and the GSX-R. The Suzuki topped the ZX-7 in almost every area: power band, peak power and smoothness. It also scored well on handling capabilities straight out of the box. But in terms of street and track the Kawasaki won. The test concluded that the V4 RC30, at $14,998, did not show any appreciable advantages in performance over either of the in-line fours, which sold at just over $6,000. Suzuki won the price tag war too – at $6,199.

If 1990 was an interim year, with little to shout about apart from putting the R

Doug Polen overcame a serious foot injury sustained during pre-season testing to win the AMA national at Road Atlanta after being drafted from Japan back to the injury-hit Stateside Yoshimura R & D effort for a one-off race appearance. (Colin Fraser)

Mick Grant's UK-based Durex Suzuki team fielded Roger Burnett in 1990 and took in a World Superbike race at Jerez. Team Grant with Mick (second from right), tuner Ron Grant (far right) and Burnett (second left) (Kel Edge)

back on track in terms of offering a more tuneable engine and lighter chassis, the same was true of its racetrack performances: there was little to shout about.

It did not help that in the US the AMA rewrote their rule book. Instead of having to import at least 200 units, large manufacturers now only had to import fifteen units of the model in question for Superbike homologation – and small manufacturers only had to bring in seven. The weight limit was also dropped to align with the WSB rules: 370lb (168kg) for four-cylinder bikes and 320lb (145kg) for twins. And the teams could use carbs and camshafts other than those on the imported machines, providing the parts were homologated separately.

Costs went through the roof. Vance & Hines used magnesium carbs worth £3,200 per set; their Yamaha OWO1 cost around $16,000. That was the initial purchase price; the bikes then had to be race-kitted. The public also had to pay dearly for the intricacies of Honda's V4 RC30s – around $15,000. Both bikes were very rare in the US but were 'must-haves' for racers.

THE YOSHIMURA BIKE

In the US Suzuki refused to import the limited edition GSX-R750R but instead opted to continue their policy of building a race bike from the base model, which retailed at $6,000.

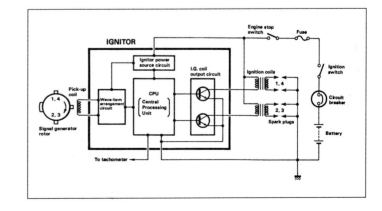

Suzuki's Digital Ignition Advance System – the microcomputer-controlled ignition system designed to match ignition advance to the engine rpm.

113

Burnett on British championship duty. Note the blanked-off air intakes on top of gas tank. (Clive Challinor)

Yoshimura stripped the stock frame of all unnecessary bracketry, then fitted KYB forks and a Fox rear shock, bolted to a different rear linkage. Wheels were either Marchesini or Technomagnesio. Yosh fitted their own lightweight bodywork.

Cycle World pointed out that while the Yosh bikes might have looked more exotic than their rival's machines, they actually used a lot of proprietary parts. For example, the triple oil-cooling system was made by Earls. Much of the trick-looking ancillaries like exhausts, engine cases, air scoops and so on came straight out of the Yosh catalogue, as did the beautifully louvred fairings.

Sven Seidel finished runner-up in the 1990 European Superbike championship. He matched Champion Rich Arnaiz on points but lost the title on the number of race wins 3–4. Seidel, though, was in spectacular form to win the wet Donington round. (Kel Edge)

SERT's bike at the Suzuka Eight-Hour. (Kel Edge)

Many of the engine internals were Yosh too. The RS40 flatslide carbs were tricked out in-house. And the fuel tank, based on the 1989 RR alloy tank, was also made by Yoshimura, incorporating a built-in ducting system to channel fresh cool air to the carbs. And what Yoshimura could not produce in-house, they bought in – Cosworth pistons, Carillo rods and so on.

With regard to riders, Yoshimura had lost James to the Ferracci Ducati team and Russell to Muzzy's Kawasaki outfit. Signed to fill their slots were Canadians Miguel Duhamel (twenty-two) and Steve Crevier (twenty-five). Both crashed out of qualifying for the Daytona 200, Crevier breaking his ankle and Duhamel damaging his right hand. The best Suzuki rider at Daytona in 1990 was Jay Springsteen in eighth place.

Tommy Lynch finished third on a Yosh Suzuki in the Supersport race behind Chandler and Russell on the Muzzy Kawasakis. Lynch would go on to finish third in the championship behind the two Kawasakis.

For the second round at Road Atlanta Yoshimura R & D flew Doug Polen in from Japan to join Duhamel on the grid. Polen, contracted to Dunlop for his Japanese racing, ran Dunlops at Road Atlanta although Yoshimura had a Michelin contract. The team experienced a lot of rear-wheel chatter during testing and Polen was forced to run an Endurance Monster Bike Shoot-out heat race in an attempt to sort it out.

Under normal circumstances this not have been a problem, but Polen was hurting. He had suffered a serious crash in February, losing four toes from his left foot after getting his boot jammed between the chain and sprocket in a pre-season test at Willow Springs. He had since fought back with incredible determination, but still suffered in protracted races.

Although in pain by the end of the twenty-four-lap race, and though the gear shift had worn through the skin graft on the end of his foot, Polen won a thriller from Kawasaki's Doug Chandler, Jamie James (Fast by Ferracci Ducati),

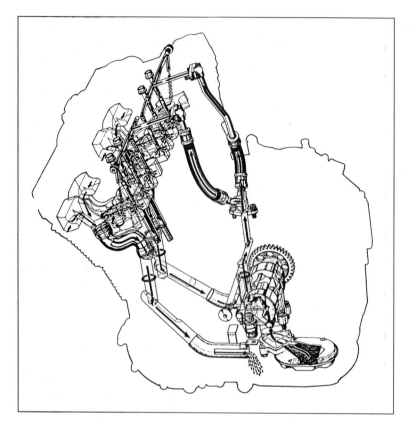

SACS, Suzuki's Advanced Cooling System in detail.

Thomas Stevens (V & H Yamaha) and Honda's Randy Renfrow. Duhamel finished back in tenth.

Duhamel, however, did win the Supersport 750 race, holding off a late charge from Russell. But in the same class at Loudon he crashed, breaking his leg, when the bike popped out of gear.

Crevier, back from injury but with his ankle still very sore, finished sixth after a smooth, sensible ride at Loudon. Unfortunately, Yoshimura R & D vice president, Suehiro Watanabe, wanted winners so Crevier was released from his contract.

At Road America old Yosh favourite Scott Gray was brought back into the team to replace Crevier, and Duhamel did not race because of his injured leg. Gray was battling with Ducati rider Jimmy Adamo when the V-twin blew up. Gray, right behind, could not avoid Adamo's bike and crashed at 140mph (225km/h), breaking bones in his hand. Another rider tried by Yosh was up-and-coming Rick Kirk.

Duhamel returned for the Mid Ohio race and finished fifth – not a bad result in only his second AMA Superbike start! Then in the penultimate Topeka round the Canadian scored his first AMA Superbike win after holding off the Muzzy Kawasaki duo of Russell and Chandler, the latter being content with third to sew up the title. Mike Crompton, the experienced Canadian tuner who had fettled GSX-R750s when they first appeared in Canada in 1985 was in Duhamel's corner that weekend.

Duhamel failed to score in the final round at Willow Springs when his engine expired. He wound up tenth in championship.

Russell won the Supersport 750 series crown for Kawasaki. Chandler finished second. The leading Suzuki rider was Lynch in third place overall.

ENDURANCE RACING

On the world stage Suzuki did not figure too well. In World Endurance SERT's number two team of two Britons, Roger Burnett and Steve Chambers, teamed up with Miguel Duhamel to finish second to Honda at Le Mans. The number one bike for Moineau/Igoa/Graziano succumbed to engine failure with five hours to go.

Duhamel, just back from his Loudon injuries and riding with a rod inserted in his injured femur, scored a confidence-boosting personal result by finishing sixth with Doug Polen on a Yoshimura

Suzuki at the Suzuka Eight-Hour. Moineau and Igoa finished tenth.

There was no Spa 24-Hours – cancelled at the insistence of Bernie Ecclestone since the traditional 24H date was considered by the GP mogul to be too close to the F1 car race. This meant the only other big Endurance event of 1990 was the *Bol*, where Burnett, Duhamel and Thierry Autisier finished fifth on the SERT bike.

Duhamel also raced in the Canadian Nationals. He won the final race at Shannonville and set a new lap record the week before the AMA National at Topeka, but was pipped to the title by rising star Pascal Picotte, who won five rounds on a Yamaha.

EUROPEAN SUPERBIKE

Suzuki continued to shun World Superbike but Sven Seidel scored a memorable runner-up slot in the new European Superbike Championship after tying with Rumi Honda's Richard Arnaiz. The American was awarded the

Compare the SERT bike with this Lucky Strike factory machine at the Eight-Hour. Note the very different top-frame spar on the 1990 factory bikes – nothing like the stock GSX-R frame. These were still the heady days of TTF1, when manufacturers could experiment with different chassis designs! (Kel Edge)

Doug Polen and Miguel Duhamel finished sixth on the Yoshimura number 12 bike at Suzuka. (Kel Edge)

title on the most wins decider by four wins to three.

In Britain Whitham had moved to Honda UK so the Durex-backed Heron Suzuki outfit fielded Roger Burnett on a bike fettled by Ron Grant, himself a former factory Suzuki rider in the US during the early days of Formula 750 in the 1970s. It was a curious set-up, with Mick Grant (no relation to Ron) still overall team manager but with the bikes based in Ron's Humberside workshop.

Their superbike, an RR model, had special cams, cylinder head, pistons, valve springs and cotters, allegedly from the Suzuki factory in Hamamatsu. The bike weighed 363lb (165kg). The stock frame weighed 33lb (15.5kg) but Grant had got theirs to 28lb (13kg). The stock swing-arm weighed 14lb (6.5kg) but theirs weighed 3.2kg and was made by JMC. The exhaust was titanium and weighed 7lb (3kg). It had a carbon-fibre muffler made by Carbon Tech in San Francisco. The brakes were PVM 310mm steel rotors with Nissin four-pots early in the year, but after the Donington World Superbike round Burnett brought some six-pots back from the Le Mans 24-Hour.

Mick asked Ron to do a lot of work to improve the air flow through the engine.

At Jerez he ran the original air scoops through the gas tank but then fitted special ducting. As a result the motor produced 125.6bhp at the rear wheel, even though it had over 600 miles on the motor!

The engine, according to Ron Grant, pulled well from 9,000rpm and produced 105bhp right up to the rev-limiter at 13,250rpm, where it produced maximum horsepower. Burnett finished tenth in the Shell Supercup TTF1 class.

THE SUZUKI WORLD CUP

The Suzuki GSX-R750 World Cup entered its third year – this time backed by Lucky Strike and held at the Paul Ricard circuit in Southern France during the *Bol d'Or* weekend. It also reverted to the original format of two races with all thirty riders from fifteen different countries on identically prepared production machines. Yet again an Australian carried the honours, this time Matt Blair, who qualified on pole and won both races.

8 Final Makeover

The writing was on the wall for the air/oil-cooled GSX-R750. Suzuki had already introduced liquid-cooling for their domestic market GSX-R400 and the problem of maintaining working engine temperatures, especially during racing situations, led everyone to expect a new liquid-cooled 750 to be imminent.

GSX-R750M

Not for 1991, though. Instead, the new GSX-R750M was refined further whilst retaining SACS air/oil cooling. There was a new cylinder head with blended valve seats, smoothed into reshaped intake and exhaust tracts – all ported by

hand – the rib dividing each port being lengthened and gradually tapered. The aim was to improve gas-flow velocity and cylinder charging and scavenging.

Instead of individual cams operating two valves via a forked rocker arm, as in previous R motors, there was a new lightweight valve train with one cam lobe operating one rocker arm per valve. Valve lash was adjusted by a shim atop the valve-spring retainer rather than the previous threaded adjuster system. The new set-up reduced inertia, especially at high rpm and, to improve valve control at higher rpm, stronger valve springs from the 1100 were used. The changes did not increase horsepower but Suzuki claimed that the engine could

New cylinder head, new valve train, very few chassis changes. The 1991 GSX-R750M represented the final makeover for the air/oil-cooled machine (Courtesy Superbike Magazine)

Riding for Suzuki Canada, Jeff Gaynor won the Canadian Superbike title in 1991 on an old-style GSX-R750R. (Colin Fraser)

The 1991 model GSX-R750M. (Colin Fraser Archive)

US-spec models got inverted Showa forks on the 750 for the first time. (Colin Fraser Archive)

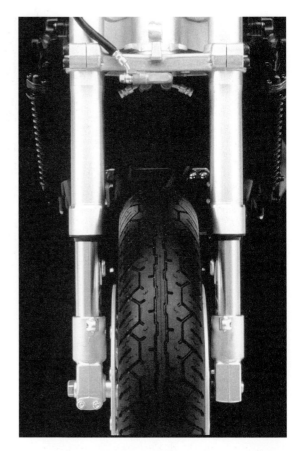

now sustain its peak power for longer periods.

The chassis remained unchanged except for the US-spec models, which now featured inverted Showa forks (the 1100s used Kayaba equipment), which had appeared on GSX-Rs in other markets.

Braking distances were improved thanks to the fitting of Dunlop D202 Sport Radials, even though the braking system was the same as the previous year. In a back-to-back test with a new GSX-R1100, *Cycle World* claimed the 750 reduced its 30mph stopping distance from 26ft to 22ft, and its 60mph stopping distance from 124 to 101ft!

Visually the 1991 R had redesigned bodywork with a more slanted nose, flush-mounted headlight and raked screen, smaller frontal area and reduced drag. The design, claimed Suzuki, was lifted straight from their 1990 racebike blueprints. There was also a wider seat for increased pilot and passenger comfort.

KEEPING THE RACING FLAME BURNING

Racing success was thin on the ground but at least enthusiasm still burned in some quarters to see the GSX-Rs out on

Cam lobes operated direct onto the rocker arm with the shim under the bucket valve adjustment. (Colin Fraser Archive)

the track. No one could fault the enterprise of the British effort. James Whitham was back on Suzuki in a low-budget, semi-official team run by Mick Grant, with Butch Cartwright looking after machine preparation.

Whitham was riding the bike Roger Burnett had used the previous year but the young charger was certainly producing some more exciting performances than Burnett had the previous year in the twilight of his career.

Whitham was rebounding from a dismal year with Honda – and a total loss of confidence in the front end of the RC30 after numerous crashes. Many felt the poor season was caused by the differences in handling characteristics (Whitham's Honda team mate Carl Fogarty also had problems early on but seemed to ride around them as the season progressed).

But Whitham did not let it bother him. Back on the in-line four he was soon per-

The French Suzukis were garbed in Lucky Strike livery at Le Mans. This Moineau / Igoa / Mattioli machine went out early with one of the GSX-R's infamous gearbox failures. Mertens led on the other bike until team mate Battistini crashed. (Kel Edge)

At Spa it rained for over 23 hours but through the gloom of the Ardennes monsoon came the Suzuki of Stephane Mertens, Dominique Sarron and Christian Lavielle to score a famous victory – back in the more traditional Suzuki blue and white. (Kel Edge)

forming at his wild best and finished fifth overall in the Shell Supercup, winning the final two races at Mallory on what was, essentially, and obsolete machine. Whitham admitted in a *Road Racing Monthly* interview:

I just couldn't get on with the Honda. It just didn't suit me. I had eleven front end crashes and never knew why. Carl [Fogarty] had the same problems but didn't crash as much. With the Suzuki I can ride harder and push the front end to my limit.

Grant claimed that the Suzuki was the best-handling bike in the field – it was up against the front-end funny RC30s, rocket-ship Norton rotaries (with awesome power but flexy handling) and OWO1 Yamahas – but the fact remained that it was an ancient charger. The chassis came from a 1987 XR55 Suzuki TTF1 racer but had inverted front forks from the later GSX-R750RR with different weight springs. Steering geometry was

adjustable through sleeves in the headstock.

The bike weighed 341lb (155kg) – the same as the Suzuki France World Endurance factory bike although that had lights, generator and various other ancillaries required for long-distance racing.

Rear suspension was by Ohlins, in preference to a factory Kayaba that was also tried. Front brakes were twin ISR six-piston calipers with 320 PVM discs. Wheels were also PVM: 3.50 x 17in front and 6.00 x 17in rear with Dunlop tyres.

The motor with its dry clutch was reputed to have special kit parts, direct from Japan, but was not a Suzuki France endurance unit as many at the time suspected.

'There wasn't any point in getting one of their engines just for one season,' said Grant in *RRM*. 'We're expecting a new model next year so it wasn't [1992] sensible economics to get that and spend money developing it for just one season.'

The motor was in fact an RR unit with a capacity of 756cc – and a bore and stroke of 70.3mm x 48.7mm. The bore was 0.3mm oversize, something which caused controversy at Pembrey when it was stripped since the ACU rule book of the time stated that the previous one per cent oversize rule had been quashed and motors had to conform strictly to the rules of the TT/Superbike class. The ACU met later and agreed to allow the one per cent rule to remain. Grant reckoned that the extra 6cc gave them less than one horsepower advantage!

Compression was 13:1 and the rev limiter cut in at 13,000rpm. Maximum power was said to be 118bhp at 12,000rpm. Ignition was a Nippon Denso system. Carbs were four magnesium flatslide 34mm Mikunis – but the team also experimented with fuel injection. Grant explained at the time:

Top speed has never been a problem for the Suzuki. Where we are losing out is coming out of

the corners. Yamaha have the EXUP system. Honda have 4-2-1 exhausts to aid mid-range. We think fuel injection will be the answer to improve our mid-range.

The injection did produce a clean-running engine but the team never found any appreciable gain in performance in the range.

Across the English Channel, Stephane Mertens, Dominique Sarron and Christian Lavielle won Spa on Meliand's SERT entry – even though the bike lacked the power of its rivals. They also finished second at the *Bol,* but still finished only ninth in the championship.

Stateside, Yoshimura lined up for the 1991 season with Mike Smith – previous year's F-USA Champion on a Suzuki – and Tommy Lynch (eighteen), but it was a lacklustre year. Lynch managed a fifth at Charlotte, but Smith was injured in a big crash at Loudon that sidelined him for most of the year so that he never got a chance to show his true potential. His best result was a fifth at Texas World,

The ageing XR55 TTF1 chassis was back in action for Team Grant in 1991 and Whitham, back from a disastrous year with Honda, proved how competitive the bike could be. He won British Championship races – and was a major player in the overall points chase. (Clive Challinor)

Grant reckoned that getting cool air to the carbs was the secret of horsepower longevity – hence the huge scoops cut into the screen. (Clive Challinor)

and there were some other lower-order top ten finishes for both riders.

Scott Russell won every Supersport 750 race for Kawasaki. Britt Turkington finished a distant second overall in the championships – the top Suzuki result - riding out of the Yoshimura team.

Turkington grabbed seconds at Daytona, Topeka and Texas World, third at Road America and fourth at Charlotte and Mid Ohio. Jeff Heino also scored some good results on a Suzuki, giving Russell a run for his money in the rain at Loudon. The GSX-R was not done yet.

9 Grant's Team Suzuki

MICK GRANT – FROM RIDER TO MANAGER

Mick Grant has unique experience of Suzuki's GSX-R750s, having successfully raced them in production, Superstock and TTF1 specification and then, having quit racing himself, turned to team management also using GSX-R750 machinery.

Honda dominated the 1984 British season with their exotic TTF1 bike and their 500. But could Suzuki alter the balance of power in 1985 with the new GSX-R750?

With the Formula One bike the answer was no. Grant recalls:

It was an awful motorbike. At the North West 200 it wasn't good. There was some sort of misunderstanding between the factory and the suspension people. Someone got the figures wrong and we ended up with 30 per cent less rear travel than it should have had. We went harder and harder on the spring to get it to work. The bike was sliding around all over the place. Hondas were fairly dominant at that time and our bike just wasn't up to it.

Furthermore, the engines were not reliable. Grant adds:

Rods were breaking because the engine kept seizing. We had a lubrication problem with the F1 engine. We were under contract to Shell at a time when synthetics and semi-synthetics were starting to show up. We were using the very best Shell had got but it wasn't synthetic oil. Motul jumped the gun with the synthetics so we tried that and it cured it.

But the F1 still wasn't the best thing. It was a trick bike, nicely done, but not in the same league as the Honda.

Grant's TT was far from competitive, with the F1 bike spitting its internals out each time he tried it. However, he did give Suzuki a hugely important 750cc Production win on the new GSX-R – but even that was not without controversy:

We had a wobbling problem. We were contracted to Michelin but the bike wasn't handling good. The tyres were the problem. I'd done my homework and Metzelers were the best tyres on the day for the Suzukis. I tried to be loyal but it got to the last practice session on the Friday and I knew by then I wasn't going to win it. I said to Suzuki, 'If you want to win the race we have got to change tyres.' So that's what we did.

Obviously Michelin were not very happy but Suzuki wanted to win. I went to Metzeler and said I wanted tyres. They offered them free but I didn't wanted them to advertise the fact I was on Metzelers if I won so I offered to pay. They said it was OK, that [success advertising] wouldn't happen but I won and they advertised the fact. A bit naughty really. But the tyres certainly cured the high-speed wobble.

Grant says that the problem would not have been so pronounced on a short circuit – and also points out with more adjustability built into the chassis (as on modern sportsbikes) it could probably been have been overcome with a chassis change. 'There was nothing wrong with the tyre grip, just a high-speed stability

James Whitham (left) with his mentor, Mick Grant. (Mick Grant Collection)

problem because the tyres didn't suit the chassis geometry.'

In the damp, Glenn Williams shocked everyone with the fastest lap on lap three but, as Grant points out, the journals of the time overlooked that Williams stopped for fuel after the first 37.73-mile (60.71km) lap to get a flying third lap with improved weather! Grant pitted at the end of lap two.

Superstock on the short circuits was Grant's glorious swan song, although he had initially resisted the idea of racing this production-based class.

Denys Rohan was in charge of Suzuki racing at that time. We had a 500 and a 750 and like everybody, I enjoyed riding the 500 the most. You think that's the bike to be on. But then Denys asked me to ride the production-based thing, and like everyone else, I said I didn't want to!

But my arm was twisted and against my judgement I agreed to ride it. We got the very first GSX-R that came into the country. In fairness we got ours a fair bit earlier than everyone else. We did work on it pre-season – we had a nice professional team with Rex White in charge. We did what the rules allowed – fitted 16in wheels, trick magne-

sium forks and a White Power unit. But the engine was absolutely stock, contrary to what the accusations were.

Then we went to Donington and within a few laps it spit me off. I thought, 'What am I doing here?' The oil filter came loose – we were the first ones to come across this problem. Later on the GSX-R it had a different thread. For the rest of year we wrapped a jubilee clip around the filter – and lock-wired it.

Grant's early domination of the series immediately got the tongues wagging, suggesting an illegal motor – and Grant says that lax policing of the series early on did not help curb the negative rumour mill:

Bruce Cox was running the series and he seemed to live by the seat of his britches. Initially it had been announced that bikes would be stripped every meeting. But it didn't happen. People said I was cheating. I knew who was making the noises but they would not come forward and put their money where their mouth was.

Rod Scivyer was series co-ordinator working under Cox. So, after my fourth race win, I insisted it be stripped and sure enough it was completely legal. The advantage was that we had tested it and got the thing right!

The Suzuki GSX-R750R was marketed as a base model for superbike competition. It came up short on spec against rival Japanese machinery – and the Ducatis. (Glenn Bayly Collection)

The 1996 GSX-R750 factory bike was raced in 'striking' Lucky Strike livery at Daytona by Scott Russell and at the Suzuka Eight-Hour. (Glenn Bayly Collection)

Below: Grant's TTF1 and Superstock GSX-R750s. The Superstocker looks huge in comparison. (Alan Cathcart Archive)

A youngster by the name of Kevin Schwantz made his British debut on a Suzuki borrowed from Tony Rutter's backers, Motorcycle Mart of Kidderminster. Schwantz was a sensation, topping the score chart for the eight-race Donington Match Race programme. (Kel Edge)

Anders Andersson was a key player in the final years of the TTF1 World Championship riding for Suzuki Sweden. He was placed fifth in this event at Assen and was third in the series. (Kel Edge)

Yoshimura's Suzuka Eight-Hour bikes of 1987. (Kel Edge)

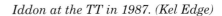
Iddon at the TT in 1987. (Kel Edge)

Andersson's GSX-R sported new-style Ohlins forks and ISR brakes during the 1988 season. (Alan Cathcart)

Andersson in action during 1988. Even with Thomas Klarkner (of drag racing tuning company Moto Speed) fettling the motor it was tough to get the short-stroke competitive enough for WSB racing. Andersson took in several TTF1 races as the season wore on and won the Kouvola round. (Kel Edge)

Suzuki's new GSX-R750R launched in early 1989. (Kel Edge)

Thierry Crine finished equal fifth with team mate Herve Moineau in the 1989 World Endurance Championship. (Kel Edge)

Ron Grant fettled the Durex Suzuki. Their British TTF1 bike was competitive enough to finish in the top six with Burnett on board at national level but the superbike did not make the grade at world championship standard. (Kel Edge)

The Ohshima/Takayoshi Yosh Suzuki at Suzuka. (Kel Edge)

Whitham on the Suzuki was always fun to watch! (Clive Challinor)

Patrick Igoa on the SERT bike. (Kel Edge)

Sven Seidel showed up at the Hockenheim WSB round with this kitted Suzuki Deutschland machine – note the airbox system. (Kel Edge)

James Whitham, letting it all hang out as usual trying to keep ahead of the green meanie duo, John Reynolds and Brian Morrison, at Mallory. (Clive Challinor)

Herve Moineau, on the gas at the Bol in 1989. He finished third with Crine and Morillas. (Kel Edge)

The US-model GSX-R750WR being put through its paces. (John Flory / Colin Fraser Archive)

Arty views of Suzuki's alternative colour scheme for the GSX-R750T. (Alan Cathcart Archive)

Scott Russell took time out from his GP500 campaign to contest the Suzuka Eight-Hour during 1996. (Kel Edge)

The Reynolds/McCarthy Eight-Hour bike. They finished ninth. (Kel Edge)

Pascal Picotte's Yoshimura Suzuki at Daytona. Note the Ohlins suspension and Dunlop tyres. The bike was good enough to win AMA Superbike races for Picotte and Aaron Yates. Maybe the WSB team should have adopted the same set-up? (Kel Edge)

Grant says that he ran all season on the Superstock without crashing, apart from the pre-season testing incident.

Handling was nigh on perfect. It was a nice, big, soft lump. Obviously what any racer likes more than anything else is winning. And even if it [riding a production bike] didn't seem a right good idea at the time, once we started popping all these wins in, it didn't seem that bad!

Grant won the title and then quit at the end of the year. It was his nineteenth year of racing yet he had not entered the season with definite plans to end his illustrious career at the end of 1985 – even though he admits to having thought about 'retirement' some four to five years previously:

I didn't really know what I wanted to do but I had started to think about it. I was a professional sportsman – but I would have almost raced for nothing. I loved the sport and I was worried because I knew it would be a hell of a let-down when I had to stop and do something else. I was worried sick about that. When do I stop? What do I do?

Ironically, it was reflecting on a tumble at the TT, one of his favourite racetracks, that ultimately convinced Grant it was time to quit, even though he did not think so at the time.

At the TT I was riding a 500 [in the Senior – after his Production TT win] and it spit me off straight line. I still don't know why. I was lucky to get away with a broken thumb. Then at Macau, at the end of year, the bike didn't finish though I'd won the previous year, no problem. That same season I'd been building the house [where he still lives]. I'd be working on Friday and Carol [his wife] would remind me it was time to get ready to go racing – and I didn't really want to. And that was not right because I'd always been really enthusiastic about my racing. So after the second Macau race I got to the pits and told Nigel [Everett, his long-serving mechanic], 'I'm finished.' Then I thought, 'What have I said?'

Any chance of Grant going back on the decision was ended when he went to see

Heron Suzuki's Denys Rohan to discuss 1986 racing prospects:

Denys, a lovely guy, said, 'I don't want you to race again. I'd like you to stop before you hurt yourself. You've had a good run but it's getting to the end.'

I've always believed in not being too greedy. Carol and I talked the night before I went to see Denys about 1986 and I'd planned to ask for enough money that they wouldn't be able to give me and that would stop my career. I didn't have the balls to admit I'd had enough. But Denys did that for me – and he offered me a job in marketing for Suzuki, so I shook on the deal there and then. And there was the option of me taking the race team over in the future. So when Rex finished I took over. I've never ever regretted the move.

In 1986 Grant attended just four meetings, and only then at the request of Rohan. In 1987, though, he became more involved, arranging a GSX-R750 for James Whitham to run in Superstock. Grant left Whitham to chase a steep learning curve and the youngster finished seventh in the series – his rookie year on a 750. It turned out to be a precursor for the 1988 season, when Grant would take up the reins as Suzuki race team manager.

British Championship racing was changing. The heady days of grids boasting exotic factory TTF1 or 500GP-type machinery were disappearing fast. Bike sales were plummeting and the future was Production racing – to keeps costs down. Grant saw this coming:

What Rex had over a number of years was big money, big budgets, he had Crosby, Mamola, he had GP bikes coming out of his ears – big team, big transport. Suddenly the market wasn't so big, and I'm sure [Gerald] Ronson [Suzuki boss at the time] must have been questioning why was so much being spent on racing when the company was only selling 10,000 units per year!

They [virtually] stopped the racing thing when Rex had run it. It went from mega-big budget to me starting with a clean sheet of paper and a smaller budget – and the budget got smaller and smaller each year. Eventually I said enough is enough. I think when I took over it was the beginning of the end for Heron Suzuki and racing. It was a very tidy way for them to pull out.

Taking Over from Rex White

But the first indications had been that Grant would step neatly into White's shoes:

When I took over it looked brilliant. We had a sponsor who was going to come in over a three-year period. I could have continued in the same vein Rex had. But in the very late stages of negotiation it fell through. I can't comment exactly why, even now, but it was down to personalities – and nothing to do with me.

This left Roger Marshall, one of White's Skoal Bandit riders of 1987, with no ride. He had gone to compete in the Australian Swann series with a 500 Suzuki and came back to the sour news.

Roger said when he left, 'Whatever happens, I'm not riding a production bike.' It all looked so good – a million pounds over three years; then the budget disappeared and we got some production bikes and a few quid out of the Heron slush fund to go racing with.

Roger was out and he was my mate and we had a big problem. Maybe Roger has mellowed since but at the time there was a lot of hostility. He felt that as soon as his back had turned we sorted the job out. There was no one more upset than me. I would rather have had a big team and plenty of money to do the job with. We were now looking at Superstock, production racing and whatever we could afford to do. We ran James and Mez [Phil Mellor].

That year Whitham won the Production title riding a GSX-R750 when most riders opted for 1100 Suzukis or 1,000cc Yamahas. It looked a vain gamble until Carnaby, the third round, when Michelin provided Whitham with new Hi Sport rubber. Grant comments:

James, one of the last of the great brakers, tried this new front tyre and said, 'I can win on the tyre.' I thought, 'Get the painter ready', [to patch up the crash damage] but he did win – his first win in the series. The front tyre transformed the bike to suit his riding style.

There was controversy because other riders claimed the tyre was not freely available, as it should have been according to the loosely written rules, and there was yet more trouble when there were claims that the 750 was not stock.

But, as Grant maintains, the 750 worked well on the tight British tracks: 'Out and out speed was not that much of a problem. The 750 really put the power down good and handled well.'

It was a banner year for Grant's small troupe. Whitham finished runner-up in the British F1 series, and Mellor was third. It was a moral victory since they only lost out to a 500cc two-stroke ridden by Darren Dixon – a bike with a much more favourable power-to-weight ratio. Furthermore, Grant recalls that their Suzuki was virtually a kitted production bike:

It was basically standard GSX-R. It even had a production chassis. We knocked it into race trim with some Yoshimura kit parts but it was nothing special – it even had a wet clutch! We were struggling [against the 500]. We didn't have it too easy! I've always believed in showing the product in a good light and if you can win as well it's a good thing. The Suzuki road bike at that time was just unbelievable.

While Suzuki's UK bosses might have had little interest in the sport, Grant still felt they could have done more to capitalize on such impressive track performances:

Our F1 results were bloody good. But I could never understand why we could do so well with what we had. Suzuki never capitalized on the successes. At the time Denys Rohan left there was a power struggle between him and John Norman. Norman won it and was never in favour of racing. He had been the boss of Kawasaki when I racing for them between 1975 and 1978 and he was against racing then. Always has been. When Denys went I knew it wasn't good news. They cut me down and down [in budget] until the final year when I used a fair bit of my own money to keep racing.

Every time we went in [to negotiate a new annual contract], the people in Suzuki were very keen, people like Steve Kenwood the sales director, but the guy at the top [Norman] put the chop on it each time.

I think I was good at running racing teams and sorting the sharp end of it but I've never enjoyed chasing the money side of it. But I went to Suzuki and said, 'Why don't you give me £10 for a racing budget for each bike you sell?' I would have had £100,000 for my budget and there would not have been a dealer in the country who would have objected. But I was told, 'No, we can't do that.' I couldn't understand why not.

I was going to prospective sponsors in my underpants and socks [he had no money from the manufacturer he was representing]. They were jittery. You could imagine them thinking, 'If he's only got his underpants and socks, and he's come on the bus, it can't be that good a deal.' But if I could have had the basis of a budget from Suzuki (the £100,000) I could have got as much again. The second 50 per cent would have been easy. I was never able to give a prospective sponsor any confidence.

Despite that, Grant took Suzuki racing again in 1988, but not in Superstock, which had a new Dunlop control rule. That angered Grant:

I've got serious principles. I've never, ever, believed in a one-make tyre series, I've never believed in one-make series really. There are times you have to use your feet and I didn't agree with Superstock rules.

Nowadays, with the CB500 series for privateers, no one's on a tyre deal, but back then in Superstock, all the manufacturers were involved. There were lots of people getting free tyres – or at least a deal on tyres. The rule meant the other tyre manufacturers could not compete and it cost the competitors a lot more money. You could understand that they [Cox, the series organizer] felt they had done a brilliant marketing job but it actually did harm because it stopped competition.

The Death of Mellor and Beyond

For 1989 Grant secured backing from Durex, but what looked like a huge financial deal turned out not to be: it amounted to around £25,000! But the name of Durex gave Suzuki access to a much wider market. Grant recalls:

Hang in there! Typical all-action Whitham style on the 1992 water-cooled bike. He had to ride it 110 per cent – the bike was never as competitive in the handling department as the old TTF1 chassis and Grant never got the backing the small team deserved from Suzuki. (Clive Challinor)

I had to run the team – and find the money. I was still on Suzuki payroll at that stage and I just suddenly thought, 'I'll go and see the London Rubber Company.' So I marched into their office and we did a deal.

Was it really that simple? Grant says it was.

Not far off. The deal wasn't like anything like as big as everyone though. They spent far more on a hot-air balloon than they did on the race team. But it was a good image for us and lifted our marketing image. We sold over £100,000 of merchandise! But neither Durex nor Suzuki did enough with the marketing.

Even on the limited budget, Grant signed up four riders:

With all of them on production bikes it didn't really cost a lot. We had something like seventeen bikes at the TT. Take machines out of the crate, run them for a year. It wasn't going to cost a great deal. It was actually very uncomfortable from their [Durex's] point of view but I thought it was brilliant. The problem we had, and I anticipated it but hoped it would never occur, was that their motto was 'safe sex' and what they didn't want was anything that wasn't seen to be safe. Tragically they got it anyway.

Mellor was killed in the Isle of Man Production race. Whitham also crashed in the same race but in a separate incident and another rider, Steve Henshaw, died in the following melee. Even in 1996, mention of Mellor's death brings Grant to an melancholy moment: 'It was not good,' he murmurs, and then goes quiet. It had been a close-knit outfit.

At the time, many said it was a mistake running big production bikes at the TT, and that the 1100s simply did not handle. Grant still refutes this:

What was said was rubbish. I looked into the crash very closely. It was a series of events that led to the crashes. Yes, the ACU stopped production racing after that – and they had to do that to be seen to be doing the job right. But it wasn't the bike. For sure they were a handful but I've ridden 500 singles around there that have been a handful.

Mez tried to pass someone in a bunch, got off line and fell off. That was that. James [Whitham] was in the [following] pack, he saw it and, in my mind, it upset his concentration a bit. He clipped the kerb going into Quarry Bends – just like Hislop did on the 250 the year after. James fell off, it was a racing accident. James had got to his feet by the time the other two came around. They came around the corner not seeing the flag and Henshaw sat up and Seward hit him.

There were suggestions that Mellor was not fully fit after a crash in practice. Grant also refutes this:

I don't recall anything like that. If he had fallen off in practice and I had been worried about Mez's condition I would not have let him ride. I've ridden with broken bits and pieces. And I would have been very pissed off if a team manager had told me not to ride. But at the same time, if I had been worried about the situation I would not have let Mez ride.

The team kept going, and some might have felt that Grant's attitude at the time was cold. But that is far from the truth.

It was the same as when John Newbold ran into the back of me at the North West and was killed. I went out next race and won it. I think you've either got to piss, or get off the pot. We know racing is dangerous and if things go wrong we can feel sad about it.

Rex wanted to pull out of the North West but I said no, lots of people come to see Suzuki race. I still felt very sad – not that it had hit me at that stage – but if you don't race that weekend, you'll never race again. You give the respect at the right time. It may seem hard but it's the only way I can cope with it. Just get on with the job.

The team did pick themselves up after the tragic TT but the level of success was not the same as the previous year. Engine problems spoilt the short-circuit year and it was finished altogether when Whitham broke his ankle at the Ulster GP after a brake rotor allegedly broke up.

Whitham then signed for Honda, breaking the long-term partnership.

James had a long time to think about things after the crash and he chose Honda. I don't blame him for what he did. Yes, I was disappointed. But he was obviously talented and went where the grass was greener. He eventually came back and we finished the job off.

Whitham had time to reflect on the politics of the sport – having been denied a GP500 earlier in the year by Grant, the very person who everyone thought had been nurturing the career of the fast-rising youngster. So why hold him back? Grant explains:

James had an opportunity to ride a 500 at the [British] Grand Prix but I was the bastard who said no. I had a meeting the previous January to discuss the GP ride with Suzuki and, for all the right reasons, decided not to do it.

The reasons were: (1) He wasn't ready for it; (2) I think it's wrong to jump in front of your own crowd when your head's not at a stage when you can actually cope with it; and (3) Suzuki were not going to give him the same bike as Schwantz had got. If they had done, it would be finely tuned and running it would be a pain. They would have given bikes that kept on running. Detuned ones. So then you get punters who think the bikes are the same and wonder why the rider is going three seconds slower.

What we did agree with Suzuki was for James to do World Superbike the following year with factory help. James may or may not have known this at the time. The way I saw it was that James was going to get help from the factory. We were committed to go Superbike on a bike that was not really competitive, the RR, but the way I saw it was that if he did that and was reasonably competitive, then Suzuki would look on him as a man to put on the 500.

Whitham had a disastrous year on the Honda RC30 with a catalogue of front end crashes. Meanwhile Grant signed Roger Burnett and the Suzuki team had a lacklustre season – even though Grant had dusted off the old lightweight TTF1 chassis from the Skoal Bandit days to build a very competitive power-to-weight ratio machine. The budget was restricted, the bikes were kept at mechanic Ron Grant's house in Lincolnshire and the best results all year were two thirds. Burnett seemed

to lack the aggression Suzuki's previous rider exuded.

Roger was a nice guy but his basic problem was that he knew the danger side of it. He had so much ability it was untrue but he didn't want the pain of it. James never gave a shit about the pain – he accepted that pain was part of it – like we all do.

The bike suddenly sported huge air scoops in the fairing screen, connected by hoses to the airbox via the dummy gas-tank front. Mick Grant claims to have discovered something most other Suzuki teams, including the mighty Yoshimura company, had overlooked with the GSX-R750 – that heat build-up within the engine was not the cause of horsepower loss during a race! He explains:

Brian Crighton [who developed the Norton rotary racer] had kept saying we should get some cool air to our carbs. We already had noticed a situation with the 600s when James and Mez raced, where the bike would be competitive for several laps then go backwards.

To try to discover why, we went on dyno after asking Shell what temperature the oil would go to. We were on the dyno for what seemed like an hour without having the fan on. The engine was so hot it was glowing and we lost half a horsepower. It proved heat build-up wasn't the problem! We could have run the engine to almost melting point and with a good oil it would not have mattered.

I also remembered reading that Polen was racing a Suzuki GSX-R750 in Mexico and it was stinking hot. The bike was going slower and slower in practice and they added radiators and it didn't make any difference. So then I thought about what Crighton had said about cool air. What Polen's lot [Yoshimura] appeared to be doing was creating a heat dam [with the extra radiator surface area] so any air passing into the carbs was actually hot air. I reckoned they would have gone a lot quicker with no radiators and cold air in the carbs.

My old sponsor Jim Lee [who died in 1996] had a racing car shop and his staff engineered some ducts and suddenly Roger [Burnett], from being fifth or sixth, was getting third. You couldn't see it [the maintained power] on the dyno – you can't simulate it. But we did have consistent power throughout a race. Sometimes you do tuning mods and you

By 1997 Whitham got a full factory ride in the Suzuki World Superbike team. This shot was taken in pre-season testing. (Courtesy Redcat)

maybe pick up a little bit here and there – this was a stark difference like between black and white. I think best power we had was 138bhp – but with hot air I reckon we lost a fair bit during a race.

The Early 1990s

For 1991 Whitham was back on Suzuki with Grant, who was now running his own team, without the Durex cash.

I'd got the brown envelope from Suzuki saying, 'We don't want you on the payroll anymore but it's not that bad because we'll continue to support you. It won't make any difference.' I set my own little racing company up and from there I was on my own.

The Whitham deal had been finalized months ahead of the new season.

James came to me half-way through the season, to my house, and said, 'I think I have made a mistake.' And we did a deal there for the following year. We used Roger's bikes (with the 1987 Skoal Bandit chassis) and had a brilliant year. James was never out of top three and never failed to finish a race. We just used Yoshimura bits. Basically it was just me, Butch Cartwright [team mechanic] and James – a great little set-up. It was so much fun, we all worked together so well. But the budget was so small.

And the following year it got even smaller. I did the whole thing for £60,000. And when you look around at the opposition, like Kawasaki, they must have been on £250,000–£300,000.

We also had the brand-new water-cooled bike the following year, and it wasn't happy motoring. We had no money for development. I was up half the night making little bits and pieces. We couldn't afford to go and buy them. We had a deal with Dunlop but not enough for the full season so we were taking John Reynolds's cast-off tyres after he had run maybe three or four laps and we were using them for all practice!

Grant only continued into 1992 in the hope that a GP deal he was working on might pan out for 1993.

It was looking good with South African contacts and I was hoping to take James with me. I hired a Padgetts/Harris bike for Russell Wood. I promised the backers we would finish in the top twelve. We did. They were delighted with that. But the deal fell through.

I went to Macau with Foggy [Carl Fogarty] and James end of 1992 with borrowed Padgetts/ Harris bikes. But the only reason I went for the full 1992 season was that while I knew it might cost a bit, I knew if we could keep up there and fighting, we'd be away on the GP deal in 1993. It was a gamble that didn't come off but I've no regrets.

It was not an easy year. The brand-new water-cooled bike needed development. The German Suzuki team had an airbox. We couldn't afford it. We got very limited tune-up parts. I worked all night making titanium parts and then all day chasing sponsorship from dealers. We got £11,000 out of dealers – twenty-one dealers at £500 each. I felt totally wrong about it. If I had been a dealer I would have said, 'Get stuffed, get Suzuki to pay!' But thankfully the dealers kept us going. I'm eternally grateful for that.

So why did Grant, obviously as talented a race team manager as he was a racer, stay with Suzuki so long?

Nothing else came up: the honest answer. I liked the people in Suzuki. There was always light at the end of the tunnel, hope that the job would come right. I liked working at home. It worked well. If Honda had offered me a job running a team from Chiswick, I would not have done it. The Suzuki deal also suited Suzuki because it got the race team out of their factory.

Grant thinks, however, that Suzuki could have done a much better job, in racing circles, than they actually achieved. He points to the errors of the company's thinking:

It's taking a long time [for Suzuki] to get there with the GSX-R750. It started good in 1985, but then they produced the short-stroke engine. The press said it was good [initially] but it wasn't. But all the time Suzuki have been doing the R, Honda have been better.

When Suzuki produced the RR, they did 1,000 bikes, so we could go WSB racing. The RR was crap. It had so much potential but at the end of the day it was a standard GSX-R with a close-ratio box and bigger carbs to get around the homologation. What they should have done was made an 'RC30' version of the GSX-R. And instead of £8,000 – which was a lot of money for what it was – it should have been tricked right out and cost £16,000. They would have sold all thousand of them – and we could have gone WSB racing and won!

The RR model was too standard. Even when the RC30 arrived years earlier at £8,000, and we all laughed saying they would never sell them, they had all gone before the containers had hit the shores!

What Honda have always done is looked where they wanted to go, assessed how to get there and done it. Suzuki [in racing terms] always seem to have fallen short. But I think now they've got a chance with the machine they have ...

WHITHAM – SUZUKI'S LONE STAR

For five seasons James Whitham, Mick Grant and mechanic 'Butch' Cartwright were family – family as much as a racing team can be. They raced Suzukis – at first as the official importer team in the UK, with a decent budget and a more extensive personnel line-up; but when the budget virtually dried up the three of them did it alone with bikes supplied by Suzuki.

Whitham became a folk-hero. He was the action man on the track but was also a free-speaking personality that everyone could identify with, always quick with a lucid quote and a personality to match his nickname – 'Whit'. He told it how it was – yet you never heard him whinging or whining.

And he has never changed. At the time of writing, in 1997, he is back on a Suzuki riding for the factory-backed team in World Superbike – and he is still one of the most approachable, most likeable figures in the paddock.

Whitham only won one major title whilst racing Suzuki GSX-R750s – the British Open Production Championship in 1988 – yet he was a threat every time he swung his leg over a Suzuki, even if the bike was not always as competitive as those raced by his rivals.

Whitham first rode a GSX-R750 in late 1986 – thanks to a test lined up by Grant. Whitham recalls his own 1986 season prior to the test session:

I'd done four or five Grands Prix and the European championship in the 125 class that year with mixed success. I had a fourth in Vallelunga on my MBA in first round of the Euros. I had my moments but broke down a lot and ran out of money generally.

He was forced to pack up early that year after the continental season had sapped his limited finances: 'I figured I regroup for the next year but then I got a phone call from Mick asking if I would be interested in testing a Skoal Bandit Suzuki.'

The bike had become available after the death of Neil Robinson at Scarborough. Two days after the test Whitham was invited to race in the final Brands Superstock round. He finished eighth – his first race on a big four-stroke! Whitham explains what happened next:

To be honest I thought nothing more about it until Mick rang me couple of weeks later and said Suzuki would supply me with a GSX-R750 to run me in the Superstock 750.

Mick helped out with a lot of the bits, and his old sponsors also helped with making special bits (yokes etc). Mick organized me some brake discs, got Tony Dawson (of Astralite) to make me some wheels and basically we got a little team up with the 750 instead of the 125.

Mick really helped me out a lot by coming to my house late at nights with bootloads of swag. But he never came to that many meetings. Off we went. It was an H model – a good bike. Virtually a street bike with slicks on. It had standard carbs, cams – but you could machine the pistons, put exhaust on it and a race-kit ignition. Superstock was a good class of racing.

In the late 1990s taking a step out of GPs and back into national racing on a glorified prod bike would be considered a retrograde step but not then:

I didn't really think like that. At that time the 125 class was in turmoil. It was going between twins and singles. It was not the best class then and certainly wasn't that strong in England at that time – and I couldn't afford to do it competitively.

And the Grant connection went way back before Whitham's racing career even started. Whitham says:

I've know him since I was a kid, since 1980 maybe. When he finished racing the NR500 Honda he got his own team together with a Harris F1 Suzuki engine. He also ran a Harris TZ350 in the George Beale series. He used to come and test on my dad's airfield – he's got a little tarmac airstrip. Mick tested gearboxes there. I was probably about fourteen when he first came to do that. I went to a couple of meetings with him.

When I started racing he helped out with helmets, leathers and stuff. He never gave me much advice though. He just let me get on with it really and he's taken an interest in my racing ever since.

After Whitham's successful first season – he finished a promising seventh in the Superstock series, winning two of the final three races – he picked up full support for the 1987 season.

At the end of 1987 Skoal Bandit decided they didn't want any further part for whatever reason – and I don't think Suzuki were even going to run a team at one stage. Rex had stepped back from it. He had run a fairly decent-sized team up to then.

Suzuki eventually decided they were going to run a smaller team. Grantie persuaded them he could run it and away we went – me and Phil Mellor. We had two F1 bikes each from 1987, which were endurance-spec chassis with F1 motors, and we ran two proddies which were the 750s, but we ran in the unlimited class. We also had two Senior Sport bikes.

The outrageous thing was that Whitham and Grant opted to run the GSX-R750 in the big Production series against 1100 Suzukis and 1000 Yamahas. This was essentially a marketing ploy to assist Suzuki, but it went deeper than that:

We did it basically because it was a good bike. It was new out, the new Slingshot model. The 1100 Suzuki had been around for a couple years or so.

The J-model Slingshot was definitely up to the task although I struggled in the first couple of rounds with the tyres we had. Then Michelin brought some tyres to Carnaby. They looked the same but as soon as I tried them I knew I could do well. Instantly, I was two or three seconds faster every lap. They transformed the whole bike.

I won at Carnaby, then won at Mallory. From then on I knew we would be challenging for the

Mick Grant – one of Suzuki's top riders – became the man who kept the race effort going when Suzuki GB lost interest. (Mick Grant Collection)

championship. The only places the 750 didn't work were Snetterton and Thruxton. We used the 1100 there – tracks where top speed counted.

If he was impressive on the prod bike, Whitham was outstanding in his first year on a fully fledged TTF1 machine: 'I loved that thing. It was excellent. I finished second to Dixon [in the series]. Mid-season I beat him every time out. But he had better results early in the year.'

Many felt that the lightweight 500 had the aces stacked on its side but Whitham does not feel the need for excuses. He says: 'I don't think it had that much on us. The bikes we had were really good. I had a cracking season. I was dead chuffed. We had good bikes.'

Whitham also had a good TT: 'I didn't ride the F1 bike because they had done a deal with Roger Marshall for that year but I finished fourth in the 750cc Production. The first three were all RC30s so I considered my ride to be a decent result.'

Whitham fitted well into the team set-up alongside the experienced Phil Mellor:

It was great to be in the same team as Mez. He was a great bloke, you couldn't fail to get on with him. There was no angle with him at all. He was just such a nice bloke – and fast too. I actually got to know him in '88. The sad thing was that by the time he had finally got really good bikes, he had missed the best years of his racing. By then he was thirty-odd years old.

For the following year things looked even better, with Durex coming in as team sponsor. Whitham and Mellor had the same F1 bikes and the same 600s (long in the tooth by then but they struggled with it), but there was a brand new 1100, which was a Slingshot-shaped 1100K.

But it all turned sour at the TT as Whitham recalls:

The TT was not going bad for me until the big Proddie. I was second quickest in the big Proddie

during practice, which I was pleased with. I finished third in the 600 race, which was a real good result for me. In the F1 I was in the top five or six in qualifying and finished sixth but the bike didn't seem so quick for whatever reason.

Then came the 1100 proddie race. I saw Mez crash in front of me. I knew he was really badly hurt. I thought he was dead [straight away] to be honest. I knew he wouldn't be in such a good way.

Really, I lost a bit of concentration. I thought about pulling in. I wasn't enjoying riding the bike anyway. But I decided to keep going and got my head down again.

I crashed at Quarry Bends – just clipped the engine cases. Certainly the bikes were difficult to put them where you wanted to within a foot. I just got it wrong. Luck was with me that day and I slid up the middle of the road. I opened my eyes and I was sat on the white line.

I picked myself up and got off the road. Behind me, and seeing my crash, Steve Henshaw panicked and sat up and Mike Seward hit him from behind. Henshaw was dead and Seward didn't look very well. It was a complete disaster.

I got back to the hotel and asked Mick how Mez was. 'Still fighting,' he said. Then Mick went back to the hospital and when he came back he just shook his head. That was the low point. By then I'd figured I didn't really want to go back to the Isle of Man.

I told Andrea [Witham's girlfriend] I didn't think I was going to come back to the TT. She had never said anything to me before (of her feelings about the TT) but when I told her that she just said 'good'. She never used to like it.

Whitham admits, for the first time publicly, that the mountain course used to frighten him:

It wasn't that I didn't like it. It used to scare me little bit. It didn't really suit me. I never thought it was worth the risk.

Thing is, when you are riding there, you never say it anyway because you know you have to ride there. You put a brave face on it. But the fact of it is that I always enjoyed coming home from it more than I enjoyed going. Once I had survived and came home with everything intact I used to think, 'Shit, yeah, it wasn't too bad' – but a month leading up to it I was shitting myself. So much more can go wrong. It's less of a calculated risk [than short circuit racing].

Back on the mainland Whitham was back to his best form and, before the team set off for the Ulster Grand Prix, he was leading British TTF1 and Production Championships, and was in the running for the 600 series too: 'We had been having quite a decent season up to that point but then we went to the Ulster. It would probably have been my last road race anyway. I didn't want to get involved in it.'

It was ironic then that Whitham was involved in a big crash – through no fault of his own – and was forced to miss the end of the short-circuit season through injury. Whitham says of his Dundrod accident:

We had a brake problem and crashed it in a big way. It was a big crash and broke my ankle fairly severely. That was 12 August. I missed the final three rounds of the season and I ended up third in Production, fourth in the TTF1.

This was also the year that Grant turned down a chance for Whitham to race in the 500GP aboard a works Suzuki. So does Whitham look back with regret at not having had the opportunity to race a full factory 500?

At the time Mick said he didn't think it was the right thing to do. I believed him and didn't do it. Garry Taylor [the GP500 race team manager] rang to say I was daft not to do it. Looking back I don't think it would had done any harm. But I'm not going to be spewing about that now.

When Suzuki lost Whitham to Honda for the 1989 season, many felt that the GP500 issue was part of the reason. But Whitham refutes this:

I got a decent deal to ride Hondas. I knew Suzuki didn't have a bike to go Superbike racing but Honda did. I knew I was going to be stuck racing in Britain for another year. It had nothing to do with the 500 ride.

Whitham went to Honda knowing that Grant was trying to secure him a World Superbike ride on the new RR model:

He had mentioned it but I didn't know how strenuously he had been working on it. They got Roger Burnett to do some World races but he did nothing on it.

Honda offered me a decent deal. The bike looked good on paper – it was winning everything. So I went for it. But at the end of the day the bike wasn't for me and I didn't have a result all year.

Whitham quickly lost confidence after several crashes and became disillusioned with the Honda team set-up. Throughout the year he had talked with Grant about a possible return to the GSX-R750 the following season.

By the end of the year I didn't really know what I was going to do. I even thought of packing it in. I'd been talking to Mick and he knew I was spewing too. But he was missing me and much as I was missing him.

Mick put a deal together for me to back to Suzuki. He said there weren't any wages but he could probably get a bonus deal sorted out – which he did. I got £500 for a front row – £500 for a win – but not one of us got any wages. Mick got a fairly meagre budget to run the team. I ended up not doing too badly that year financially.

The old F1 bike came out of mothballs. I had a steady start to the season but turned in some decent rides by the end of the year. The bike was good, the '87 chassis was perfect and I was running right up there with Rymer, Rob Mac, Reynolds.

It was like I'd never been off the bike. I jumped on it and it did everything I really wanted. You could ride the wheels off it. You could try your nuts off and get away with it. With the Honda you had to be really precise – both set-up and the way you rode it. The only thing I liked was the Honda engine – it was dead reliable too. But with the Suzuki you could get away with so much more. And it was quick enough too.

And I was in a perfect position. With Roger not doing much on it the year before, and him being held in high regard by some people, I was in a no-lose situation. I loved the bike but everyone thought the bike was shit. It wasn't! It was so good.

At the end of 1991 had a bit of a head-to-head with Rob Mac [McElnea – one of Yamaha's top riders and British Supercup Champion that year]. I ended up beating him in the last race of the series. Suzuki were cock-a-hoop. There was a big party. They were so pleased to have won it but had no idea what they were going to do the next year. Mick said there was this new bike coming. Water-cooled, going be the business, fastest thing ever seen, so good – but it wasn't. He persuaded me to stay but again there was no money [wages]. I was on the same deal again – bonuses, that's all.

The new water-cooled bike subsequently arrived but was nowhere near the highly competitive mount Grant – and Whitham – had hoped for. Being all-new it meant a steep development curve was required yet the team had no money to spend on the much-needed aftermarket parts. Whitham recalls:

We struggled with the bike. The series was a bit more competitive that year. John Reynolds was on the case with the Kawasaki. I reckon I could probably have gone a bit better on the old bike. I know I could have still won races on it. In fact, I did win the first two rounds on the old bike in the rain at Thruxton when we didn't have the new bike ready. I was off to a cracking start but never really got with it with the new bike.

The GSX-R750W was lacking in many departments as far as racing was concerned:

It was too big, too long. It just didn't feel like a race bike. We struggled with it all year. We had no trick stuff. Mick and Butch had to make all the bits themselves. At the end of the year a couple of people had a go on the Suzuki and one magazine test rider said it was a bag of shit. That made me feel a little better. I had started thinking maybe it was me. But no one was doing anything on them anywhere in the world anyway!

It marked the end of the line for Whitham and Suzuki – and Suzuki and Grant – and Grant and Whitham, for that

matter. Whitham went to Yamaha the following year in search of a competitive mount and won both British Superbike championships. Grant quit team management. The Suzuki name would not grace the British championship grids again until a young enterprising dealership owner by the name of Paul Denning flew the flag for the company in 1996.

Whitham says: 'I knew Suzuki didn't have a new bike coming out in 1993. I got chatting to Rob [McElnea, the Yamaha team manager] at the end of the year and we did a deal.'

However, he looks back on his Team Grant Suzuki days with affection:

I always enjoyed working with Mick and Butch. The Suzuki people down at Suzuki GB were good people and really keen. The trouble was the people who controlled the money side of things weren't interested. But I never look back and think, 'I could have been doing World Superbike.' In five years time or whatever, when I pack in, I don't want to be sat at home thinking 'if only'. I don't think like that. I may have made mistakes but I'm happy.

I enjoyed my times on the Suzuki. I've always been happiest when I've been in teams with a family atmosphere. Certainly with Mick, and with Rob Mac, and now with the Harris's, it's been that way. It doesn't mean you don't want to win, but it's a good atmosphere. Everyone gets on well together. Everyone pulls that same way. I'm happier in that sort of atmosphere.

Looking back, I think Suzuki got a lot of results for not an awful lot of money when I was riding and Mick ran it. Certainly none of us got rich. But I was in a position where I was living at home and when I met Mick it was costing me a lot of money to go racing. So I was happy to be making some money, enough to buy a car and so on. It was ace to be making a bit of money out of racing even if I wasn't getting rich.

Maybe I should have had my sights set a little higher but I didn't. I was grateful to Mick for what he did. No regrets. I enjoyed it.

10 Water-Cooling for the Third Generation

Seven years after the launch of the original air-assisted, oil-cooled GSX-R750, the machine that set new standards for sportsbikes, Suzuki unveiled their third generation GSX-R, the GSX-R750W – W for water-cooled.

Suzuki never denied that the GSX-R was designed with racing in mind and marketed the 'racer image' to the masses. And, even though the marque had lost its competitive edge in the later years with the rising tide of opposition from other manufacturers, the Suzuki's racetrack-honed handling and competitive horsepower, plus its competitive price, still made it a big seller in the sportsbike stakes on a global basis.

In their GSX-R750W press hand-out, Suzuki reiterated:

Our aim in introducing the GSX-R750 to the 750cc class was to bring to the large-displacement class a pure-bred, high-value, circuit-bred racer replica. To fully integrate sporty styling and high performance with precision handling standards and high reliability in a street bike, we had to look no further than the machines on the circuits to find examples. Superb engine performance. Superb handling qualities. Such qualities are really the basic requirements of a motorcycle, and they are brought together at a new level of effectiveness in the 1992 GSX-R750 ...

The new water-cooled GSX-R750W being put through its paces.

*Water-cooling for the
1992 GSX-R750W.*

It is built to open up new horizons for four-stroke 750cc-class road-going racer replicas, on the road and on the circuits, for years to come.

And Suzuki declared their racing ambitions thus:

The 1992 model, the third generation GSX-R750, newly unleashes onto the road – both straight and winding – the full force of racing confidence won on the circuit battlefields, while the factory racebike of the 1992 GSX-R750R will go for more victories in the 1992 racing scene.

The street bike won accolades – especially in *Cycle World,* which opened its test by stating: 'One of the world's most exciting, most important motorcycles is not sold in the States ...'

Just as in 1985, American Suzuki had opted out of importing the new model. They reasoned that the air/oil-cooled model was competitively priced and still sold well. But most tuners and racers lusted after a water-cooled engine. The

*The new cylinder head
featured cams operating
directly onto the valves.
The number of cam
journals in the water-
cooled engine was
reduced from five to four.
(Colin Fraser Archive)*

142

Water-cooling allowed a more compact, lighter and slimmer engine unit. The new motor retained the 70mm x 48.7mm bore and stroke of the previous year's model. (Colin Fraser Archive)

air/oil-cooled model simply did not dissipate the heat quickly enough under racing conditions. Heat build-up was thought to sap as much as 30bhp from a Suzuki motor during a typical Superbike national-length race.

What made it all the more frustrating was that Suzuki had already launched a water-cooled GSX-R600 in the States, which, while a little heavy and tardy under acceleration, impressed in the handling stakes. The Americans were

The huge, curved, Radial Flow radiator had a heat-dissipating capacity of 24,000 kcal/h. (Colin Fraser Archive)

looking forward to the zip an extra 150cc would provide. They would have to wait – once again.

While America lusted for a new GSX-R model, Canada, Europe and Australia were on-line. *Cycle World's* test bike was a Canadian model and the magazine had to venture north of the border to the Shannonville race circuit to sample it. And tester Don Canet liked the machine so much that he returned to Canada to race a test bike in the National race at Shannonville!

The GSX-R750W may have had the now-familiar trademark look of the GSX-R750 – cradle-frame, similar body-work and graphics – but was essentially a brand-new motorcycle. New engine, new chassis.

NEW ENGINE

The powerplant was redesigned throughout, incorporating water-cooling but still retaining some aspects of the

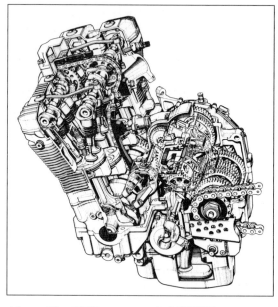

Above: The 1992 water-cooled GSX-R motor: lighter in weight, slimmer and more compact compared to the previous model.

The 1992 bike had a brand-new frame design utilizing pentagonal-section tank rails as part of the aluminium double-cradle frame. (Colin Fraser Archive)

original oil-cooling principles. The water-cooling system featured a curved core Radial Flow radiator (320mm x 318mm) with a heat-dissipating capacity of 24,000Kcal/h. Compared to a conventional flat radiator of the same width, Suzuki reckoned the curved shape had the advantage of a larger effective surface area for cooling without increasing the drag-inducing frontal area of the bike.

There had also been another problem with the flat radiator: it offered poor cooling efficiency right behind the front wheel. The air flow was improved with the new curved design, which directed cool air into this area.

Three quarts of coolant circulated the system, pushed through the engine's water-jackets by an externally mounted water pump driven off the oil-pump shaft on the rear section of the crankcases. This high-performance pump had a maximum capacity of 80l/m at 10,000rpm.

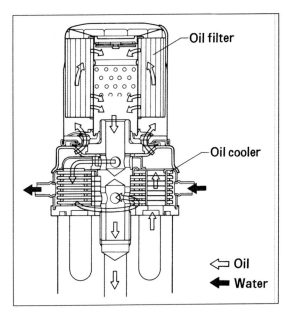

Above: Even the oil filter was water-cooled in the new 1992 GSX-R750W.

The front brakes incorporated twin 310mm-diameter, 5mm-thick rotors gripped by four-piston Nissin calipers. (Colin Fraser Archive)

145

The GSX-R750W featured a slimmer and more compact crankshaft. (Colin Fraser Archive)

A slim 210mm-diameter electric fan behind the radiator directed the cooling air passing through the radiator out through the fairing. The optimum operating temperature of the engine was 170°F. The fan would switch on if the coolant temperature reached 220°.

The engine also featured a water-cooled oil-cooler, combining with the oil-filter element and sharing the water pump. The system was designed to cool the lubricating oil effectively despite the extra heat generated by the supposedly more powerful new engine. The engine

The gear cluster had wider spaces between each transmission axle – increased from 58mm to 68mm for greater strength – but the transmission, as a whole, was reduced in width. (Colin Fraser Archive)

The right-side swing-arm aluminium pressing allowed room for the exhaust pipe to be tucked right in. (Colin Fraser Archive)

now required 4.2 quarts of oil, compared to 5.4 for the previous air/oil-cooled machine.

The original oil-jet piston-cooling system – first developed in 1983 for the GSX750E and utilized in the GSX-R for seven years – was the result of a quest to cool the pistons directly, and this system was retained in the new water-cooled engine. The cooling oil was jetted from small nozzles installed in the crankcase to cool the lower sides of the pistons.

In producing the new water-cooled engine Suzuki engineers were able to design a more compact, lighter unit. The cylinder block, incidentally, still sported the trademark GSX-R outer finning seen on the air/oil-cooled engine. The proven

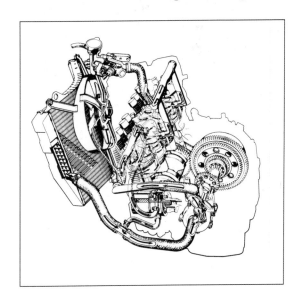

Water-cooling for the GSX-R. The 1992 design incorporated water-cooling but retained certain aspects of the old motor, like the oil-jet cooling of the pistons.

147

The camshafts pushed the valves directly in the new GSX-R750W engine.

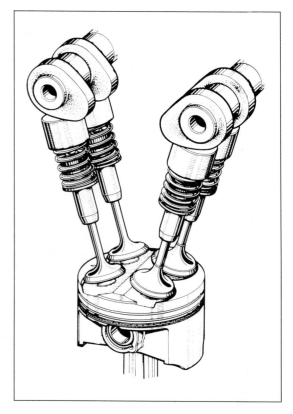

over-square 70mm bore and 48.7mm stroke was retained but the width between cylinders was reduced by 10mm. The crankshaft section was similarly slimmed down and made more compact. The total width of the crankcase covers was narrowed from 490mm to 433mm. The crankshaft journal diameter was increased from 32mm to 34mm for higher rigidity.

The starter clutch was repositioned from the left side of the crankshaft to the generator shaft side, and the starter motor and generator were positioned above the crankcase behind the cylinder – both moves contributing to a reduction of engine width.

The newly designed valve-driving system in the cylinder head of the new engine had the camshaft lobes operating directly on to the valves. This system was considered more accurate at higher revolutions. Other new ideas included single-valve springs and a reduction of valve stem diameter from 5mm to 4.5mm – to save weight. Valve sizes were 27mm for the inlet, 24mm for exhaust. The shim-under-bucket valve operation also increased valve adjustment intervals from 3,500 miles to 7,500 miles.

The new system also required a redesign of the camshafts, with profile design drawing directly on racetrack knowledge. The number of cam journals supporting the camshaft was reduced from five to four, minimizing mechanical losses caused by friction between the camshaft and the cam journals. As a

GSX-R750WN (1992)

Four-cylinder, four-stroke, water-cooled, DOHC, TSCC, four valves per cylinder

Engine

Bore and stroke	70.0mm x 48.7mm
Cubic capacity	749cc
Compression ratio	11.8:1
Carburettors	4 Mikuni BST38SS
Ignition	Suzuki PEI
Starter system	Electric
Lubrication system	Wet sump

Transmission

Clutch	Wet, multi-plate type
Gearbox	Six-speed, constant mesh

Suspension

Front suspension	Inverted telescopic, coil spring preload fully adjustable, rebound and compression fully adjustable
Rear suspension	Link-type, gas/oil damped, spring preload fully adjustable, rebound four-way, compression twelve-way

Brakes and Tyres

Front brake	Twin 310mm floating disc, Nissin four-piston calipers, hydraulically operated
Rear brake	Single 240mm disc, hydraulically operated
Front tyre	120/70ZR-17
Rear tyre	170/60ZR-17

Dimensions (in/mm)

Overall length	81.5/2,070mm
Overall width	28.9/735mm
Overall height	44.9/1,140mm
Wheelbase	56.5/1,435mm
Ground clearance	5.1/130mm
Seat height	30.7/780mm
Dry weight	458lb (208kg)

The GSX-R750R version was meant to 'go for more victories in the 1992 racing scene'. (Colin Fraser Archive)

result, the camshaft length was shortened by 40mm to 360mm compared to the 1991 model.

The valve-included angle was reduced from 40 degrees to 32 degrees to offer a more compact combustion chamber. The surface area of the piston head section was reduced and the shape was much smoother. The compression ratio was 11.8:1. The compact combustion chamber provided a better heat efficiency while the higher compression ratio raised combustion efficiency – both contributing to the engine's improved performance over the 1991 R.

The intake port shape was smoothed to minimize turbulence – which may otherwise have arisen in the transition from relatively slow in low-to-mid rpm to faster flow in high rpm ranges – and intake resistance, further increasing charging efficiency. In addition, a clearance groove was cut into the intake side of the cylinder block sleeve to decrease

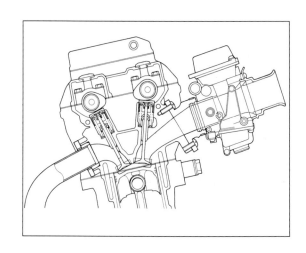

The combustion chamber was more compact in the GSX-R750W, with a narrower valve-included angle of 32 degrees (compared to the previous model's 40 degrees), reduced piston head section and higher compression ratio.

intake resistance still further. A lightweight piston, reduced in weight by four per cent compared to the 1991 model, was also necessary because of the higher rpm performance of the new engine.

Since the 1988 model the GSX-R conrods had been assembled with bolts threaded upwards from the bottom of the rod. This design reduced the concentration of load on the big end of the conrod and increased the con-rod's strength.

The 1992 R had 38mm Slingshot carbs without the power jet circuit used on previous models. The 6.7-litre airbox was positioned below the fuel tank.

There was also a new six-speed transmission with the space between each transmission axle widened from 58mm to 68mm for greater strength. The clutch was redesigned to cope with the engine's improved output and incorporated eight composite material drive plates and seven steel-driven plates.

NEW CHASSIS

The aluminium double-cradle frame retained the GSX-R look but was said to be stronger and thicker than before, with new 60 x 45mm pentagonal cross-section main spars. The problem was that without the spar-type chassis other manufacturers had opted for, Suzuki

The all-new GSX-R750W. (Courtesy Superbike Magazine)

Cutaway of the 1992 GSX-R750W.

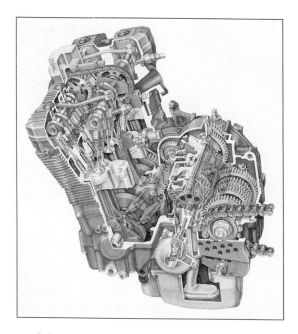

were forced to continue locating the carburettors directly behind the cylinders instead of switching to downdraught carbs with the straight inlet shot preferred by their rivals.

Suzuki claimed the new frame offered five per cent more torsional rigidity than the old frame. The frame's body section, running from the tank spar down to the swing-arm pivot section, was a forging created by a special three-step process from extruded aluminium bar material to ensure optimum balance of sideways rigidity and torsional rigidity. The frame headstock, created in a sand-mould casting process, offered a balance of light weight and high rigidity.

Since Suzuki intended that many GSX-Rs would be used on the racetrack, the aluminium box-tube seat sub-frame was bolted, not welded, to facilitate race maintenance.

Up front were inverted forks, which had been first seen on a GSX-R750 in 1990: 41mm Showas with altered spring

and damping rates. The rear suspension, with a Showa shock, was a refinement of the system Suzuki first used on the R back in 1985. The swing-arm, though, was completely new. The left side was a one-piece aluminium box-section of 71.6mm x 38.6mm, while the triangulated right side arm was specially shaped to allow the exhaust to be tucked in closer to the centre of the bike.

'Slim and compact' was how Suzuki described the new bike. The engine was inclined at 18 degrees to the front of the bike and was mounted in a position that achieved optimum front-to-rear weight distribution and a lower centre of gravity. This location, together with the engine's compact design, allowed more freedom in positioning the carburettors, airbox, fuel tank and other components.

Slim and compact it might have been but light it was not. At 525lb (239kg) wet the latest model tipped the scales approximately 60lb (27kg) more than the original 1985 GSX-R750 and 15lb

(7kg) more than the previous year's model. Even Kawasaki's ZX-7, which was regarded as the heavyweight in the class at the time, weighed no more! When bikes such as Honda's 1992 CBR900RR Fireblade weighed in at around 432lb (196kg) dry, Suzuki's new 750 was positively porky in comparison.

Compared to the old GSX-R, steering geometry was quickened up by reducing rake to 24.5 degrees from 25.5 and shortening the trail to 3.7in from 3.9. The possible loss of stability was countered by increasing the wheelbase to 56.5in (1,435mm). The bike was also fitted with a non-adjustable hydraulic steering damper.

Braking up front was from two 310mm, 5mm-thick slotted and floating rotors gripped by Nissin four-pot calipers with 80mm leading pistons and 34mm trailing pistons. The rear brake was a 240mm disc with a single two-piston caliper. The bike rolled on 17in low-profile, hollow cast aluminium wheels shod with Michelin radials mounted on 3.5in front and 5.5in rear rims.

The bodywork was completely redesigned but retained the distinctive GSX-R look. Close attention was paid to keeping the frontal area small, effectively shielding the rider from the wind, increasing stability at high speeds and reducing drag. The front-end design had a slanted windshield and flush-fit dual headline similar to the previous year's fairing nose. The front fender had an aerodynamic design, 'reflecting the front fender of the factory race bikes', according to Suzuki hand-outs. Its shape not only reduced turbulence but also directed more air into the radiator. The new R also sported bold new graphics!

TESTERS' OPINIONS

Cycle World's test in Canada showed the bike to have a top speed of 158mph (254km/h), enough to make it the fastest production 750 they had ever tested and a full 8mph (13km/h) faster than they had achieved with the previous GSX-R – and only 1mph slower than the 1991 GSX-R1100.

The magazine's testers were unable to put the engine to the test on their own rolling road dyno but *Cycle Canada*, whose test bike they borrowed, carried out a test on a similar Dynojet rear wheel dyno and came up with 100bhp, 18 horses short of what Suzuki had claimed – and the same horsepower figure *CW* had come up when they tested the previous year's GSX-R on their own dyno. Even given the differences of machines and conditions, the tests indicated the latest GSX-R750W was no more powerful than the air/oil-cooled mill it replaced.

On the road, the stock motor would start making usable power at 7,500rpm, considerably earlier than the old oil/air-cooled plot, which came on strong at around 9,5000rpm. The racetrack power kicked in at 10,000rpm. With regard to top speed, the new model scored over the old one by as much as 3mph (5km/h) but quarter-mile times were similar. *Sport Rider* claimed a time of 11.12 secs at 121.5mph along a 1,320ft drag strip when they tried the new-to-the-States W model in early 1993. Their 1992 air/oil-cooled test bike ran 11.15 at 122.3mph.

Sport Rider suggested replacing the Dunlop D202 rubber with more performance-orientated rubber to maximize the handling characteristics of the chassis. *CW* agreed that the new model did

Herve Moineau put in a stirring performance on the new water-cooled GSX-R at Spa in the World Superbike round. If only Suzuki had had the budget to mount a full Superbike campaign that year ...(Kel Edge)

have a better chassis and improved handling over the old previous model – and that the cooling system had been over-engineered for road use – suggesting the bike would lend itself to race-tuning more readily than the air/oil-cooled bike.

With Suzuki keeping the price increases to minimum, *Cycle World* concluded that Suzuki were 'on the right track' with the W. However, in 1993 when *CW* did get an opportunity to dyno test a W, they discovered the new engine to be no less than nine horses lacking compared to the 1992 air/oil-cooled model they had tested on the very same dyno!

Superbike magazine in Britain performed a back-to-back comparison shoot-out with the Suzuki, Kawasaki's ZXR750J and the more touring-orientated VFR750 Honda. The magazine concluded:

In terms of outright performance, there's a clear winner, the Suzuki. Not only does it smoke the other two bikes at the strip, but the suspension means that the engine and stiff chassis are usable on real roads with bumps on. This year's water-cooled variant has lost a little of the traditional GSX-R rort: it feels smoother, less refined and less psychopathic.

Superbike found the Suzuki to be some 10mph (16km/h) faster than its rivals and it was half a second quicker over the drag-strip quarter and beat them to the 100mph mark – by one and a half seconds. 'Revs harder, peaks higher, goes faster,' the testers said.

However, they did not score the bike quite so high in the handling stakes, pointing out the machine's obesity and its rather soft suspension; in the same breath, they marked its handling qualities as 'excellent', whilst warning readers that the GSX-R was not the extreme race replica others had suggested it was.

Maybe the Suzuki had initially impressed the magazine testers but Suzuki's racing efforts during 1992 did not, mainly because of the company's apparent lack of interest in using racing success to promote their wares.

WATER-COOLED RACING

While the new Suzuki was raced in domestic competition world wide, the company still declined to take the bike into the Ducati-dominated World Superbike arena – and none of the importer teams had the budget to contest the series.

In England the UK importer did not even attempt to drum up the budget to run a team in national competition and it was left to Mick Grant to run a shoestring effort with donations from Suzuki dealerships in the country to ensure the Suzuki name was still in competition!

Grant fielded Whitham once again but with such a small budget that the bike could never be fully developed. They started the year with the old oil-cooled bike then switched to the water-cooled version, which was furnished with kit engine parts. With 39mm CV carbs the power delivery was a lot smoother than the old flatslide-carbed version and low-down torque was said to be impressive.

However, the handling took a lot of sorting. Showa inverted forks and triple clamps were borrowed from the F1 bike while the stock rear swing-arm was replaced with a British-made JMC unit with underslung triangulated bracing. An Ohlins rear shock was also used.

Whitham was placed sixth overall in the Supercup series – thanks largely to his inspired riding. The following year he would win both major British Superbike titles for Yamaha on their YZF750!

Grant did enter Whitham in two World Superbike rounds, where he scored eleventh and fourteenth places at Donington against the world's top four-stroke factory race bikes. A couple of weeks later he was blown off on the long straights of Hockenheim and failed to qualify!

The following year, when Whitham raced a Yamaha, he was interviewed by *RPM*, the British road-racing fortnightly publication of the period, and only then did he reveal some of the problems he and Grant's outfit had faced with the GSX-R750W:

The engine was the strongest part of the bike. With the chassis it didn't matter where you had the settings to a degree, we could never get it just right. It wasn't the shockers and stuff that were limiting the Suzuki, more the general design of the bike. It took us all season to get the thing handling properly and even when you'd get it feeling nice going into corners, it didn't steer quick enough and you couldn't get through chicanes. But I don't want to take anything away from the

Yoshimura R & D's David Sadowski leads Freddie Spencer (Honda) and Mike Smith (Camel Honda) at Daytona in 1992. Strange not to see a Yosh GSX-R covered in air scoops! (Colin Fraser)

The new-style graphics were also available in black and pink. (Colin Fraser Archive)

effort. It think we did quite well with the limited money we had in '92.

ENDURANCE RACING

It was interesting to watch Herve Moineau's performance at Hockenheim on the SERT bike – essentially a factory GSX-R750W. No spring chicken, veteran Moineau nevertheless finished an impressive seventh in the first leg and tenth in the second. At that same meeting in Germany, local star Sven Seidel finished fifteenth in the first leg to record points on his Suzuki Deutschland entry – a big-budget outfit compared to Grant's shoestring effort.

Seidel's bike was equipped with an RGV500-type rear unit, suspending a works endurance swing-arm. The team opted for kit forks and Seidel said the handling was perfect. Braking was from PVM six-piston calipers. The bike ran on RVM wheels too.

But the motor was down on horses and many reckoned the 39mm CV carbs restricted performance. Seidel reckoned they were some 6–8bhp down, and the weight did not help either at 374lb (170kg). The motor was fitted with kit transmission, special cams and crank, a '91 dry clutch, and a cylinder head ported by the factory in Japan. The team later did work on an airbox system that was integral with the bodywork to do away with the unsightly air hoses running along the fairing, which Seidel squashed with his knees!

Moineau also raced at Spa – a circuit he always excelled on. He shocked everyone by qualifying front row and ran with the fast guys in the freight train until his motor popped! That excellent effort was never followed up and SERT went back to Endurance racing. It would be nice to feel that Suzuki management look back and think, 'if only …'

Kawasaki won the World Endurance title but Suzuki were not disgraced – thanks to a privateer team. Moineau,

A Real SERT

A typically Gallic pose of Dominique Meliand – headset on, totally immersed in a world that encompasses only his pit box and SERT's bikes on the track. (Kel Edge)

In 1980 former racer Dominique Meliand established his own race preparation shop, Meliand Production, in partnership with Suzuki. The Japanese factory supplied Meliand with works machinery, which his race shop then developed further for long-distance racing.

And from this partnership SERT, Suzuki Endurance Racing Team, grew. The team is based at Le Mans, the move to new premises coinciding with the launch year of the new GSX-R750. The workshop facility is located very close to the famous Bugatti circuit, which hosts the annual Le Mans 24-Hour race. Meliand's race shop houses its own dyno.

In fifteen seasons (1981-95) Meliand's team won 3 World Endurance championship titles, started in 84 races, scored 18 wins, 22 second places and 18 third places.

The championship years came in 1983 with the old GS1000, then with the GSX-R750 in 1987 and 1988. The latter two titles also brought the World Constructors title.

Then in 1996 the team debuted the brand new GSX-R in long-distance competition with Terry Rymer, Bruno Bonhuil and Juan Eric Gomez in the saddle. Rymer grabbed pole but the bike suffered valve-seat leakage. Rymer, injured during GP duty with the Lucky Strike Suzuki team, was replaced by Doug Polen for the Liege 24-Hour and the team finished second behind the rival Kawasaki outfit. Polen, Peter Goddard and Rymer also finished second at the *Bol*. Rymer recorded the fast race lap at Le Mans and the *Bol*. Polen recorded the fastest race lap at Spa, breaking the lap record by over two seconds.

The list of *pilotes* who raced in SERT colours reads like a Who's Who of long-distance racing: Thierry Autissier, Jean-Fançois Balde, Bruno Bonhuil, Roger Burnett, Steve Chambers, Thierry Crine, Eric Delcamp, Jean-Marc Deletang, Jehan D'Orgeix, Miguel Duhamel, Gilles Ferstler, Peter Goddard, Juan-Eric Gomez, Michel Graziano, Ernst Gschwender, Patick Igoa, Hubert Jund, Christian Lavielle, Bruno Le Bihan, Andre Lussiana, Jacques Luc, Jean-Michel Mattioli, Stephane Mertens, Herve Moineau, Jean Monin, Phillipe Monneret, Adrien Morillas, Jean Pierre Oudin, Dominique Pernet, Doug Polen, Terry Rymer, Eric Sabattier, Pierre-Etienne Samin, Dominque Sarron and Jean-Louis Tournadre.

For the water-cooled machine, the Slingshot carb size was increased to 38mm. (Colin Fraser Archive)

Herve's Adventures of Moineau

Herve Moineau. (Kel Edge)

Herve Moineau is a legend in France, though not a GP star or even a Superbike star. Moineau earned fame racing Endurance and the French have a passion for long-distance racing. Most of Moineau's career was spent racing factory Suzukis for Dominique Meliand's SERT team.

Born in April 1955, Moineau, from Heyers, was one of the mainstays in Endurance racing right through the 1980s and up to the mid-1990s. He won four World Endurance titles – three of them with Suzuki and two of those on GSX-R750s – and won no fewer than fifteen major long-distance racing events during an illustrious career.

He started racing in 1974 and rode his first endurance race in 1977. The following year he switched to open-class machinery, finishing eleventh in the F750 championship, mainly thanks to a second place at Zolder in Belgium. He also scored points in the 250 Grands Prix.

In 1979 he raced for Performance Kawasaki alongside Christian Huguet and won the Assen Six-Hour and the Brands 1,000km, but their bid was overshadowed by the outstanding efforts of eventual title winners, Honda's Christian Leon and Jean Claude Chemarin, another of long distance's great champions.

For 1980 Moineau switched to Jean Louis Gilliou's Minolta Honda France team and completely upset the form book, beating Kawasaki's Huguet to the title, winning the Assen Eight-Hour, the Liege 24-Hour at Spa and the non-championship *Bol d'Or*.

Moineau joined Suzuki in 1981, but that year was dominated by Kawasaki. Moineau's only win came at Donington, teamed up with Belgian Richard Hubin when they beat team mates Pierre Etienne Samin and Jacques Luc by 23 secs.

Moineau and Hubin repeated the Donington win in 1982, but were out of luck in the big-league races; however, the duo won the title in 1983 on the HB-liveried Suzuki, winning at Silverstone, Jarama and Suzuka to claim the crown.

In 1984 the rules changed for World Endurance, downsizing the engines to 750cc, and Moineau's career took a different track, into 500GPs with Cagiva. After a fruitless year on uncompetitive machinery, though, Moineau returned to long-distance racing in 1985 with Suzuki on the brand-new GSX-R750 factory bike.

He finished fifth in the championship, again with Hubin, and rode with SERT right through until his retirement in 1995. His third World title came with Bruno Le Bihan in 1987 to give team manager Dominique Meliand, another long-serving Suzuki man, his first championship title since 1983.

On his way to the title Moineau won at Donington, the last major league endurance race held in the UK. The French ace won every one of the international Endurance races held in the UK from 1979 on – a unique record. Moineau added his fourth World Endurance championship title in 1988, this time with Thierry Crine.

Moineau continued to race with SERT right through until 1995. There were some lean times in the early nineties when the air/oil-cooled Suzuki engine was stressed beyond its limits, but while he did not win another race, the Frenchman continued to qualify near or on pole in most races and finished his career with flourish: third in the 1994 *Bol*, second at Le Mans in 1995 and third at Spa the same year. Moineau was still one of the fastest in the sport when he called it quits.

Lavielle and Graziano finished second at Le Mans but the SERT bikes had major engine problems the rest of the year.

Graziano, however, went back to his privateer roots and finished fourth at Spa with Michel Simeon and Mario Duhamel on an old 1991 bike. The trio then captured fourth place at the *Bol* on the same bike and suddenly Graziano had an outside shot at the title with Terry Rymer and Carl Fogarty also in the running on the works Kawasaki.

Graziano's team could not afford to go to the final two races at Phillip Island and Johor so Suzuki arranged for him to team with Steve Martin on a local bike in Australia, where they finished fourth. Fogarty and Rymer won, so it was all on the last round.

Graziano then teamed with his regular partner, Simeon, for the final race and took third but Rymer and Fogarty won again to clinch the title – with 160 points to Graziano's 114.

In the US Yoshimura soldiered on for one more year with the old air/oil-cooled motors but with two new riders: David Sadowski and Supersport charger Britt Turkington. Their bikes, even with larger finning on the barrels, extra rads mounted on the seat rails and a new ram-air induction system, were never fully competitive and their best results were one top ten placing apiece in Superbike. They did not score any wins in 750 Supersport either and finished outside the top ten in a Kawasaki-dominated year.

11 Supersport Swan Song

From 1993 through until 1995 Suzuki faced a tough battle in the 750cc sportsbike market – especially since their GSX-R750 received little more than detailed alterations in the final three years of its life.

Furthermore, Suzuki took no interest in racing – at least as far as the burgeoning World Superbike Championship was concerned. Instead, they appeared to be putting all efforts into Grand Prix racing. In 1993 Kevin Schwantz finally clinched the World 500cc title for the Lucky Strike Suzuki team – an accolade that would win both rider and manufacturer publicity world wide. But did GP success relate to shop sales?

Superbike was the marketing class for sportsbikes. If that was not so, why then did Honda, Kawasaki, Yamaha and Ducati spend so much money on developing such fire-breathing sportsbikes – and then racing them?

The World Superbike Championship was gathering momentum. Kawasaki came close to the title in 1992, Australian Rob Phillis giving the dominant Ducatis a tough time. He eventual-

Thomas Stevens (11) on the front row at Road Atlanta in 1994 with Miguel Duhamel (Harley-Davidson 17), Pascal Picotte (Ducati 19) and Jamie James (Yamaha). (Colin Fraser)

The 1994 Yosh Suzuki. Note the airbox, Suzuka endurance fork, and steering head bracing. (Colin Fraser)

ly wound up third in the series. By now Honda's RC30 had seen better times, as had Yamaha's OWO1.

In 1993 Kawasaki claimed the crown thanks to the efforts of Scott Russell, who defeated Ducati's new signing, Carl Fogarty. Kawasaki were also third with Aaron Slight in the saddle, and Yamaha presented a strong factory-supported challenge through the Italian BYRD (Belgarda Yamaha Racing Division) team and Fabrizio Pirovano on the new YZ750SP.

Suzuki were nowhere. Not entered. The company declined to mount a serious effort (that is, factory team) in the series and importer outfits did not have the budget to sustain a full season of World Championship competition. At domestic level, though, the GSX-R750 could not yet be written off – a hard-ridden, well-prepared bike could still occasionally spring some surprises. Perhaps Suzuki were concentrating their efforts on preparing the new-generation GSX-R750?

THE GSX-R FALLS SHORT

But while racing success could be attributed to the ingenuity of the crew chiefs, the determination of the racers – the showroom ethics that the original GSXR-750s were built on in 1985 – had gone. Suzuki's lean and mean sportsbike had long since strayed from its initial heritage. It was light and fast in 1985. By 1992 it was heavy and not so fast compared to its rivals. So for 1993 the GSX-R750WR went on a diet.

Suzuki went for an improved power-to-weight ratio rather than seeking more power from the ageing design. The process involved weight reduction to motor and chassis. No less than sixty detail changes were incorporated into the 1994 bike, with thirty engine components being reduced in weight.

The dry weight for the 1994 model was 439lb (200kg) – 20lb (9kg) less than the 1993 version – but engine performance remained the same. The diet included lightweight magnesium valve covers

Britt Turkington carried the number 1 plate during 1994 after winning the 1993 AMA Supersport 750 title on a Yoshimura GSX-R750. (Colin Fraser)

and side covers, hollowed transmission shafts, and machined transmission gears. The frame-wall thickness was also reduced but chassis rigidity was maintained by fitting cast-aluminium head stays, one on each side of the engine.

But after pitting the 1994 Suzuki against a Yamaha YZF and Kawasaki ZXR750, *Superbike* magazine commented: 'Suzuki weren't that bothered about mass reduction when they built this bike. How else do you explain the glass headlight cover, the bulky tail light and the cosmetic extra body plate under the tank?'

The latest model sported Tokico six-piston front brake calipers from the GSX1100 (with sintered metal pads to bite on the drilled rotors) and a wider rear wheel to carry a 180/55 tyre. The brakes drew great reviews from *Superbike* in their four-way test (GSX-R, Ducati 750SS, ZXR and YZF) published later in the year: 'Monster braking? Oh yes … The result is a massive amount of power at all speeds but with enough feel to pick the front end up just for fun on the national speed limit.' But as *Superbike* succinctly pointed out,

Kawasaki achieved similar braking performance from four-piston calipers.

There were also new 43mm inverted front forks from Showa (an increase of 2mm in stanchion diameter from the previous year), altered suspension rates front and rear and different box-section bracing on the swing-arm. The arm had previously been made from a pressed construction; now it was made from extruded aluminium. The pivot shaft was increased from 20mm to 22mm.

Superbike added in their early three-way test:

I'd still rate it behind both the ZXR and the YZF in the handling stakes, but the Suzuki has the neutral steering that gets lighter as velocity rises … Ridden in isolation you'd be convinced by the Suzuki, but of course we didn't do any such thing … both the Kawasaki and Yamaha have a rigidity to them that the GSX-R can't quite compete with in standard form.

The rear tyre size was increased to 180/55-ZR17 (170/60-ZR16 in 1992), matched to a front 120/70-ZR17 on the three-spoke rims.

In 1995 the GSX-R got different colours and graphics. It was the final year of the R as everyone knew it – the

Sports Production

In 1994 Suzuki also released the GSX-R750 SP – SP for Sports Production. It was aimed at Superbike racing – just like the ill-fated RR in 1989 – and only 200 found their way to Europe, 150 for the German market (which still boasted a huge GSX-R market) and fifty for France (where a lot of interest centred on the two major endurance races).

The SP had three major differences from the stock GSX-R – carbs, pipe and gearbox. Because World Superbike forbade the replacing of stock carbs, Suzuki homologated this bike with flat-slides; replacing the CV carbs were 40mm Mikuni TMR40 smooth-bores with resin slides rather than alloy to offer a light throttle action.

The exhaust had 35mm stainless steel header pipes (3.2mm bigger than stock), with a huge polished aluminium muffler joining the four-into-two-into-one collector. And finally there was a close-ratio gearbox with deeper-cut hardened cogs – and a taller first gear.

The other difference between the two models was in the suspension; the SP handled better and steered quicker than the stock model.

The net result of the package was increased street performance and improved handling at the cost of glitches such as sluggish take-off from the lights and a typical flatslide flat spot in the carburation. And the price was an extra £2,500 over the standard model: the idea was for this bike to see action on the racetracks …

Merkel finished an incredible fourth in the 1995 AMA Superbike series. He finished sixth in this race at Laguna Seca. Sadly his illustrious career came to an abrupt end after an end-of-season crash at Firebird Raceway. (Colin Fraser)

new generation was on its way and scheduled for a 1996 launch.

In *Sport Rider*'s three-way '750' test in August 1993, comparing the GSX-R with Ducati's triple-eight and the Kawasaki ZX-7, the Suzuki was blasted for its undersprung suspension and poor carburation while the ageing twin-cradle frame was described as feeling 'dated' compared to the opposition. The GSX-R came third in the shoot-out but the revvy motor, gearbox and ground clearance earned plus points.

The 1993 bike – essentially the GSX-R750W the rest of the world saw in 1992 – was slowest over the quarter mile (11.37 secs at 119.5mph compared to the Kawasaki's 11.30 secs at 122.5mph and the Ducati's 11.33 at 120.6mph) but posted second fastest top end of 155mph compared to the Kawasaki's 157 and Ducati's 154.

But by April 1994 the GSX-R got a better vote in the same magazine – even if it still ended up last in a four-way Superbike shoot-out that included the Honda RC45, Kawasaki ZX-7 and Yamaha's YZF750.

Dyno tests carried out by SR showed that the Suzuki, still the only non-downdraught engine in the class, came out third in a comparison of peak horsepower (105.4bhp at 11,000rpm) and third in peak torque (54.9 at 9,000rpm). Honda's RC45 topped both charts, and the Yamaha was bottom in both yet was still voted the winner of the shoot-out thanks to its agility, ergonomics and power output – it had the best overall package.

The Suzuki did come top in one department – price. At $8,099 its suggested retail price equalled that of the ZX-7 and was $1,700 less than the Yamaha. The

Merkel celebrates an oh-so-close Supersport 750 victory at Daytona over Yamaha's Tom Kipp in 1995.(Colin Fraser)

Yoshimura's Britt Turkington (28) and Gerald Rothman (5) launch the 1993 Daytona Supersport 750 race with Tadahiko Sohwa (41) and Fritz Kling (43). (Colin Fraser)

RC45 price tag was $27,000 – and there were even fewer of them in northern America than there had been of its predecessor, the RC30.

Sport Rider said of the GSX-R:

The excellence of the Suzuki's revised GSX-R750 make its fourth place ranking patently unfair. The '94 is probably the best GSX-R to come across the ocean and certainly among the top ten best sport bikes available in the world. Unfortunately the competition is better.

Sport Rider still did not like the suspension: 'The front end feels oversprung and too harsh on compression,' they said. 'Last year's GSX-R ate bumps for breakfast, this year's will have you aiming for the smooth spots. But if you hit them, you're on one of the best sport bikes in the country.'

Cycle World also carried out a comparison test, employing three-time World Champion Freddie Spencer and World Endurance Champion Doug Toland to help staffer Don Canet put six superbike-class street bikes through their paces.

The test covered Ducati's 888LTD, Honda's RC45, Kawasaki's ZX-7 and the limited-edition, race-orientated (105bhp) ZX-7R, Yamaha's YZF750R and Suzuki's GSX-R750. *CW* said: 'If performance-per-dollar is your yardstick then the $8,099 GSX-R750 is a winner. Clearly Suzuki's lightweight, impressive performance and price make it a viable choice.' In monetary terms, the closest rival was the YZF at $9,799 or Kawasaki's base model ZX-7 at $10,699. But in lap times only the ZX-7 was slower than the GSX-R!

In August 1995 *Sport Rider* carried out yet another comparison of 750s with Suzuki again coming in last – even though the bike had won the AMA Supersport 750 title on the track for the past two years. On the street, it seemed, the GSX-R was still not up to scratch.

The brakes again scored well, as did the free-revving motor, but the nervous chassis and poor carburation let the package down. And the Suzuki was slow (149mph) – but so too was the Yamaha YZF (146mph) compared to the 155mph clocked by the Kawasaki ZX-7! The Kawasaki also tripped the lights quicker at 11.22 secs, 121.80mph. The Suzuki's 11.37 secs at 118.25mph was marginally better than the Yamaha. The Kawasaki was heavy, though. At 496lb (225kg) dry it was over 20lb (9kg) heavier than the GSX-R at 473lb (215kg). The Yamaha was the lightest at 467lb (212kg).

Street racing at Alma, Canada, in 1993 with Mario Duhamel leading on a Suzuki ahead of works Yamaha racers Linnley Clarke (26) and Benoit Pilon. (Colin Fraser)

Motorcyclist set up a similar head to head, this time pitting the GSX-R against the Kawasaki ZX-7, Yamaha YZF750R and the Ducati 916. The Duke produced the most horsepower (105.8bhp), most torque (63.1ft/lbs) and highest top speed – 156mph. Suzuki came in last in horsepower (98.7), placed third in the top speed figures with 153mph compared to 151mph for the Yamaha (the Ducati clocked 156mph) and only just bettered the ZX-7 in torque delivered (52.3 versus 52.2). The Ducati did have an outrageous price tag in comparison, though, of £14,975. The Suzuki cost the least – £8,499 – to put things into perspective!

Despite its faltering credibility on the street, the GSX-R750 was still scoring on the racetracks, winning back-to-back AMA Supersport 750 titles. And in 1995 the marque enjoyed a superb final season Stateside – in Superbike as well as Supersport 750 – thanks to Fred Merkel's stirring efforts.

THE W IN AMERICA

The arrival of the GSX-R750W into American showrooms for 1993 coincided with a rejuvenation of the GSX-R750 in racing – at least as far as the US was concerned. Yoshimura Suzuki bounced back into the winner's circle courtesy of Britt Turkington, who won the AMA Supersport 750 title.

Yoshimura had not fielded a bike in the series since Russell and Chandler had dominated the 1990 season with Muzzy-prepared ZX-7 Kawasakis.

From 1988, when it was introduced, right up to 1990, Supersport 750, a class for mildly modified street bikes (as opposed to wildly modified street bikes, which were raced in Superbike), had been a stomping ground for the air/oil-cooled GSX-Rs.

It did not look too promising for racing when magazine tests revealed the new W to be heavier and less powerful than the previous air/oil-cooled GSX-Rs yet

Turkington was able to lift the Supersport title – arguably proof that the Suzuki was a better machine than any other in the class.

GSX-R riders shared five wins with those on Kawasakis during the ten-round programme, Turkington taking three races and team mate Gerald Rothman winning the other for Suzuki. Turkington's Daytona victory broke Kawasaki's twenty-six-race winning streak.

How come? Yoshimura's title-winning effort was based on building a winning power-to-weight ratio – something the factory copied when they produced the 1994 street bikes! With titanium and carbon fibre being banned from AMA Supersport competition, Yoshimura's team still managed to strip 68lb (31kg) from their 1993 race machine and reports suggested that they prepared a machine capable of turning 122bhp at the rear wheel – with strong mid-range, too, and a good degree of reliability. The mid-range was no doubt helped by Yoshimura's titanium exhaust system with special canisters welded to the 1/2

and 3/4 headers. The bike had Ohlins rear shock (stock but re-valved), stiffer sprung forks and Dunlop tyres.

Turkington's pole position at Daytona, at 1m 56.8s, was an impressive squashing of Russell's 1m 58.2s lap record. Turkington – a thirty-one-year-old Texan – led the fifteen-lap race from start to finish and later took victories at Laguna Seca, Elkhart Lake and Brainerd and finished on the podium in nine of the ten races.

While Turkington put a smile back on the faces in the Suzuki camp, there was little grinning from the Superbike corner. Building the Superbike was not as easy as it might have appeared. The team had years of experience with the old air/oil-cooled bike but this baby was brand new. When Stevens rolled out of pit lane for the first practice at Phoenix, the opening race of the year in mid-February, there had been merely three months of development time on the brand-new water-cooled bike.

The bike was based on the machine developed in Japan by the Suzuki factory team and raced by Akira Yanagawa,

The 1994 GSX-R750WR.
(Colin Fraser Archive)

but the AMA bike had many parts developed by Yoshimura. Stevens finished sixth at Phoenix after running in the leading pack early on. Then he crashed out in the chicane at Daytona in March. The twenty-one-year-old Japanese pilot, Yanagawa, gave an impressive performance on his Daytona debut, out-qualifying Stevens with the best Suzuki grid slot in seventh overall. He finished sixth in his qualifying heat and ran as high as fourth until an expensive-looking oil leak sidelined him.

Early in the year Thomas Stevens's best efforts seemed hampered by tyre problems – due, it was thought, to the Suzuki's abrupt power delivery. If that was the case, Yoshimura had dialled it out by mid-season. Stevens qualified a strong third at Road Atlanta and finished fourth in the race. Brainerd showed that the bike lacked acceleration – but Stevens still qualified seventh, then crashed out on team mate Donald Jacks's oil, along with three others.

In the penultimate round of the series – Mid Ohio – Stevens finished fifth. And then came a sixth place at Sears Point with yet more tyre problems to finish the year.

THE 1994 SEASON

Yoshimura continued with Thomas Stevens in 1994 and signed Tom Kipp from Honda. He became their number one Supersport 750 contender, repeating Turkington's 1993 feat of winning the AMA Supersport crown, defeating his team mate Turkington in the process. Kawasaki, with an overweight and under-powered ZX-7 in comparison, did not get a look in – and were in any case not helped by Kawasaki management putting less emphasis on Supersport racing.

The defending champion, overlooked by Yoshimura Suzuki when the team decided its Superbike line-up, dominated Daytona, and won round three at Pomona but Kipp's four-win mid-season streak set him up for a shot at the title. Merkel had battled hard on the porky

The factory Suzuki entry at Suzuka 1994. Akira Yanagawa and Thomas Stevens finished eighth. (Kel Edge)

Kawasaki, which weighed 25lb (11kg) more than the 407lb (185kg) Yosh Suzuki.

Merkel won one race, but the Suzukis were too strong. The weight advantage, plus Yoshimura's experience in extracting horses from the now ancient design, gave the GSX-Rs the edge – and the Yosh team continued always to experiment with cam timing, new valve jobs and exhaust pipes in a constant effort to remain ahead of the game. Kipp's Yosh bike turned 116bhp at the rear wheel on the dyno.

Going into the final race at Atlanta, Turkington and Kipp tied on points. Turkington led after passing Kipp early on but, with two laps to go, Turkington lost third gear and pulled out when the gearbox finally locked up after fourth had also failed.

Kipp – a twenty-six-year-old from Mentor, Ohio – won the race by over two seconds from James Randolph on yet another Suzuki to clinch the title – his second Supersport crown. He had won the AMA 600 title in 1992.

Stevens, meanwhile, finished ninth in the AMA Superbike series after a consistent string of finishes in the top ten. The bikes appeared at Daytona in full Lucky Strike livery and looked reasonably competitive too. Stevens said that the 1994 bike had come a long way in development terms since his 1993 Daytona outing. According to him the team had worked hard all winter, aiming to get more drive off the turns, especially for the tighter tracks later in the year.

One of Stevens's Daytona bikes had a traditional black motor with a plain rocker cover, while the other had an unpainted engine and finned rocker covers. Stevens said Yoshimura Japan sand-blasted Eight-Hour engines to remove the paint – but whether Stevens's unpainted engine was actually a trick 'works' engine specially for Daytona remained unclear. Lap times and trap speeds suggested not (Stevens clocked 169mph (272km/h) through the speed trap – 6mph (10km/h) slower than the fastest bike – Pascal Picotte's Ducati. The Donald Jacks and Tom Kipp Suzukis were even slower). Stevens said:

The motor is a lot stronger [than the 1993 bike's]. Last year I couldn't even hold the draft. At least now I can, even if it's hard work. The chassis is the same as last year. It could be improved and that's one area we're working on with Suzuki.

The Suzuki lacked punch off the turns, which in turn hurt terminal speeds at the end of the straights. Stevens's best results came at Loudon (a really tight track) and Mid Ohio, where he finished sixth both times. Seven times in the ten rounds, Stevens was placed in the top ten.

The bike was trimmed down to 375lb (170kg) by extensive use of titanium, magnesium and carbon parts. There was additional bracing along the top frame rails and at the steering head and swing-arm pivot. Forks were 43mm factory Showas with separate compression damping adjusters for different positions of travel. Rake and trial were 24.7 degrees and 90mm respectively. Stevens ran a cocktail of one steel rotor and one carbon with Nissin calipers. Carbon brakes were outlawed for AMA competition in 1995.

The motor had a dry clutch, 41mm smooth-bore Keihins and was said to produce 145bhp at 13,200rpm, the side-draught head sacrificing mid-range to the downdraught opposition.

INTO 1995

Stevens stayed on the team for the 1995 season but was joined by Jacks again – and new signing Fred Merkel from Kawasaki. The former World Superbike Champion had returned to the US to race full time the previous year after seven years' absence was determined to out-score his established team mate.

Merkel was on a two-year deal and it was common knowledge that he had been hired specifically with the new bike in mind. He told *American Road*racing:

My contract with Suzuki is for two years, 1995–6. After that, who knows? When I signed on the dotted line with Mr Itoh, 'Nabe' [Suehiro Watanabe] and Don [Sakakura], we pretty much had an understanding that we're just going to do our best this year – it's a low-pressure thing. I want to get a good understanding of the motorcycle. Try and make as many improvements as we can and make it handle as best we can – even though next year's bike is going to be different.

Early in the season it was Stevens who set things rolling with a third place at Daytona. With it came a desperate late-race charge that took the Suzuki past the tyre-spinning Honda RC45 of Doug Polen and the Yamaha of Colin Edwards. It was a charge not normally associated with the 'consistent' Stevens – a millstone the Suzuki rider had carried ever since the days of his AMA Superbike National Championship title in 1991, when he won only one race all year.

'Consistent finishes is the old Thomas Stevens,' he told *American Roadracing* from the podium. 'All I care about now is winning. A lot of people had written me and Suzuki off, but I think they are eating their hats right now.'

Merkel finished eighth in the race but it was to be Merkel who shone for the remainder of the year to put Stevens in

the shade. Flyin' Fred finished sixth at Pomona while Stevens limped home with a damaged rear sprocket. He trailed in eighteenth and dropped to fifth in the points. Donald Jacks, also on a Yosh bike, was thirteenth.

Jacks, who had conserved his wet tyres on a drying track, finished fifth at Laguna Seca, having passed a sliding Merkel late in the race. Stevens had run off the track whilst leading Merkel, and finished eighth. Jacks later died in a road traffic accident.

Yosh Suzuki briefly held first and second during the Mid Ohio race but Stevens had gambled on soft-compound tyres and he dropped back to seventh. Merkel, though, was involved in a race-long duel with the Smokin' Joe's Hondas, ridden by eventual winner Miguel Duhamel and Mike Hale. Merkel lost ground with two laps to go when his bike tried to highside him. He finished third – his first Superbike rostrum placing since joining the team. It was a surprising yet impressive effort.

Stevens beat Merkel at Road America (fifth and seventh respectively) but after that Merkel was always the leading Suzuki rider, with consistent sixths and a fifth in the penultimate round at Sears Point.

In Supersport Merkel was the man to beat – even if he ultimately did not lift the title. He started out hot, winning Daytona after a hard-fought scrap with Tom Kipp. Jacks finished third on another Suzuki. Team Suzuki Sport's Aaron Yates had made a good start and led for most of the first half of the race but then collided with Scott Zampach's Buell and broke both forearms in the accident.

Merkel qualified in pole at Pomona but crashed in the race, handing victory – and the points lead – to rival Kipp. It

Nial Mackenzie raced this Yoshimura Suzuki at the Suzuka Eight-Hour in 1994. He finished eleventh teamed with Australian Shawn Giles. (Kel Edge)

was Yamaha's first-ever Supersport 750 win. Kipp won the next round too, at Laguna Seca after Merkel crashed on the first lap. But at Mid Ohio Merkel scored a resounding win – by over 6 seconds from the now-recovered Yates. Kipp finished fifth on the partially wet track. Mid Ohio was the start of a six-win streak for the Californian but he was not destined to win the title.

Firebird, Arizona, hosted the final race of the season. Merkel was quick in Superbike, leading practice and most of the first timed qualifying session, only to be pipped late on by Kipp. But Merkel would never take his second-place, front row start. He had taken an early lead in the Supersport race but crashed into a concrete retaining wall. He was air-lifted to hospital with multiple injuries, the worst being partial paralysis of his left arm.

The injuries led to his retirement from the sport. The announcement came on 24 October. Thirty-three-year-old Merkel still had a year of his contract to run with Suzuki and had been slated to race the brand new GSX-R750 in AMA Superbike and Supersport 750 competition during 1997. He had injected new fire into the Yoshimura racing effort; the most successful Superbike rider in AMA history (nineteen victories) would be sadly missed.

SERT FIGHT ON

In World Endurance SERT continued to battle on with the ageing war horse and even showed up at the Hockenheim WSB round, but were never competitive. However, they scored a memorable win in the final round of the 1993 season at

SERT's bike at the Spa 24-Hour in 1995. Bonhuil, Gomez and Monneret took second place. Note the airbox. Compare this bike with the bike they had for the Bol d'Or *later in the year. (Kel Edge)*

the *Bol d'Or* with the team's number two pairing of Dominique Sarron, Jean-Marc Deletang and Bruno Bonhuil taking the honours. Moineau, Lavielle and Graziano finished fourth after Graziano had crashed with British rider Simon Buckmaster and had to push back to the pits. Buckmaster's foot was severed in the accident.

At the prestigious Suzuka Eight-Hour earlier in the year, a factory Suzuki actually qualified fourth, but the Akira Yanagawa/Noriyasu Numata entry DNF'd in the first hour. Alexandre Barros and Peter Goddard, on a Lucky Strike Suzuki, qualified eleventh, however, and finished seventh in the race after seventh-hour low-side. Their bike sported trick 40mm carbs, and a special one-off frame with steeper steering geometry. It also had larger radiators, twin six-piston Nissin brakes, and a new intake system.

The bike was said to be the basis of a new RR model for the showrooms – but the 1994 production version was expect-

ed to appear with a different frame. The expected 1994 'special' appeared as an SP model (see p.165).

In Japan things were changing. The end of 1992 had seen the axeing of the F3 class. The following year was the last season of TTF1, which Keiichi Kitagawa won for Kawasaki in a year when Suzuki and Yoshimura developed different versions of the GSX-R. Suzuki switched from Keihin flatslides to new-style Mikuni TMs, while Yosh continued to use the older-style Mikunis with their own MJN system; the teams also had a different approach to airbox systems. Suzuki also opted for Kayaba suspension, Yoshimura went for Showa and in the national series both used Michelins.

For 1995 Japan adopted Superbike as the premier class of racing in Japan, which was bad news for Suzuki and Yoshimura. They would face a tough battle until the new GSX-R appeared in 1996.

In 1994, the first year World Endurance ran to full World Superbike regulations, only Suzuki and Kawasaki contested the four-race series with two-bike teams. Honda declined to take part in the 24-Hour races and instead concentrated their efforts on winning the Eight-Hour with Aaron Slight and Doug Polen in the saddle. And Ducati only fronted at the *Bol*, with a pair of bikes with very short fuses.

SERT's Bruno Bonhuil, Juan Eric Gomez and Phillipe Monneret finished equal second in the championship after third place at Le Mans, third at Spa and fourth at the *Bol*. Moineau – who suffered a fearful crash at Spa at Eau Rouge with Rachel Nicotte but got away without serious injury – Lavielle and Jehan D'Orgeix also finished third at the *Bol*. In the Eight-Hour, the best Suzuki finish was achieved by Yanagawa and Stevens in eight place.

With Honda returning to the series and the Kawasakis very strong, many felt the Suzuki was way past its best for the rigours of 24-hour racing in 1995 – but the critics had been saying that for years. True, it lacked top speed but at Le Mans Moineau, Lavielle and Juan Eric Gomez finished second. At Spa they were third. At the *Bol*, Moineau, Bonhuil and Gomez were seventh.

The truth was that none of the factory bikes had the good fortune bestowed upon them all year and could not run with the pace of the privateer RC45 that won the title. Suzuki simply hung in there. Moineau and Gomez, with fifth place in the series, and Meliand looked forward to 1996 and the brand-new machine. They were not the only ones!

The SERT bike at the Bol, *1995 – which Meliand took delivery of at the Eight-Hour. Note the black frame, specially coated forks and boxed-in swing-arm. Moineau, Lavielle and Jehan D'Orgeix finished third. (Kel Edge)*

12 New Design – New Benchmark

In 1985 Suzuki created the benchmark race-replica sportsbike with the new GSX-R750T. Ten years and 138,000 GSX-R750s later they launched their all-new GSX-R750, a four-cylinder sportsbike that again set out to establish new standards in race replica development.

Suzuki started the project on 8 April 1993, aiming to grab a slice of Superbike glory with their all-new GSX-R750 – a compact, lightweight package that had the look of a Bimota and the profile of a GP500!

There were two basic goals in mind. One was to build a machine capable of winning World Superbike and World Endurance races. The other was to produce the lightest, fastest, best-handling street bike in its class.

Alan Cathcart tested the exciting new GSX-R750T at Misano and pronounced the new bike to be a phenomenal road rocket. (Alan Cathcart Archive)

Transparent bodywork allows insight into the airbox system, including the SRAD ducting to the 39mm flatslides. (Alan Cathcart Archive)

Suzuki said their engineers began with the basic dimensions and profile of the RGV500 GP design and then created a new engine design that delivered more horsepower than existing rival designs.

ENGINE REDESIGN

The liquid-cooled, sixteen-valve, double overhead cam, 749cc, four-cylinder engine, designed by Masahiro Nishikawa, was incredibly compact (18.46in/469mm at the widest part of the cases – 1.2in/30mm narrower than the previous GSX-R), short-stroke, high-revving (13,500rpm) but with slower piston speed for reduced friction and more durability, with a bore and stroke of 72mm x 46mm – the same short-stroke dimensions as Yamaha's YZF750 and Honda's RC30. And it weighed 20lb (9kg) less than the 1995 GSX-R750W unit.

The chain drive for the camshaft was located on the end of the crankshaft, which allowed the use of just five bearing crank journals instead of six as in

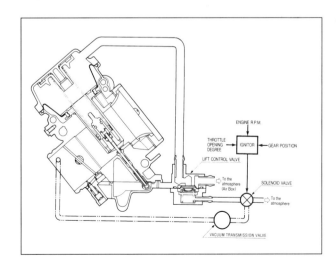

A new vacuum chamber pressure regulating system controls the carburettor piston slide lift.

Unclothed, the huge spars of the beam frame become more obvious. It may be a Superbike but the chassis has GP500 proportions and razor-sharp handling to match. (Alan Cathcart Archive)

the old GSX-R – thus narrowing the overall engine width, reducing mechanical losses and saving 3.3lb (1.5kg) in weight.

The outer camshaft drive also allowed a much straighter shot at the inlet ports. The inlet valves were 29mm, the exhaust valves 24mm – all with double valve springs and bucket tappets – sitting at an included angle of just 29 degrees (compared with the 32 degrees of the old water-cooled engine it replaced) to offer a very short, downdraught intake port.

Pistons were flat-topped with a 15cc combustion chamber, and the compression ratio was 11.8:1.

Replacing the cast-in cylinder liners was a nickel silicon-carbide plating (SCEM – Suzuki Composite Electrochemical Material first used by Suzuki in the RE5 rotary back in 1974!) applied directly to the aluminium-alloy cylinders, which allowed the bores to be moved 5mm closer together.

Additionally, Suzuki concentrated on a shorter front-to-rear crankcase length to

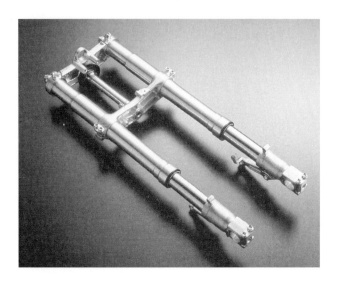

Forks are 43mm Showas. (Alan Cathcart Archive)

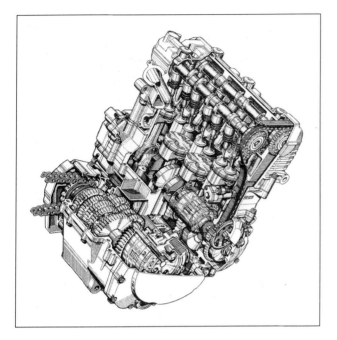

This cutaway of the 1996 GSX-R750T clearly shows three horizontal splits of crankcases.

permit a shorter wheelbase whilst concentrating engine mass closer to the centre of the wheelbase. This was achieved by locating the transmission shafts below and behind the crankshaft, on a separate split in the crankcases, thus creating a three-layer crankcase with the cylinder assembly bolting to the upper case, the next layer supporting the crankshaft, and the gearbox shafts sitting in the lower case. The transmission could, therefore, be removed from the engine unit without disassembling the crank. The engine still had to be removed

Rear Showa shock has an electronically controlled temperature compensating device to ensure consistent response. (Alan Cathcart Archive)

The crank journals have been reduced in number from six to five by switching the cam chain drive to the outside right on the motor. (Alan Cathcart Archive)

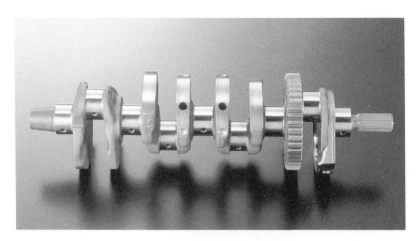

from the frame, but even this job was made easier since the engine was a stressed member of the chassis and there were no downtubes.

To reduce the size of the primary gears still further, there was a bolt-on counter-weight, which also reduced crankshaft weight by another kilo. The motor sat

with the cylinder inclined forward by 25 degrees in the frame.

The downside to this incredibly compact engine design was that Suzuki would not be able to produce a larger-capacity version of this design – although they could go smaller, as the launch of the 600 version a year later showed.

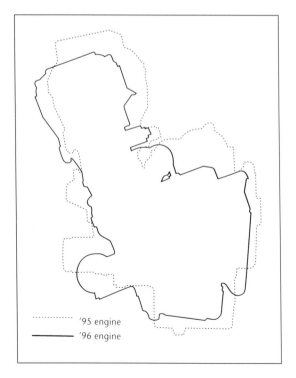

········· '95 engine

———— '96 engine

The difference in size between the 1995 GSX-R and the new 1996 motor is obvious.

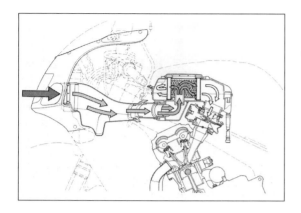

Suzuki Ram Air Direct (SRAD) takes air through two ducts, one on each side of fairing nose, to feed pressurized air to the airbox.

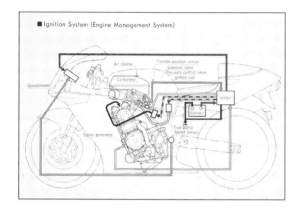

The engine management system of the 1996 GSX-R

Carbs on the 750 road bike were new downdraught 39mm CV Mikunis, with what Suzuki claimed to be a new semi-flatslide shape and new vacuum chamber pressure control system to improve throttle response and 'driveability'. Suzuki dubbed this electronically enhanced carburation SRAD, Suzuki Ram Air Direct. The airbox was fed by two large intakes, one inlet on each side of the twin headlights. The system was controlled by an electronic management system that monitored throttle angle and engine rpm. The black box also controlled the ignition and low-pressure fuel pump.

NEW FRAME

Suzuki engineers knew they needed a new rigid chassis to be competitive in current Superbike competition, hence the all-new aluminium perimeter beam frame, based on dimensions taken from the RGV500 – although the new 750 was actually slightly shorter than the GP bike (and shorter than a 600 Kawasaki ZX6R by 15mm!).

The wheelbase was 55in (1,400mm) with a steep rake at the steering head of 24 degrees, plus 3.8in (96mm) of trail. The main frame was fabricated from aluminium alloy sheet stampings with

GSX-R750T (1996)

Four-cylinder, four-stroke, water-cooled, DOHC, TSCC, four valves per cylinder

Engine

Bore and stroke	72.0mm x 46.0mm
Cubic capacity	749cc
Compression ratio	11.8:1
Carburettors	4 Mikuni BDSR39SS
Ignition	Transistorized
Starter system	Electric
Lubrication system	Wet sump

Transmission

Clutch	Wet, multi-plate type
Gearbox	Six-speed, constant mesh

Suspension

Front suspension	Inverted 43mm telescopic, coil spring, adjustable preload damping and compression damping, 43mm stanchions
Rear suspension	Link-type, gas/oil damped, adjustable spring preload, rebound damping and compression damping

Brakes and Tyres

Front brake	320mm twin floating disc, four-piston Tokico calipers, hydraulically operated
Rear brake	220mm single disc, hydraulically operated
Front tyre	120/70ZR-17
Rear tyre	190/50ZR-17

Dimensions (in/mm)

Overall length	80.9/2,055mm
Overall width	28.3/720mm
Overall height	44.7/1,135mm
Wheelbase	55.1/1,400mm
Ground clearance	5.1/130mm
Seat height	32.7/830mm
Dry weight	394lb (179kg)

The front brakes are 320mm cast iron rotors with six-piston Tokico calipers. (Alan Cathcart Archive)

die-cast aluminium sections – carrying the steering head bearings and swing-arm pivot shaft – welded to the main spars. The bolt-on rear sub-frame was of extruded aluminium alloy tubing. Suzuki claimed the frame to have twice the torsional rigidity of the previous GSX-R750 – yet its structure weighed 7.5lb (3.4kg) less than the previous year's. Even the wheels, outwardly similar to the Marchesinis, represented a

weight saving of 3lb (1.3kg) over the 1995 wheels! And the wheels, including a full six-inch wide rear, were shod with radials.

Up front were fully adjustable Showa 43mm upside-down forks, while the rear swing-arm, in extruded aluminium alloy and braced up, was 12 per cent more torsionally rigid then the 1995 model. The rear ride height was adjustable and the Showa piggy-back shock was some 7oz

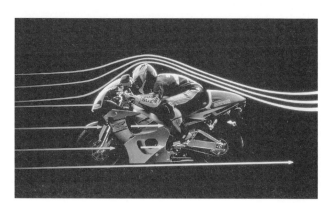

Suzuki engineers made much of the 1996 GSX-R750T's aerodynamic efficiency.

The engine measures just 39mm across the cylinder head. (Alan Cathcart Archive)

(200g) lighter then the remote reservoir unit used on the 1995 GSX-R.

The front brake discs, at 310mm, were 10mm bigger in diameter than on the 1995 bike, but also 0.5mm thinner at 4.5mm. The discs were lighter, however, since the inside diameter was larger with the brake swept area moved outward. The cast-iron rotors were gripped by six-piston Tokico calipers.

The slender yet stubby new GSX-R also looked a lot sleeker as the result of extensive wind-tunnel testing, and at 394lb (179kg) presented owners with thoughts of racing the new bike with no problems in reaching the official Superbike weight limits.

Much of this low weight was achieved by attention to design but Suzuki also included magnesium clutch, camshaft, starter and engine sprocket covers. The stainless steel exhaust was 3.5lb (1.6kg) lighter than the previous model's. The valve-spring retainers, large-diameter (but hollow) axles, swing-arm spacers, wheel-bearing spacers, fairing brackets,

The cylinder bores have a special coating that does away with the need for iron liners. (Alan Cathcart Archive)

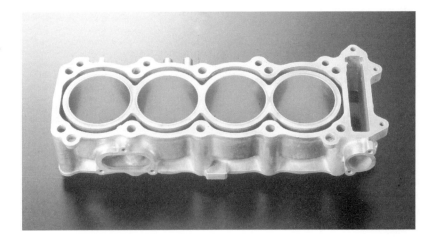

Carburation is optimized by SRAD ducting and these 39mm flatslide Mikunis. (Alan Cathcart Archive)

triple-clamp spindle rear shock rod and the mirror brackets were all fabricated from aluminium.

PRESS REACTIONS

The new bike wowed the magazine staffers. American-based *Sport Rider* voted it number one on both their com-parison bike shoot-out against the Kawasaki ZX-7R and Yamaha YZF750R. And it topped their bike of the year poll ahead of Ducati's 916, Honda's CBR900RR Fireblade and CBR600F3.

In *Cycle World*'s 'Ultimate Sportbike Challenge' the Suzuki bested Honda's Fireblade and the 916 in an overall rating. *Cycle World* said this:

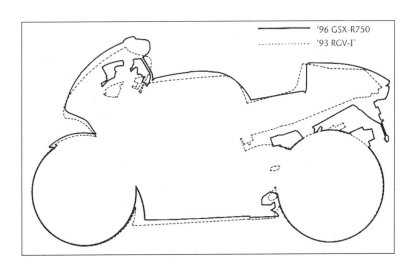

'96 GSX-R750
'93 RGV-Γ

The profile comparison of the new superbike and Suzuki's RG500 GP bike, on which the GSX-R750 dimensions were based.

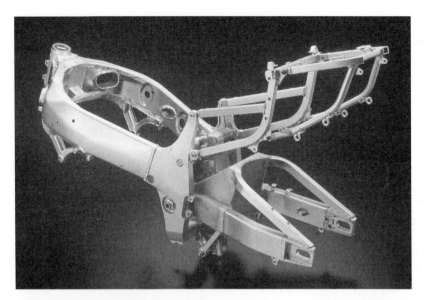

The frame is based on RGV500 dimensions with huge slab-sided, aluminium main spars. (Alan Cathcart Archive)

... the Suzuki GSX-R750 [is] the closest thing yet to a street-legal GP bike. No, the Gixxer isn't perfect, but it picks up where the CBR left off in the power-to-weight department. Not only is the GSX-R impressive for a 750, it out-performed the 900RR in nearly every aspect of our performance testing.

In *RPM,* the British road and racing magazine, Alan Cathcart enthused:

It changes direction so fast yet so precise is the steering – but it's nimble without being twitchy. You hardly need to move a muscle to make it turn into an apex, while flip-flopping from side to side through the Misano chicanes is as easy as on a four-stroke supermono racer.

The Suzuki's handling is completely neutral. It's just that everything happens so quickly, just like on a works 500GP bike.

... But the real peach is the fabulous motor, undoubtedly the best four-cylinder 750cc motorcycle engine yet put into production. It'll pull cleanly from as low as 2,000rpm, which with a 13,000rpm red line gives a pretty outrageous usable power band.

With the new GSX-R750, Suzuki took the race replica concept to a new level. But would it work on the track?

13 Tough Track Baptism

The 1996 racing season started with so much promise for Suzuki. Scott Russell came within inches of giving the machine what would have been an incredible win at the rain-delayed Daytona 200 but was pipped on the line by a hungry Miguel Duhamel. The Smokin' Joe's Honda rider risked all with a late lunge around the banking wall to win a ferocious drag race to the tri-oval stripe.

Peter Goddard won on his debut for Team Ansett Air Freight Suzuki in Australia (their bike had Ohlins and Dunlops). Meanwhile Terry Rymer demonstrated how fast the Suzuki France factory bike (with Ohlins and Michelins) was in World Endurance trim

when he set a blistering pace after being left on the line at the start in the Le Mans 24-Hour World opener – although the team were dogged with front-end push all race (which chewed tyres dramatically) – but eventually went out with a valve-seat failure.

WORLD SUPERBIKE

But in World Superbike – the very stage Suzuki needed big results to capture the public's imagination – there was little to shout about. It was a tough call: new team, new bike, one experienced rider who had some dire luck and one rookie who was trying to learn the tracks as

Doug Polen and Eric Gomez finished ninth in the Suzuka Eight-Hour. (Kel Edge)

The SERT factory GSX-R at Spa. Polen, Gomez and Bonhuil finished second to the works Kawasaki. (Kel Edge)

well as feel his way around an untried machine. The wisdom of the entire set-up was questionable.

The season began well enough for the GSX-R750 at Daytona – the launch-pad for the new model. To cover all bases Lucky Strike GP star Scott Russell was enlisted to ride a specially prepared factory bike (the basis of the company's Suzuka Eight-Hour bid) in the colours of the GP500 team backer.

The three-times Daytona 200 winner, shooting for a record-breaking fourth victory, led the Suzuki charge of no less than six factory-supported riders. This was the first big race for the new GSX-R750. Suzuki wanted Daytona badly.

In addition to Russell, Briton John Reynolds and Australian Champion Kirk McCarthy were on the World Superbike Team, and another Australian, Mat Mladin, Canadian Pascal Picotte and new signing Aaron Yates formed the three-man Yoshimura team for American Suzuki. Lester Harris, World Superbike Team Suzuki Manager, said at the Florida track:

This event is very important to Suzuki – globally. They feel [success at] Daytona would be a good springboard to the season. Logistically, for us, it's a bit of a problem. You can never do enough testing and as we started the programme late: there's still so much to do. We'll still be doing testing and development right until the middle of the season I would guess.

How prophetic those words became. Good springboard for the World Championship team Daytona was not. All week Reynolds and McCarthy fought high-speed stability problems around the banking while the Lucky Strike and Yosh teams got on with dialling themselves in. When the race was postponed due to heavy rain, the British-based team licked their wounds and scurried back to the UK to get in some serious testing. Russell, meanwhile, ran strongly in the re-scheduled race, but just missed out on the race win, coming second. Picotte was fourth, Yates seventh.

Harris said there was absolutely nothing wrong with the horsepower on hand with the new bike – or its reliability:

The Suzuki engine is very strong – with a good spread of power. Daytona showed how fast but we were having to work on set-up. The new bike was very much based on 500 geometry. It proved critical on set-up. A little bit out and it was way off – and that was down to the radical steering geometry.

Despite there being three distinctively different teams at Daytona, all the Suzukis looked very similar, Suzuki being keen to foster a reputation for a successful kit package. 'Nothing you see on our bikes is any different to what is in Suzuki's kit part catalogue,' said Harris, who estimated the full kit to cost over £75,000. Yet if they were only running kit parts what marked the Harris-run team 'factory'? He revealed:

Not everyone has access to the full kit parts. The factory kit parts are only available to top-level importer teams; obviously, Suzuki would have liked successful race teams in each country where they had a major importer. But what the other teams didn't have was the direct access to the factory. We had the Suzuki infrastructure behind us.

The kit parts were said to give 150bhp and lower the overall weight to bang on the FIM minimum Superbike weight limit of 356lb (162kg).

At Daytona Russell was armed with a pair of Lucky Strike bikes straight out of Japan. Russell's 500GP crew chief Stuart Shenton oversaw the effort, while the rest of the crew was largely made up of Japanese mechanics.

Apart from different paint, Russell's bike did not outwardly show any signs of 'factory special' equipment compared to the other works Suzukis, except that, since Russell tested with Showa suspension in the December Michelin tyre tests, the team had switched to Kayaba, the same company that equips Suzuki's Grand Prix RGV500s.

Officially the team switched since they were used to dialling the GP kit. 'We ran 50s with the Showas and couldn't get the handling sorted with the Kayabas early on,' Russell admitted during practice week. 'Then on Thursday we found something and got the bike working a lot better.'

Shenton, used to playing the balancing act with the set-up on a 500, disagreed

John Reynolds had a tough year on the brand new GSX-R750 in World Superbike but looked to be on the up towards the end of the season. (Courtesy Redcat)

Long-Serving Sakakura

Don Sakakura, race team manager for Yoshimura R & D of America, has been with the company since 1979, when the team won the first of two straight AMA Superbike titles with Wes Cooley. He was also with the team when the team lifted the title again in 1989 with Jamie James.

That year Yoshimura R & D was still using the short-stroke engine. Sakakura reflects:

It had its merits but also had its pitfalls. Overall, with the two-year development programme we had, it seemed to be fairly competitive at the end of the first year – almost. Changing the torque band around we needed with various carbs settings, exhaust pipes and internal engine modifications, we got it to work pretty well.

It was a banner year for Suzuki in the US. James also won the Supersport 750 title, with GSX-Rs winning all but one of the championship rounds. But surely everyone was slamming the short-stroke motor's inability to deliver competitive horsepower? And one would have thought if it was going to show its short-comings anywhere, Supersport would have been the class?

The AMA regs didn't – and still don't – allow you to do too much [tuning]. Mainly it consists of carb tuning and exhaust pipe exchange. Other than that you're pretty limited to what you can do. Stock carb body, standard slides. You're allowed to do jetting. Fujio [Yoshimura] developed the MJN [Multiple Jet Nozzle] jetting kit. It's a multi-jet needle design that really helped us out a lot. It gave us better fuel atomization (the fuel/air mixture) before it hit the venturi of the carburettor. We're continuing to use that even now but back in 1989 it really helped us.

So why do not all the manufacturers use an MJN system? Sakura replies: 'I'm not really sure why other manufacturers are not using it, except that it is customized specifically to each application.'

The Long-Stroke

In 1990, though, it was back to the long-stroke engine.

We took up where we had left off in 1987, incorporating some new cylinder head refinements. It was that year when we started getting into the pressurized airbox systems. That gave us the biggest advancement in terms of horsepower.

As far as internal engine modifications were concerned we continued a basic programme that we had been running the past few years. I think when you get a new model you have to find what the engine is lacking. Whether it's cylinder head work, internal friction. Try to focus on these areas. You have to work on one area at a time and then move on.

1990 was a difficult year in terms of riders getting hurt. Both Duhamel and Crevier were injured at Daytona. Duhamel would go on to race at Road Atlanta but was not fully fit. Crevier missed the race and would not ride for Yoshimura again. Polen – by now racing full-time in Japan and back in action after missing Daytona through his Willow Springs testing crash – was brought in for the Road Atlanta race. Sakakura's memory is a little clouded on this subject – and what he does recall seems to contradict with Polen's recollection of the event: 'One year we had one rider on Michelin and one on Dunlop. We hired Doug and he's always been contracted on Dunlop. I can't recall the race ...' Was it Road Atlanta?

Yeah, he won there on Dunlops, I'm sure..and Miguel won Topeka. I'd rather not get into that [the tyre saga]. It brings up bad memories. We were looking for a rider at the time and Doug was available. It was unfortunate that he was contracted to a different tyre manufacturer than we were contracted to. Michelin could have said no way, but they were gracious enough to allow it to happen.

In 1991 Suzuki introduced a single-rocker design, which was said to improve valve control at higher rpm. Sakakura says otherwise: 'We had reliability problems with the single-rocker design. The head design was OK [Fujio Yoshimura, listening to our discussion, interjects: 'the valve geometry was wrong'] but to get the reliability back [into the valve train] we used a lot of the older parts.'

The other pressing problem by now was excessive heat build-up:

The main problem for us was trying to keep the head temperature down. We got into a lot valve seat distortion due to heat, and cylinder distortion. We were losing [piston] ring seal and valve seal. Keeping power constant throughout a race weekend was difficult to do.

There were suggestions that the team attempted to build more tolerances into their engines to account for the heat build-up. Sakakura dismisses this with a smirk:

Not really. We didn't have a reliability problem as such but we did lose power. It was something we knew was happening so we tried to overcome it by raising the whole power up so if (or rather, when) it did drop off you were at a higher level to start with.

A typical AMA Superbike Yoshimura Suzuki of the time looked incredibly cobby, with oil radiators and braided hoses in every conceivable spare space.

We tried placing them in different locations trying to keep the oil as cool as possible. We had a separate cooler just for the head and then a sub-cooler for the lubrication. We started that as early as 1990. We had coolers all over. At one time we had three! We were trying to keep the head temperature as cool as possible. All the oil remained in a common sump but before it went back to the sump it would cool the other circuits. The bike was kind of a mess – it had braided lines all over.

A fully kitted Suzuki GSX-R750 superbike. (Alan Cathcart Archive)

Kirk McCarthy's first international season was traumatic: new bike, new team, new tracks. A lot to learn in one short season. (Courtesy Redcat)

with Harris on the 'critical' set-up: 'Each bike throws up different problems but I wouldn't say the set-up of this bike is that critical. We tested at Daytona in December then came here for the 200 with different suspension and got it working OK.'

Russell's bike and the Yosh bikes had a cockpit-mounted three-position switch for three different ignition curves. Shenton insisted that the options were to aid set-up and that Russell was not switching between curves from infield to banking.

Russell had a digital read-out panel (for a real-time lap time read-out) above the switch and to the left of the tach, while the Yosh bikes had all information feeding through their Pi display. The WSB team bikes also had the 1,2,3 switch but it was taped in position on 'two' all week.

The Lucky Strike and Yosh bikes ran similar Yosh titanium exhaust systems, which had tapered elbows exiting the head but had parallel headers down to the collector. On the Yosh bike there were the familiar small interconnecting tubes welded between cylinders 1/2 and 3/4, approximately 3in (75mm) from the exhaust port. The Lucky Strike bike had a titanium muffler but Yosh opted for

Lester Harris, team manager of the Suzuki WSB effort. (Courtesy Redcat)

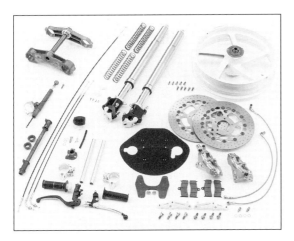

Front end kit included: new forks, triple clamps, Marchesini front wheels, cast iron rotors and new six-piston calipers. (Alan Cathcart Archive)

Other kit parts included: titanium exhaust system, carbs, large capacity rad and magnesium engine covers. (Alan Cathcart Archive)

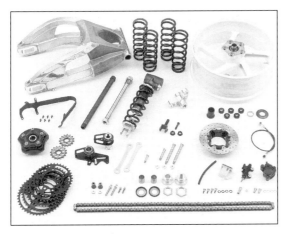

Rear end kit upgrade included: new swing-arm, shock, selection of springs, ride height adjuster and Marchesini wheel. (Alan Cathcart Archive)

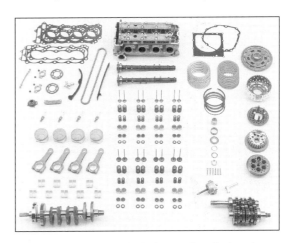

Kit engine parts included: new head, titanium rods and valves, forged pistons, and dry clutch. (Alan Cathcart Archive)

carbon. The Harris bikes sported kit exhausts.

But a great opportunity to pool information was squandered at Daytona. There was no possible way to glean meaningful feedback off each other. The World team ran Showa suspension and

Michelin tyres. The Lucky Strikes had Kayabas and Michelins while the Yosh team toped for Ohlins and Dunlops!

In 1995 Russell had won Daytona on a Muzzy Kawasaki. So how did the new Suzuki perform in comparison? During Bike Week he said:

The New W

Britt Turkington gave the team the AMA Supersport 750 title in the first year of the water-cooled GSX-R750. Sakakura says:

Struggling with the air-cooled system for as long as we did helped us look into other areas to develop our speed. We knew other areas that needed development faster. 1993 [the water-cooled launch year as far as the US market was concerned, remember] was basically the same as the previous year [in terms of engine spec] but with water-cooling. The bore and the stroke was the same. We had a good feel for what was needed – other than the water-cooling. There were quite a few things we needed to change internally due to the cooler temperatures.

While the bike won the title, the press criticized the stock machine for being overweight – especially when compared to the ultra-light concept of the original GSX-R in 1985.

It was the first year of the water-cooled and I'm not sure they [Suzuki's engineers] really knew what was required. You could shave a lot of weight off and that's what eventually happened. [In the launch year] they added quite a few pounds to the motorcycle with water-cooling. But it didn't affect us too much. At that time we were fairly light anyway. We were underweight and adding weight to the motorcycle anyway.

Sure, the machine itself was a little heavier than the air-cooled model but the power stayed good all the way through the event – really close numbers to when you started whereas the old air-cooled would lose as much as 5 per cent. It's tough to be there at the end when you give away that much.

We were working within very limited areas that we could modify – and those were the areas we always strove to perfect. It's all down to accurately measuring all the bearing clearances. Spinning friction has a big effect on overall power. People don't realize that.

Production units can be fine-tuned and that's what is needed in Supersport. It's a close form of competition. And to have a good pilot is the number one thing.

We're not allowed to do much to the chassis at all. Aftermarket shock. At the time we were using Ohlins. Front forks mods? We always did a lot in the area: valving, spring rates, oil viscosity. Production racing shows a lot more what the motorcycle is all about. If they [the manufacturer] produce a good motorcycle – like the current models – we don't have to do a lot to them to get the result. It's showing up right now [in 1997]!

In '93 we did as well as we were hoping to do – simply because it was the first year of the water-cooled system. We were learning what to do. it was the same in 1994 but by 1995 we were starting to be real competitive.

We had three years of refinement on the new liquid-cooled bike and lot of works-style pieces from Japan. That made a whole of difference to us. Fred [Merkel] also is a world-class champion. He helped us in the development process.

Fred was on a two-year deal and towards the middle to end of the year we were already testing the new machine. He'd been on it and was licking his chops waiting to go racing on it. He knew it was going to competitive right out of the crate. It was just a shame about the accident – he never got a chance to race it.

Sakakura has worked on each model year of the GSX-R750 and is still heading the Yoshimura R & D race effort in the AMA Superbike Championship. He has never been more impressed with a stock production bike than he was with the new Suzuki GSX-R750.

As a production bike out the crate we were surprised how bad it made us look. Out of the crate it would produce power in stock trim almost the same as we were getting out of our 1995 Superbike! With an 18lb [8kg] advantage in weight too. It made our job that much easier. Suzuki fully supported us with full-factory pieces that they had been developing over the 1995 year.

We had options to test other suspension product but ended using Ohlins. That worked well for us. For the riders we had they preferred the Ohlins. I'm not saying that it's a much better product but it suited them.

Engine-wise we fitted the normal hop-up pieces: stronger pistons, valve train, con-rods etc. Overall, the engine design surprised us. We were expecting a high rpm, peaky engine but it was the complete opposite with the downdraught engine. Lower rpm has very, very high torque numbers. RPM was about where we were with the 1995 bike but we had a lot more mid-range torque. It made it that much easier to control for the riders. It was easier on the tyres, easier on the chassis. It's hard to compare the two [old GSX-R and latest GSX-R]. They are two very different motorcycles.

And we're just getting started with this bike. It's got so much more potential. Next year [1998] I expect us to win quite a few more races than we previously have.

Internal engine reliability is good. We've not found a real problem yet. It was refined in Japan with the racing kit pieces – they are available through Suzuki's kit part network. Ninety-nine per cent of what we run is on the kit part list that anyone can buy – it's expensive but you can buy it. There's not the unobtainium like some of the other manufacturers' equipment. [Suzuki do choose who have the parts though!]

It's been stated in the past that some manufacturers do use parts [in Superbike competition] that are not available. But our parts are. Doug [Polen] is one who is getting support with kit parts.

Sakakura has always worked with Suzuki. He says:

We've been with Suzuki as long as I've been with Yoshimura and I've been here since 1979. They've always given us 100 per cent support, as far as the race product goes. I think you have to have that – without official factory manufacturer backing nowadays it's impossible to be competitive. It's tough. Maybe back in 1986 it wasn't quite so bad.

From the first 1985/86 model it was something Suzuki had brought out that was two steps ahead of everyone else at the time. A real lightweight, higher horsepower. It had a great power-to-weight ratio. Then 1990 through 1995 it was kind of unchanged. Now the new bike is really looking in the direction of the original bike with the new model – real lightweight, high horsepower. It's working. It's selling really well. It's a proven winner. And what they give us to race is a proven winner.

Sakakura dismisses suggestions that Yoshimura R & D's race effort has produced very tricked-out race bikes. He says that it is down to the original product from the manufacturer:

It's amazing what they can do with production bikes now. Ten years ago we weren't even thinking of bikes on this level. The level of quality is a race bike with lights. It make our job easier.

There's nothing special what we are doing. It's down to what you get from the manufacturer. You get the base starting point and build from it. Suzuki have a good base model and can build a Superbike off that. It's a good philosophy that obviously works. And it's proven in the sales.

Factory Suzuki superbike. Lester Harris claimed all the equipment they used was on the Suzuki kit part list ... (Kel Edge)

193

The Kawasaki always worked well at Daytona. I'd say last year's Kawasaki was more peaky. The Suzuki delivery is more linear – with more [power] on top.

The Suzuki chassis is stiffer. I'd say we got it better than the Kawasaki. We ran Dunlops last year. The Michelins have more grip. Compared to my 500, though, the bike feels heavy and hard to turn – and it's got no power. Hey, the only bike out there with power like a GP bike is a Ducati and they ought to be in the GPs anyway!

While Russell beefed about the alleged Ducati advantage at every opportunity, the speed trap showed his Lucky Strike Suzuki to be the fastest at 169mph (272km/h). That, however, was on Wednesday when the Ducatis were not handling owing to a rear shock assembly problem.

Speed was not something the World Superbike Team Suzukis could take advantage of most of Daytona week. Both Reynolds and McCarthy had serious stability problems on the banking with Reynolds giving up on the infield set-up right up to Thursday (the final day of practice) to concentrate on being able to run flat on the banking.

And going into the race they still had not beaten the problem. Reynolds qualified a dismal twentieth with the two works Harleys ahead of him. Demoralizing or what?

The Yosh bikes ran Dunlop tyres rather than Michelins on the other three and opted for Ohlins suspension front and rear – but even that set-up took time to figure (and Suzuki politics would later dictate that Yoshimura switch to Showa, working with factory Showa technicians, much to their riders' frustrations).

Like Reynolds, Mladin, struck down with flu, struggled. He raced a Kawasaki in 1995 and commented:

The suspension is holding us back at present. Getting onto the banking is the problem but we'll get it sorted. We've already planned a three-day test after Daytona. Right now the steering is not so nice as the Kawasaki but we've had so little time on the bike. The chassis is short, like a 500, and I think that could be causing us problems.

It certainly was. As the season progressed it became evident that the GSX-R, in racing trim, was absolutely critical on set-up.

At least Suzuki won the number-crunching game at Daytona. They accounted for thirty-two bikes, 40 per cent of the eighty-bike grid for the 200-Mile Superbike race (Kawasaki had 23.75 per cent, Yamaha 12.5, Ducati 13.75, Harley 7.5, Honda 2.5 – but the 2.5 per centers came out tops! Suzuki also dominated the Supersport 750 with 55 per cent of the entry (Kawasaki had 23 per cent, Honda 16, Yamaha 6) and boasted a one-two in the race, courtesy of Yosh duo Aaron Yates and Pascal Picotte.

WORLD CUP

The first WSC round at Misano was a disaster for the British-based World Suzuki team. Reynolds finished seventeenth after tyre problems in the first race, then crashed in the second. McCarthy crashed in the first, battling with Paolo Casoli's Ducati, but scored twelfth place points in race two.

By Donington the team had switched to Kayaba suspension and things were looking good when Reynolds clocked a 1m 35.21, tenth quickest time, and it could have been better still but for a huge crash on Saturday down Craner Curves. Reynolds sprained both wrists and tweaked his back so did not race.

McCarthy battled away for two thirteenth places.

Reynolds pulled out of the race at Hockenheim. All weekend he struggled to eradicate the same high-speed stability problem that plagued the team at Daytona. Eventually he was withdrawn from the meeting after qualifying thirty-second! Officially his back was giving him problems. Unofficially you had to wonder why the rider had been chasing a set-up so long – especially when his team mate, with no prior experience at the track, posted tenth-fastest time. McCarthy got stuck in at Hockenheim and looked far better than his tenth and ninth places suggested. Harris explained:

I think maybe Kirk [McCarthy] is more liable to accept some small problems, grit his teeth and ride around them. He's also learning his way around the tracks, remember, so needs as much track time as possible.

John's already got that database – and how he expects his bike to work. He's more experienced than Kirk and maybe more critical on set-up. He knows riding around problems won't solve them so we're happy for his critical analysis. In World Superbike there's lots of factory opposition so the bike needs to be spot-on.

At Daytona Reynolds admitted he had given up trying to run fast through the infield, simply because all the effort there was wasted once he got into tank-slappers on the banking. At Hockenheim it was the same deal: forget the stadium, work on the fast bits.

McCarthy faced the same problems:

It's OK [stability] until you get right on top end, then it starts to shake and gets worse and worse. Then you try to brake [AP Lockheed six-piston calipers gripping 320mm rotors] and there's nothing there. The pads have been thrown out so you have to pump the brakes.

Harris explained:

We made great strides forward at Donington [after switching to the Kayabas] but then John crashed. At Hockenheim we had to start out fresh. We have direction with Kirk but John's not able to set the bike up the way he likes it right now. At Hockenheim terminal speed is everything – turn 1 to the Ostkurve is critical.

Russell at Daytona, where he ran Miguel Duhamel a very close second. Russell's bike came direct from Suzuki Japan and was looked after at Daytona by his 500GP Lucky Strike crew chief, Stuart Shenton. (Kel Edge)

The 'R' from the Hot Seat

Terry Rymer is one of the most experience four-stroke pilots in international racing. He won the British championship riding a Loctite Yamaha OWO1 and has raced in the World Superbike championship from its inception in 1988, including spells with Yamaha (through Loctite), Kawasaki and Bimota factory bikes.

He also rode privateer Ducatis in the WSB (for Aldeo Presciutti's Red Devils team) and British championships (in 1996 for the Old Spice team when he had several rides on a Lucky Strike 500GP as well as acting as test rider for the team), the works JPS Norton rotary and an importer-backed RC45 Castrol Honda in the British series.

In 1996 he also raced the new Suzuki for Dominique Meliand's SERT World Endurance team and was the fastest man on the track in the opening race at Le Mans. He had this to say about the new bike:

I was one of the first guys in Europe to ride the Suzuki in November 1995. When I tested it I felt it had a really good engine but the chassis was a long way off. We were running Showa at that time and couldn't get it working so we decided to fit Ohlins. In January I ran the bike again and put the Showas aside!

Terry Rymer was the fastest man on the track at Le Mans in the early part of 1996 even though the team experienced so much front-end push that the bike chewed up front tyres badly. SERT soon overcame any handling problems with a private test session. Rymer said he could not understand why the factory team still had handling troubles going into the 1997 season. (Kel Edge)

We raced at Le Mans with Ohlins forks and a Showa rear unit. We chewed up front tyres all weekend there, which was, I suspect, a geometry problem.

Then after Spa we went testing at Nogaro and Ledenon. Polen and myself spent three days at Ledenon with a Showa technician and ended up getting the bike really good.

We went to the *Bol* and the bike was on rails. In the first hour Jamie [Whitham – on a works Yamaha] was leading. I was fifth early on but pulled through to take the lead and had 17s on the pack after the first hour. The bike was so rock steady I was able to smoke 'em!

To get the bike to work that well wasn't too hard. We changed linkages on the rear and the compression and rebound. The Showa technician had to completely re-shim the forks to change the damping characteristics to suit us. We all worked hard and did a lot of laps but nothing more that was needed. It's normal racing practice. You go testing to sort the bike.

We got it to the stage where it was stable and would track though the fast corners. Then all that was left was to get the balance of the bike right by adjusting the ride heights and so on. So I was really surprised to read in one of Jamie (Whitham's) articles [after a fruitless attempt in pre-'97 season testing to sort the WSB Suzuki's handling] that they've had so many problems. I know Endurance isn't World Superbike racing but we seemed to dial our problem out so early in the year; the WSB bikes have had a stability problem all the time.

We never had a stability problem. We did find one linkage that produced a problem so we didn't use it! One theory we had was that maybe with big riders [as on the SERT team] the Suzuki was OK and with little riders [as on the WSB team in the form of Reynolds and McCarthy] it wasn't. It's a common fact that 500s and Superbike tend to be a bit 'wobbly' with little guys on. We put it down to that. Obviously it wasn't that.

All through last season it seemed all the main development was with the WSB. We just used kit parts. It was a little bit strange was that none of the teams in the world were working together. I would have thought they would have their heads together seeing it was a brand new bike. But as far as I could see no exchange of information. All I know is that our bike was extremely stable.

Engine-wise it lacked a bit mid-range – which would have hurt in WSB – but it could have been sorted. It certainly wasn't a problem for us in Endurance racing. If I could qualify pole at Le Mans – first time out – it can't be that bad a motorcycle. It seemed like the new Suzukis always looked fast but were just a little lacking off the turns.

The big problem is that if you haven't got the stability and can't run it into the corners, you're not going to track through it and then get out of it well. If a rider hasn't got any faith in the stability of the bike, he doesn't want to open the throttle. When a bike is sliding around you know how much you can do with it but when it loads itself up and gets out of control you just don't know what it's going to do next.

I always said last year that if I could have brought the Suzuki back to the UK I could have won Superbike races on it – even in full endurance trim. The last year I rode for Kawasaki I was for ever moaning that the bike was getting more and more difficult to turn. It seemed like the Honda could flick through the Piff-Paff at Ricard so easily compared to my bike. I was finishing sessions with my arms pumped up. Hard work. It felt like a long bike. The Suzuki, though, felt short and nimble in comparison but it didn't feel unstable either. It felt comfortable to ride.

And it was reliable too. Apart from the valve seat problems at Le Mans nothing else gave real problems. Meliand's team was the strongest last year – no doubt. The Suzuki was a really good motorcycle.

Peter Goddard – Australian Superbike Champion riding a GSX-R750T. (Clive Challinor)

The biggest problem we have is trying to get enough testing. It's impossible to do at a race. You have to go for a time in the afternoon session on Friday, just in case it rains on Saturday, so you can't really try anything. You can make radical changes in the untimed session because you need to get sorted for the timed ones. It's tough with a brand new bike.

The GSX-R's saving grace appeared to be its powerplant. 'The engine is excellent,' enthused Harris. 'We've had no problems at all. You could always do with more speed and it's an on-going development programme at Suzuki. But technically there are absolutely no problems at all.'

Hockenheim also provided the opportunity to view what options another importer team, Suzuki Deutschland, had chosen. For years the GSX-R750 had been a top seller, even when the old model was in decline elsewhere. The German importer always ran a top-class outfit in the Pro Superbike series and in selected World races. For 1996 veteran Andy Hofmann was in the saddle.

His bike had Ohlins forks, Pirelli rubber running on PVM wheels and PVM six-piston calipers gripping 320mm rotors from the same company – the works team ran Tokico six-pistons. Hofmann's bike also sported a Skorpion pipe (which produced exactly the same top end but offered more 'user-friendly' power) and 2D data-logging. Hofmann qualified seventh row in Germany – ahead of Reynolds – but did not figure strongly in either race.

The World team had some respite between Hockenheim and Monza to go testing – and it showed. In Italy McCarthy got eighth place in both races, Reynolds scored a seventh in race two. In the Czech Republic it got even better with Reynolds up to fifth in the first leg. But that was as good as it was going to get. Perhaps the team's plight was underlined best when Peter Goddard finished ahead of both factory bikes in the final round at Phillip Island.

Lester Harris went shopping for new riders to continue the development pro-

gramme into 1997 and picked James Whitham and American Mike Hale.

RACING STATESIDE

In the US the GSX-R750 had enjoyed better fortunes – not great, but better. Yoshimura appeared to have a handle on development with Pascal Picotte and Aaron Yates both scoring race wins (it was Yates's first-ever Superbike national victory) and finishing fifth and sixth respectively in the point standings. Their other rider, Matt Mladin, finished fourth overall after three runner-up race finishes!

Picotte's win at a rainy, crash-strewn Mid Ohio was Suzuki's first AMA Superbike race victory since 1990. And Yosh duo Picotte and Yates dominated the Supersport 750 ranks with Yates taking the title. Suzukis won all ten races, Yates took five, Picotte (in his

The British Suzuki importers once again opted to steer clear of using racing to publicize a new GSX-R model. Instead plucky Bournemouth-based dealer, Paul Denning of Crescent Motorcycles, entered the British Championship with a TTS-tuned machine. By mid-season, the Crescent Suzuki, with Jim Moodie in the saddle, was becoming a competitive package. (Clive Challinor)

first-ever season of 750 Supersport racing) four and Michael Barnes, who was third in the series, took the final Las Vegas round.

In World Endurance the new GSX-R also came on in leaps and bounds after the Le Mans disappointment. Doug Polen teamed with Eric Gomez and Bruno Bonhuił to finish second at Spa after Polen had smashed the lap record by two seconds!

Polen and Gomez also took ninth at the Suzuka Eight-Hour but another GSX-R, ridden by Katsuaki Fujiwara and Keiichi Kitagawa, finished ahead of them in seventh. And Polen, Rymer and Goddard, a formidable combination, finished runners-up to the works Honda at the *Bol* when they should easily have won. A muffed pit-stop, when Polen tried to rejoin the race before the rear wheel was in place, cost them 16 minutes while the damaged swing-arm was replaced.

In England there was no official Suzuki effort – as usual, despite the fact that here was a brand new model to promote and a fully televised (by BBC Grandstand) British Superbike Championship.

Instead the company name was represented in the revamped British series by one inspired dealer, Paul Denning, boss of Crescent Suzuki in Bournemouth. He bought kit parts, got TTS to hop up stock internals and went racing on a limited budget and loads of enthusiasm. Club racer Denning himself took to the saddle, and signed up Ian Cobby for the other machine.

It took much of the season to develop the bikes but by season end, after Cobby had been hurt (badly broken leg at Cadwell) and Denning had taken a back seat and signed up top Scot Jim Moodie, who had parted company from Colin Seeley's malingering Ducati effort, the

Consistent finisher Matt Mladin, from Australia, finished fourth in the AMA Superbike championship on a Yosh GSX-R750. (Colin Fraser)

AMA Supersport 750 racing became the domain of the Suzuki GSX-R750T in 1996. This is the all-Suzuki Laguna Seca podium of (left to right) privateer Mark McDaniel and factory Yoshimura riders, Pascal Picotte and Aaron Yates. (Colin Fraser)

Suzuki was not far off ballpark with the competition.

Moodie put the bike into the top six four times in the four-round final (after switching from Ducati after Knockhill) to demonstrate the bike's potential, and the team looked forward to 1997 with limited factory parts for Moodie and new signing, Matt Llewellyn, to make use of.

Would 1997 promise to be the year of the GSX-R?

Index

ACU 132
Aldana, David 34
All Japan Formula One 83, 104
Alumite 110
AMA Superbike 91
AMA Superbike rules 49
Andersson, Anders 39, 51, 61–63, 71–74, 77
Andersson, Mieka 73
Aoki, Masano 26
Autissier, Thierry 117

Ballington, Kork 47, 49
Barros, Alexandre 172
Battistini, Jean-Louis 123
'Beast', the 70
le Bihan, Bruno 56, 58–61, 70, 99
Blair, Matt 119
Bolton, Paul 30
Bonhuil, Bruno 171, 173, 180, 199
Bonneville 78
Booler, Paul 107
British Supercup 140
Brown, Roland 50
Buck, David 84
Burnett, Roger 113–119, 123, 133

Camel Challenge 84, 91
Can-Am Cup 44
Carbon Tech 118
Cartwright, 'Butch' 123, 135
Caspers, Bernd 62

Chambers, Steve 117
Cirafici, Bruno 94
Cooley, Wes 11, 34
Cox, Bruce 29, 97, 128
Crescent Suzuki 200
Crevier, Steve 115, 116, 188
Crighton, Brian 133
Crompton, Mike 69, 94, 110, 116
Crosby, Graeme 73
Crine, Thierry 99

DAIS 21, 89, 113
Deletang, Jean-Marc 93, 172
Dixon, Dave 12
Don knit 104
DOP 23
D'Oregiex, Jehan 173
Duhamel, Miguel 104, 110–118, 159, 166, 188
Dunlop 591 84
Durex 131, 134, 138

Eurolantics 77
Endurance Monster Bike Shoot-Out 115
Everett, Nigel 30, 129

Full Floater 23, 81
Fuji, Tansanobu 14
Fujiwara, Katsuaki 200
Formula USA 68, 91

Gaynor, Jeff 93, 121
Goddard, Peter 172, 185, 198
Goodfellow, Gary 50, 56, 60, 67, 69, 95, 98, 104
Gomez, Juan-Eric 173, 185, 199
Grant, Carol 129
Grant, Mick 11, 30, 32, 35, 38, 75, 113, 118, 123, 127–137, 138–140, 155
Gray, Scott 68, 91, 95, 96, 116
Graziano, Michel 106, 117, 159, 171
Gschwender, Ernst 62, 63, 92, 105

Harris, Lester 186, 187, 194, 198, 199
Heasman, Wayne 56
Heino, Jeff 126
Hiscock, Dave 56
Hodgson, Grant 92, 99
Hofmann, Andy 199
Hubin, Richard 9, 39, 61

Iddon, Paul 51, 62, 63, 69, 72, 76,
Igoa, Patrick 117, 123
Irons, Kenny 62
ISR 66, 76, 77
Itoh, Mitsuo 76, 94

Jack, Donald 169
James, Jamie 101, 103

Kipp, Tom 169
Kiryu, Mr 23
Kitagawa, Keiichi 200
Klarkner, Thomas 72
Kocinski, John 34
Kosar, Richard 67, 69, 84
Kosar Suzuki 69
Kyoseki GP-X oil 92

Lance, Ottis 69
Lavielle, Christian 124, 125, 159, 172

Lewis, Paul 51
Liegibel, Klaus 92, 106
Lindholm, Christer 92, 99
Llewelyn, Matt 201
Lodge, Jason 107
LTD 42
Lucky Strike 93, 117, 172, 186, 187, 195
Lynch, Tommy 46, 115, 125

Mackenzie, Niall 172
Marshall, Roger 62–65, 69, 70, 76, 90, 96
Martin, Chris 51
Mattioli, Jean-Michel 123
McElnea, Rob 11, 51, 73
McDaniel, Mark 201
McGladdery, Andy 55, 62
McGregor, Graeme 35, 38
McCarthy, Kirk 186, 187, 191–195, 199
McLaughlin, Steve 98
Meliand, Dominique 9, 10, 38, 71, 99, 157, 186, 194, 199
Mellor, Phil 33, 55, 97, 107, 132
Mercier, Michel 29, 30, 33, 43, 68, 69, 95, 106
Merkel, Fred 163, 168–170, 192
Mertens, Stephane 123–125
Millar, Mark 46
MJN 101, 172, 188
Mladin, Matt 186, 194, 199
Moineau, Herve 9, 31, 39, 50, 56, 58–61, 70, 99, 117, 123, 156, 158, 171
Monneret, Phillipe 173
Moodie, Jim 200, 201
Morillas, Adrien 92, 105, 106
Moriwaki 25
Motul 129
Mouchet, Phillipe 92, 99
Motospeed 71
MR-ALBOX 22

Nation, Trevor 32, 38, 52, 55
NEAS 43
Newbold, John 132

Nishikawa, Masahiro 175
Norman, John 96, 130

Ogborne, Martyn 43, 62
Ohlins 66, 75, 77
Ohsaka, Kinjii 26
Ohshima, Yukiya 25, 63, 91, 106, 107
Oudin, Jean-Pierre 10, 31, 39

Padgetts 96
PDF 23
Penisch, Achim 93, 94
People's Network, The 86
Picotte, Pascal 186, 199, 201
Polen, Doug 25, 26, 44, 46, 48, 61, 67, 81,
    83, 90–92, 95, 103–107, 112, 115, 117,
    133, 185, 192, 199
Phillis, Rob 52, 55
Pro Superbike 199
PVM 118

RACE 34,106
Radial Flow 143
de Radigues, Patrick 10, 39
Randolph, James 46, 169
Reynolds, John 186, 187, 191–195, 199
RE5 Rotary 176
Robinson, Neil 'Smutty' 51, 136
Rohan, Denys 10, 96, 128–130
Ronson, Gerald 129
Rothman, Gerald 46, 166
RR 100
RS40 carbs 115
Russell, Scott 46, 101–104, 186, 187, 195
Rutter, Tony 50
Rymer, Terry 185, 195
Ryuyo circuit 28

SACS 15, 65, 88, 108, 120
Sadowki, Dave 95, 103, 104, 155, 159
Sakakura, Don 24, 82, 86, 188

Sarron, Dominique 124, 125, 171
SCEM 176
Schwantz, Kevin 24, 34, 39, 46, 47, 48,
    57, 58, 62, 63, 66, 67, 91, 106
Seidel, Sven 115, 117, 156
SERT 38–40, 56, 99, 115, 117, 157, 171,
    173, 186, 196
Shenton, Stuart 187, 195
Springsteen, Jay 115
Simeon, Michel 61, 93
Simul, Mark 61
Skoal Bandit 62, 63, 96, 130, 136
Slingshot 79, 88, 98, 100, 108, 111, 137
Smith, Mike 125
SOL-AIR 16
SP 163
Sports Marketing Company 98
Sport Production 163
SRAD 175, 179, 183
Stevens, Thomas 91, 160, 167, 170
Supersport 600 91
Supersport 750 91, 97
Superstock 29, 128, 129, 136
Suzuki Canada 69
Suzuki Cup 44, 83, 84
Suzuki Cup Finals 84
Suzuki Deutschland 198
Suzuki World Cup 119
Suzuki, Takayoshi 22
Suzuki World Cup 83, 98
Swann, Ray 55
Swann Series 75
Syfan, Bill 44

Takayoshi, Katsuro 60
Takayoshi, Katsushiro 106
Team Ansett Air Frieght Suzuki 185
Teneggi, Roberto 94
Tornado F1 78
Tourandre, Jean-Louis 59, 61
Transatlantic Challenge 68
TTS 200
TSCC 18–20, 88
Tsujimoto, Satoshi 25, 47, 49, 56, 67

Turkington, Britt 46, 126, 159, 191

Vance & Hines 27

Watanabe, Suehiro 48, 116
WERA 34, 45
White, Rex   11, 30, 35, 49, 51, 62, 96,
    128–130, 136
Whitham, James   70, 96–98, 103, 106,
    107, 118, 128–135, 138–140, 155
Williams, Glenn 62

Yanagawa, Akira 167
Yates, Aaron 46, 186, 199, 201
Yokouchi, Etsuo 13
Yoshimura, Fujio 24, 48, 101, 188, 189
Yoshimura, Hideo 'Pops' 24
Yoshimura R&D 83, 85, 116
Yoshimura Tornado 78–80
Yoshimura UK 11, 12